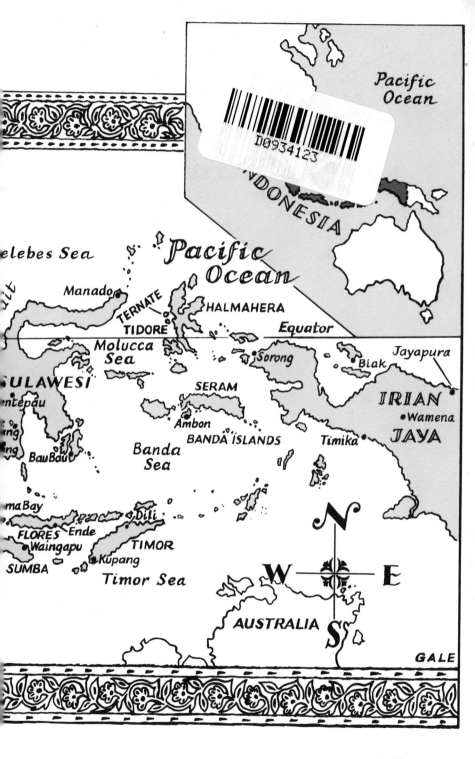

Pacific
Ocean

INDONESIA

elebes Sea

Pacific
Ocean

Manado

TERNATE

HALMAHERA

TIDORE

Equator

Sorong

Biak

Jayapura

Molucca
Sea

SULAWESI

SERAM

IRIAN

ntepau

Wamena

ng
ng

Ambon

BANDA ISLANDS

Timika

JAYA

BauBau

Banda
Sea

ma Bay

Dili

FLORES Ende

TIMOR

Waingapu

SUMBA

Kupang

Timor Sea

N

W   E

S

AUSTRALIA

GALE

DISTANT ISLANDS

DISTANT

Viking

Charles Corn

Islands

Travels
Across
Indonesia

VIKING
Published by the Penguin Group
Viking Penguin, a division of Penguin Books USA Inc.,
375 Hudson Street, New York, New York 10014, U.S.A.
Penguin Books Ltd, 27 Wrights Lane, London W8 5TZ, England
Penguin Books Australia Ltd, Ringwood, Victoria, Australia
Penguin Books Canada Ltd, 10 Alcorn Avenue, Suite 300,
Toronto, Ontario, Canada M4V 3B2
Penguin Books (N.Z.) Ltd, 182–190 Wairau Road,
Auckland 10, New Zealand

Penguin Books Ltd, Registered Offices:
Harmondsworth, Middlesex, England

First published in 1991 by Viking Penguin,
a division of Penguin Books USA Inc.

10 9 8 7 6 5 4 3 2 1

A portion of this book first appeared in slightly different
form in *The Sophisticated Traveler* magazine.

LIBRARY OF CONGRESS CATALOGING-IN-PUBLICATION DATA
Corn, Charles.
    Distant islands: travels across Indonesia / Charles Corn.
      p. cm.
    ISBN 0-670-82374-0
      1. Indonesia—Description and travel—1981–   I. Title.
DS62.2.C67   1991
915.9804'39—dc20   91-50172

Printed in the United States of America
Set in Aldus
Designed by Francesca Belanger
Map by Robert Gale

For my family—
Especially in memory of
Ernest and Polly and Thomas Lewis Pierce Corn;
Also for Thomas Seery Corn.
In memory, too, of Edwin Tribble.

And for Rosalie.

To the ordinary Englishman this is perhaps the least known part of the globe. Our possessions in it are few and scanty; scarcely any of our travellers go to explore it; and in many collections of maps it is almost ignored, being divided between Asia and the Pacific Islands. It thus happens that few persons realize that, as a whole, it is comparable with the primary divisions of the globe, and that some of its separate islands are larger than France or the Austrian empire. The traveller, however, soon acquires different ideas. He sails for days, or even for weeks, along the shores of one of these great islands, often so great that its inhabitants believe it to be a vast continent. He finds that voyages among these islands are commonly reckoned by weeks and months, and that their several inhabitants are often as little known to each other as are the native races of the northern to those of the southern continent of America. He soon comes to look upon this region as one apart from the rest of the world with its own races of men and its own aspects of nature; with its own ideas, feelings, customs, and modes of speech, and with a climate, vegetation, and animated life altogether peculiar to itself.

ALFRED RUSSEL WALLACE, *The Malay Archipelago*—1869

. . • . .

"Where do you come from?" she said, impulsive and inconsequent, in a passionate whisper. "What is that land beyond the great sea from which you come? A land of lies and of evil from which nothing but misfortune ever comes to us—who are not white."

JOSEPH CONRAD, *An Outcast of the Islands*—1896

Contents

Distant Islands

Prologue:
"Surabaya Johnny"

ON THE SUMMER OF 1952, when I was a high school student, I joined a hosteling group for a bicycle trip across England and Northern Europe, our destination the Olympic Games in Helsinki. We sailed from Hoboken and disembarked in Southampton eleven days later to discover an England still in the throes of rebuilding seven years after the end of the war.

One rainy afternoon in Newcastle, as our group awaited the next day's crossing to Norway, I went alone to a movie, *Outcast of the Islands*, directed by Carol Reed and based on the Joseph Conrad novel. The islands of the title were the vast archipelago, known by various names, that lies between Australia and Southeast Asia. In Conrad's day these islands were the East or Dutch East Indies or the Eastern or Malay Archipelago. An old Malay term called them Nusantara, or the Empire of the Islands. In seaman's argot they were often simply known as "the Malays," as were the people who inhabited them. However they have been called, the islands are spread over an expanse of approximately three million square miles and today comprise almost exclusively the nation of Indonesia.

In the film, Trevor Howard plays the opportunistic Willems and Ralph Richardson is Captain Lingard, whose secret, treacherous river, winding to the sea from the island's heartland and navigable only by Lingard himself, is betrayed to Arab traders by Willems.

At the film's end, having broken Lingard's trust, Willems realizes he is a lost man. Abandoned by his former mentor, he can only shout from the dimness of the rainforest at the retreating figure, who has left Willems to himself: "We shall meet again, Captain Lingard!"

The exotic setting and circumstances of the movie made a deep impression on me. I date my desire to go to those islands from that afternoon.

I steeped myself in Conrad and eventually came to view the archipelago as a cultural estuary where the few Westerners who ventured there became hopelessly immersed, with Willems a fictional prototype. If they were masters by virtue of the muted colonialism they represented, likewise they were slaves—imprisoned, caught up in a play of opposites, an irreconciliation assuming many forms.

"Tell me, Tuan . . . do you white people ever hear the voices of the invisible ones?"

"We do not," answered Lingard. "Because those that we cannot see do not speak."

So many years later I recognized the broader truths suggested by this exchange from Conrad's novel. As a fifteen-year-old in the England of 1952, I could only sense a keen undercurrent of kinship with his islands and with the attitude that characterized his view of the world. But that sense was sharpened in an unlikely setting two months later, in Germany.

Having reached my full growth that summer, I did nothing to discourage other people's notion that I was older than I was. One evening in Hamburg I visited a seedy, raucous cabaret to hear music. The patrons were grim-faced, especially the men, many of them clad in moth-eaten uniforms stripped of insignia, some of them missing limbs. Late in the night a woman of bizarre dress and indeterminate age held the audience spellbound with a set of songs. Afterward, I learned they had been composed by Kurt Weill with lyrics by Bertolt Brecht.

I was especially taken by one song. Though I had only phrase-book German that summer, the plaintive refrain revealed its title: "Surabaya Johnny." The strangeness of the musical idiom and the incomprehensible German lyrics only enhanced my enthusiasm for Conrad's islands. I knew that Surabaya was a port on Java's northeastern coast and that it was a place of truth and legend. I learned that the song expressed a woman's yearning for a wandering sailor, and I dreamed that the sailor was I.

"Surabaya Johnny." Today the title suggests a Western, world-weary, between-the-wars, Brechtian cynicism crossed with Eastern exoticism, but that evening it spoke to me in a way I could not explain. Puffing the pipe I affected, I applauded with the others by banging my beer glass on the table. Alone and excluded—like the subject of the song, or so I imagined—I left when drunken trouble started. But "Surabaya Johnny" stayed with me.

Baubles, Bangles, and Beads

INDONESIA ADORNS THE EQUATOR like a gigantic necklace, its odd-sized island ornaments dangling north and south of the line that divides the world into hemispheres. It is a nation of islands comprising most of the Malay Archipelago —the world's largest, with 13,677 islands that extend north to south for 1,100 miles and west to east for 3,200 miles. Indonesia stretches from the northern reaches of Borneo south to the small island of Roti near Timor off northwestern Australia, and from Sumatra in the Indian Ocean east to New Guinea, a distance comparable to the expanse between San Francisco and Bermuda. The country of Indonesia occupies some of the largest islands in the world: Sumatra, Java, Kalimantan (the major part of Borneo), Sulawesi (called Celebes by the Dutch), and Irian Jaya (the western part of New Guinea).

In addition, thirty small archipelagos are scattered here and there. The most famous among these islands to Westerners, Bali, is hardly more than a speck on the map, with less than two percent of the nation's total population. Bali is an emerald-green legend of an island (its eastern shore is the boundary between Asia and Oceania), but it is lost in a vast country made up entirely of islands and their seas.

Indonesia's diverse beauty is painted in extremes, from the snow-covered peaks of Irian Jaya, which tower above wildernesses and jungles more treacherous than those of the Amazon Valley and Africa, to the oppressive mangrove swamps of eastern Sumatra; and from the fine open-range country of Sumba to the lofty Dieng Plateau of central Java, all encircled by the awesome "ring of fire," a honeycomb of great smoking volcanoes. This ring of fire represents the voices and instruments of the gods who bring havoc, and then, as if for balance, fertility.

Today the islanders of the archipelago are predominantly of Malay stock (with the exception of the people of Irian Jaya, who are Melanesian), and it is generally held that waves of migrations occurred thousands of years ago from South China, Yunnan, and Tonkin. These bands of immigrants were a Mongolian race and introduced refined stone implements before later arrivals brought Bronze Age and then Iron Age cultures. Cohabiting with the original peoples, most of these settlers built their villages around the rice fields they cultivated. Others sought the vast interiors as nomadic hunters, while still others became seafarers and sailed west to Madagascar and east to Polynesia and the Easter Islands.

The Hindu migrations began in the seventh century, followed by the Arabs' first arrival in North Sumatra in A.D. 846; by the sixteenth century a series of Muslim kingdoms had arisen, and Islam had spread throughout the islands. Apart from the occasional traveler, the Portuguese were the first Europeans to sail into these waters, arriving in the sixteenth century in search of the Spice Islands. Then, in 1605, the United Dutch East India Company (known as the VOC, for Vereenigde Oostindische Compagnie) seized trade monopolies, increasing its suzerainty in the archipelago until a brief hiatus during the Napoleonic Wars, when Holland was occupied by the French and the islands fell under the control of the British East India Company from 1811 to 1816.

Over the centuries of Dutch colonialism, native rulers waged many wars against the VOC, which in turn visited bloody retributions upon the unfortunate usurpers. But nationalistic sentiments flourished, taking wing during the harsh Japanese occupation of the Dutch East Indies in World War II. With the official Japanese surrender on September 2, 1945, Sukarno, who would become the nation's first president, with his followers proclaimed Indonesia's independence.

Independence was finally granted by the Dutch in 1949. Indonesia's nearly 170 million people make it the fifth most populous country in the world after China, India, the Soviet Union, and the United States. Though Sukarno's successor, Suharto, has resisted pressures among his own constituency to convert his country into a Muslim theocracy, Indonesia has the largest Muslim population of any nation.

Yet reminders are everywhere that this country is an amalgamation of and an accommodation to every invasion it has suffered. Indonesians are divided into approximately 300 ethnic groups which speak about 200 distinct languages and many more dialects.

Indonesia's story tells of wave after wave of migrations, whose peoples absorbed earlier arrivals, or destroyed them, or drove them into the interiors of remote regions, where they are found to this day. Political and cultural turbulence has been the hallmark of Indonesia's past, and through the centuries these islands have amassed a history of violence. *Amok,* meaning "in a murderous frenzy," is a Malay word.

Whether the European mind perceived these islands as lying to the East (as in the case of Marco Polo) or to the West (as in the case of Christopher Columbus), the European imagination seized upon them as the repository of great riches. The promise of such wealth became justification for the hope and struggle to reach them. But if the tenor of the age of exploration demanded the material, it demanded the fantastic as well.

Landing on Sumatra during his return to Venice from China, Marco Polo noted in his journal the single-horned rhinoceros, whose tongue was "armed with long, sharp spines," as well as men with dog-like tails who ran wild in the mountains. Cosmographers of the famous journeyer's day decorated their maps with such images.

Unsurprisingly, the accounts that travelers published of their journeys prompted more doubt than admiration. Marco Polo was branded a liar and boaster. A similar fate befell the famous Portuguese Fernão Mendes Pinto, who between 1537 and 1558 journeyed through different parts of Asia including Sumatra, Java, and the Moluccas, and by his own account was sold sixteen times, enslaved thirteen times, and shipwrecked five times. The Roman Catholic Church of the day put a fine point on institutionalized skepticism in the saying, *"Qui multum peregrinatur, raro sanctificatur,"* or "He who travels much is seldom canonized."

Odoric of Pordenone, a Paduan friar and missionary of the early fourteenth century, may have been the first European traveler after Marco Polo to visit Sumatra. Presumably, he saw with more perceptive eyes than his predecessor and noted Islam's conquest of these shores when he encountered men and women stark naked from top to toe. "Seeing me appalled," he wrote, "they scoffed at me, saying God made Adam and Eve naked." If Saracen traders had brought the faith of the Prophet Muhammad to these shores, the natives in turn adapted Islamic trappings to local *adat*, or custom. Odoric, however, owes his canonization not to his travels but to his having baptized sixty thousand Saracens.

The archipelago, while exquisitely pictorial, is rife with paradoxes born of the collision of cultures, and while a visitor may see these islands with the eyes of a painter, rendering the experience of them seems more the writer's business. Small wonder that Joseph Conrad seized on these distant outposts in his fiction. Everywhere and nowhere, this part of the world was Conrad's "East." The traveler may or may not search in vain for Captain Lingard's secret river or the spot where Lord Jim celebrated his "pitiless wedding with a shadowy ideal of conduct."

The views Conrad held about his craft confirm, if only by implication, the inseparability of the novelist and his major subject, the archipelago. "I suspect," he wrote, "that the aim of creation cannot be ethical at all. I would fondly believe that its object is purely spectacular—a spectacle for awe, love, adoration or hate, if you like, but in this view—never for despair. These visions, delicious or poignant, are a moral end in themselves." Conrad's choice of the words "spectacular" and "spectacle" and "visions" strikes me as uniquely evocative. The Malays, after all, are a country of spectacles and visions.

For myself, I had traveled in the archipelago for two months nearly ten years before the travels in the late 1980s and early 1990s that resulted in this book. That first trip gave me a sort of blurred vision for the second, in turn allowing a sense of familiarity that was at times eerie.

I gradually learned Bahasa Indonesia, the lingua franca of the archipelago, and when appropriate I ate with the fingers of my right hand in the prescribed Islamic manner. As my travels took direction, they also assumed a shape and pattern that betrayed my true interests. Often the elusive horizon was a mirage—a necessary delusion, I reminded myself, to induce me to undertake the ordeal. I primed myself for the unexpected, telling myself that surprises spice a journey, taking the traveler unprepared like a sudden gust laden with a fresh, wild scent. As I traveled, I found myself drawn less to the fragments of societies purer by virtue of their isolation, and more toward the cultural estuaries where fiercely drawn divergencies were at work, resulting from centuries of trade.

The incongruous excesses and ceremonies of the archipelago, the lulling rhythms of Indonesia's contrary music, its glare and its fading light, invite a discovery that in itself is a giant puzzle, disassembling, reassembling, to be measured by curiosity as well as by the subtlety and lastingness of irresistible mystery.

Jakarta:
Victorious Fortress

"**W**HERE ARE YOU STAYING in Jakarta?" asked a Chinese businessman sitting next to me on the flight. We'd boarded together at Singapore's Changi Airport, near the prison where a gallows awaited convicted drug traffickers. He lived in Singapore and traveled often to Jakarta, dreading it each time. There was nothing to prepare you, he told me, no middle ground between the Asian extremes—Singapore's pristine, futuristic dream of a city and Jakarta's squalor—except the invisible equator and the scattering thirty-five thousand feet below of the Riau Archipelago, which sheltered as many pirates as fishermen.

My itinerary was vague, but the vagueness unbottled a genie in my gut that filled me at times with a cold, barbaric terror. I had wanted to take things as they came, but that sense of freedom, once so exhilarating, now spawned uncertainty.

"I don't really know where I'm staying," I told him. "What about this place called Bloddy Mary's Homestay?" I asked facetiously.

"Oh, for heaven's sake, don't stay there. A man's throat might be cut for his wallet. Even taxis stay away from that sector."

Sector. I envisioned a city besieged, sliced up like a pie, each piece jealously occupied by hostile forces. The businessman scribbled the names of three hotels. In a tone less a suggestion than a warning, he said, "Always insist upon a discount. *Always!* Don't let them tell you they are full. Hotels are never full in Jakarta. *Never!"*

The aircraft banked and drew a lazy circle over the flat and seemingly endless city stretching south from the coast to a range of foothills. Late-afternoon sunlight reflected off the tin-roofed mosques scattered across what appeared to be a stagnant lake of terra-cotta, green, and gray, whose colors were muted by fog rising from the surface. But it was traffic exhaust and industrial smoke that bound the red tile roofs, the bougainvillea and palm, the ribbons of avenues, side streets, and canals. I glanced over at the Chinese, who smiled grimly and held his nose.

This city of eight million inhabitants was founded in 1527, though official records point to a settlement dating from the sixth century. The Portuguese established the port of Sunda Kelapa on the swampy north coast of West Java, a concession granted by the kingdom of Pajajaran for the European spice trade; the port was in turn conquered by a rival prince called Fatahillah, who renamed the settlement Jayakarta or Jakarta ("Victorious Fortress"). The Dutch invaded a century later and erected a new town on the ruins of Jayakarta, naming it Batavia. In the nineteenth century, prompted by the British interregnum, the city's governing center moved inland several miles, where it remains today, spread over 650 square miles. The metropolis reclaimed an approximation of its earlier name after creation of the Republic of Indonesia.

When we deplaned in late afternoon, the sky was the color of mustard gas. By the time I claimed my bags and was waved through customs, it was nearly dusk. It was an hour's drive in the darkness to the Hotel Indonesia on Jalan Thamrin, the city's main boulevard, and the taxi driver covered the thirty-odd kilometers with the grim recklessness of a deranged fighter pilot.

I was arriving in Jakarta on a Sunday in mid-April, the eve of Ramadan, the holiest month in the Islamic calendar and a time of fasting and prayer. My initial impressions: it was a hellish place, dark, iridescent, and sinister.

After I checked into my room, having negotiated a "diplomatic rate," I left the hotel for a walk, ostensibly to buy bottled water and toothpaste. It was still early evening, and the streets were filled with people. A mile away was the great mosque that could oblige thirty-five thousand prostrate souls, and from its loud-speakers could be heard the nasally wailing call to prayers.

Today's Jakarta is Sukarno's legacy. In the early 1960s Indonesia's first president envisioned his city as a major trade center. The six-lane Jalan Thamrin suddenly broke out with a rash of high-rise buildings, including the Sarinah department store and the Hotel Indonesia, which figured prominently in C. J. Koch's novel *The Year of Living Dangerously*. Its bar was the watering hole of Western journalists covering the sequence of events that would ultimately lead to Sukarno's downfall. The influx of money from the Soviet Union accounted for a huge sports stadium erected for the 1962 Asian Games, as well as a collection of ungainly statues bearing proletarian messages that overlooked Jalan Thamrin and other wide boulevards.

Sukarno's fall from grace in 1965 hardly stymied development in the capital, but under Suharto, who has governed Indonesia since Sukarno, growth came with American and Japanese investment as well as multinational consortia. Today gleaming foreign exchange banks line Jalan Thamrin, now ten lanes wide, along with new office buildings for such tenants as American Express, Citibank, and IBM; expensive shops and boutiques; and a plethora of international hotels. These luxury hostelries stand grandly aloof from the squatters' hovels and food stalls of the narrow *kampungs*, or villages, behind them.

As I walked that evening, taxis and *becaks*, the motorized tricycles typical of Asian cities, congested the streets. The stench from the ancient canal dug three centuries ago by the Dutch, which bisected the city, singed the nostrils, as did its subterranean tributaries, which unexpectedly surfaced, reeking of litter and waste, to flank the sidewalks.

Jakarta was a street city undergoing constant rejuvenation—but of a cursed sort. Jackhammers sounded the hours of the night, and floodlights illuminated monstrous cranes hauling girders into place on every other corner. People were everywhere: hanging out of overcrowded buses that emitted noxious fumes or squatting on the sidewalks in circles of a half-dozen. The sarong-clad, slight, dark men played cards and talked. Women nursed babies and cooked on charcoal grills. Children played. Doorways were for sleeping and Westerners for hassling.

I did not have to walk far for my purchases. Sarinah was nearby, and it was open. An Indonesian Macy's, it seemed a sanctuary. I picked bottled water from the shelf and found the toothpaste. There were the usual containers of Pepsodent and Colgate, but one brand, easily the most popular, as its generous shelf space indicated, immediately caught my eye. Tubed and boxed like any toothpaste, in a black-and-white package with green trim, it bore the name "Darkie" and a picture of a grinning black man sporting a top hat. It was an early clue to the ambivalence with which Indonesians throughout the archipelago regard race and color. Gleaming white gnashers framed by a shining, happy black face sold toothpaste. "Darkie" would become my dental cream of choice.

A different route back to the hotel led me past a Mexican restaurant called the Green Pub and a Pizza Hut. The humidity in the streets was stifling, overriding a sea of dust. The rainy season for Jakarta was over. Across the way was a cinema, above whose marquee was emblazoned a large billboard of Charles Bronson, and near it another advertising a forthcoming Stevie Wonder concert.

I was followed back to the hotel by an insistent pimp with a frozen smile, and left him to be turned away by the doorman. In the bar, when I ordered a drink, I intercepted furtive glances from a table of astonishingly pretty, small-boned, almond-eyed girls waiting to be picked up. In the adjoining café I ordered *nasi goreng*, a reliable fried rice with meat and shrimp, and a beer.

A Western woman traveling alone in the East displays a freedom deemed heterodox, provocative, an invocation to trouble, while a

lone Western male is courted, ardently so, fawned over as a superior being and valued for his company as well as his purse. The
question of money is treated with masterful circumspection, and
the charade shrewdly casts the Westerner as gentle, civilized, open,
tall, strong, handsome, generous, deserving of the title *tuan*. This
title is used in formal circumstances with varying shades of meaning, traditionally by one of inferior social or professional status
addressing his superior.

The Western male's Malay counterpart is equally gentle but
small, servile if not obsequious, confident of his patron's gener-
osity. The elaborate interplay between Westerners and Malays (it
might be termed "the *Lord Jim* syndrome"), with its countless
variations on different social levels, springs from centuries of colonialism and white supremacy. What is harder to grasp is the
sincerity buttressing the hypocrisy.

"It is written that the earth belongs to those who have fair skins
and hard but foolish hearts. . . . You are wise and great—and you
shall always be fools." Thus was a fine point put on this prevalent
attitude by a native speaking to Conrad's Captain Lingard.

I returned to my room, and while preparing for bed, I noticed
a sign on the door in English warning guests against "unwanted
callers."

The next morning was the first of Ramadan. Over coffee I read
in the *Indonesian Times* that Stevie Wonder's concert was the talk
of Jakarta, a sellout at twenty dollars a ticket. An editorial in the
Indonesian Observer, another of Jakarta's English-language newspapers, implored militant Muslims to have a tolerant attitude toward those who would not observe the fast. Though Indonesia is
the most populous Islamic state in the world, President Suharto,
himself a Muslim with a wide streak of Javanese mysticism colored
by peasant cunning, has rejected conservative demands that his
nation become a Muslim state. Thus the *Pancasila* democracy was
created, ushered in by Sukarno over forty years ago, and carried
forth by Suharto as a sort of philosophical connective tissue to

reconcile the many cultural divergences that comprise the country.

The *Pancasila,* or "Five Principles," are nonnegotiable and at first glance seem benevolently bland cant: Faith in God, Humanity, Nationalism, Representative Government, Social Justice. But these principles have startling ramifications. For example, faith in God is not a right but a commandment to Indonesians, compelling a belief in a single supreme being, whether He be called God, Allah, or Vishnu. (There are few, if any, Indonesian Jews.)

The principle of faith in God is a veneer, overriding a centuries-old underpinning of fiercely held animistic beliefs and vivid superstitions. But in its efforts to stress unity with faith in God as an abiding principle, the government was casting its nets into more practical waters. The iron-fisted Indonesian logic has it that if you are an atheist, you are a Communist. This syllogism is closed with restrictions against the teaching of any Chinese language or dialect in any school and against the importation of attendant literature or teaching devices. Though there have been recent conciliatory gestures from the capital of the People's Republic of China, Beijing's role as instigator in what led to the bloodbath of 1965 remains vivid in memory.

It is remarkable that such a variegated country with so many violent upheavals in its last fifty years could have emerged as a nation, much less have survived. Most authorities today agree that Indonesia could not have emerged and would not have survived had it not been for the agility and resourcefulness of Sukarno and Suharto, the only two (and markedly dissimilar) presidents to have governed this nation.

After World War II the Dutch were not eager to surrender their colonial empire, and for the next three years they engaged in an unsuccessful diplomatic and military struggle to repossess their holdings. On December 27, 1949, after protracted negotiations, Holland bowed to international pressures and transferred sovereignty over the archipelago to the Republic of Indonesia. Years of internal discord marked by economic depression, separatist movements, and rival political factions followed before Sukarno with his National Front was able to assume power in 1960.

Sukarno was a curiously flamboyant figure whose political identity was rooted in abject hatred of Western colonialism, which, in his view, had been the ruin of Asia. He wore it as a personal humiliation that his state was perceived as a "nation of coolies and a coolie among nations" and resented any signs of Western imperialism: the American presence in the Philippines, the British influence in the new state of Malaysia, and above all the presence of the despised Dutch, who still claimed West Irian on the island of New Guinea.

Branded a troublemaker in the 1930s, Sukarno was banished by the Dutch to the remote port of Ende on the southeastern island of Flores, where he remained until his liberation in 1942 by occupying Japanese forces. While the Japanese coveted Sukarno's silver-tongued oratory as a force to promote anti-Dutch sentiments, the nationalist movement in the archipelago prospered during this period.

During the formative years of the republic, Sukarno carried the dual banners of Islam and Marxism, and he did so to establish a broad-based coalition that would ensure political unity and an economic stability that would lift the new nation out of its poverty. Sukarno remained in office by playing off two major rival factions: the PKI, the third largest Communist party in the world after those in China and the Soviet Union, and the army. His ultimate downfall coincided with the near dissolution of the nation he had created.

Mounting pressures from the PKI prompted the president, now in failing health in the spring of 1965, to strike a deal with Beijing to import arms. This move would gain the Communists more leverage in dealing with the army, which for its part was growing increasingly disenchanted with Sukarno's failed economic policies (the inflation rate was running at 650 percent per annum) and his inability to consolidate bitterly opposed factions. The stage was set for a major confrontation.

On October 1, 1965, Communist rebels murdered six top Indonesian army generals, threw their remains into an abandoned well, and moved on the presidential palace. The suppression of the revolt, led by General Suharto, was quick, brutal, and ultimately devastating to the fortunes of the PKI. The army slaughtered tens of thousands of Communist sympathizers as well as ethnic Chinese, as an anti-Communist wave swept across Indonesia.

Estimates vary as to how many people were killed in the purge. An official source puts the number at eighty thousand; others say the victims numbered closer to a million. Whatever the number, according to the Australian historian J. D. Legge, "one of the bloodiest massacres in modern history" went virtually unnoticed in the West, while thousands of suspected Communist sympathizers were imprisoned and many later executed. The results were the virtual annihilation of the PKI and its supporters, the discrediting of Sukarno (whose power was systematically curtailed by the army until his death in 1970), and the rise to prominence of Suharto, who was elected president of the nation by the Congress in 1968.

By all accounts, Suharto seemed an unlikely choice to succeed Sukarno. A quiet and decidedly unflamboyant family man who was more soldier than politician under his predecessor, Suharto appeared out of nowhere to consolidate the counterrevolt and effectively reverse many of Sukarno's policies. Rejecting his predecessor's isolationist stance, he brought his country back into the United Nations as well as into the Association of Southeast Asia Nations (ASEAN) as a charter member, thereby improving relations with contentious Malaysia. Suharto sought foreign investment from the United States and Japan. While Sukarno had played the juggler and managed some semblance of unity through manipulation of hostile parties, Suharto has fostered a democracy undergirded by military power. One measure of his success in binding together as a nation such disparate peoples, languages, and cultures is his nearly twenty-five years in office.

· · • · ·

As the days passed, I developed an affinity for the brooding, hot labyrinth of a city that is Jakarta. I regarded with a near-animal fascination the low-life hysteria of the nexus of neighborhoods, hearing the polyglot native tongues, and smelling the air, which stank of exhaust fumes and the refuse of the canals.

Shortly after my arrival I moved to a cheaper hotel on Jalan Salim. My preferred restaurant was a place in the next block owned by a Minangkabau family from Padang in West Sumatra. There was no menu to ponder. As was customary in Minang restaurants, a dozen dishes were placed before the diner: chicken, beef, lamb, fish, eggs, vegetable, rice, all seasoned with chilis and turmeric and simmered in coconut milk. You made your selection, ate your dinner, were billed only for the dishes you consumed, and paid the old woman keeping accounts in front. The Minangkabau were a matrilineal, if not a matriarchal, society, and women, not men, counted their gain.

What with heterogeneous peoples having drifted into the capital from all over the archipelago, Jakarta was far from exclusively Javanese, and this entire block was Sumatran. My throat invariably burned from the highly seasoned Minang food; but to quench the fire, I had to walk afield from this Muslim community, which eschewed alcohol, to find a place that sold beer.

A walker by nature, I soon discovered that Jakarta was such a bewildering labyrinth of a city that reliance on becak and taxi became a necessity. But my habitual walks through this Sumatran quarter were instructive in the varying degrees of street life so characteristic of the city at large, from the mini-entrepreneurs—purveyors of food, drink, cigarettes, and sweets; and cobblers, watch repairers, photographers, printers, and gemstone dealers who conducted their businesses on the sidewalks—to the more sophisticated shops on the major thoroughfares specializing in such fare as rock and opera tapes pirated from the West.

In my neighborhood, as in all the city, hopeless beggars lived lives of abject poverty. Daily and at the same place I passed a boy of perhaps eight, shoeless and dressed in rags, his skin nearly black with dirt. He was a wild creature but with a deadly submission to his fate, as isolated from the world around him as a wounded animal. He simply sat on the sidewalk with an absent look on his face, beyond resignation. There were thousands of children like him in the city, street urchins who knew no other life than this existence. Each time I passed, he remained as motionless as a statue, a sphinx who nonetheless tracked any movement around him. Once I looked back and felt in my pocket for rupiah notes. I placed the money in a wall crevice, and when I left it, he rose and dashed for the spot as fast as his legs could carry him.

I had no choice but to take the inconveniences of this straggly, clamoring city of villages and neighborhoods in stride. Telephoning proved a fruitless exercise in crossed lines and interminable busy signals. A call across the world from Jakarta took minutes; across the city you were lucky if you got through at all. I had hoped that official sanction of my travels from the Ministry of Tourism would prove useful in dealings with provincial authorities, but the the government offices were bureaucratized to the point of inertia, and there was no hope of assistance. The mails proved as erratic as the telephone. I learned later that a letter from the States could take three months or even four to find its way through the mysterious intercity postal system. Conversely, a letter to California took only five days.

My frustrations with official Jakarta were mollified by the occasional company of Stan, a tall, youthful American journalist in his late fifties whose firm did consulting and public relations work for the Indonesian government.

We had dinner one evening at a friendly, nearly empty place with homey red-and-white-checked tablecloths and a piano-saxophone combo that cranked up about nine. When the band took a break, the manager played Vera Lynn records dating from the early 1950s over the speakers.

"You know the real story of Indonesia is the last twenty-five years of Suharto's rule, how he's been able to govern as effectively as he has a country of thirteen thousand islands," Stan said.

"Imagine the constant pressure from fanatical Muslim factions to make Indonesia a Muslim state. Muslims are allowed to go only so far, and if you're a Christian, the five points of Pancasila are the best possible news. It allows you to worship your Christian God, but it can also tell you when to shut up, if there's a streak of the political rabble-rouser in you. But if you really want to see the forces of Pancasila at work, turn on the television for an hour or so."

The networks were government-controlled, and programming provided something for everybody: glitzy variety shows; sitcoms and movies from the United States, Hong Kong, and Japan; sporting events such as soccer and the badminton finals for the Thomas Cup held in Kuala Lumpur; cooking classes with chefs in starched white toques; the heavily censored news; and religious ceremonies.

If the Christian was called upon to endure a muezzin at early evening, he did so with the assurance that a program of Protestant hymns would follow, while Balinese could eschew a Catholic Mass but tune in the gamelan dances from the *Ramayana*, the ancient Hindu epic, the next hour. The Indonesian national anthem punctuated every evening of viewing at strategic times; it was sung over a pictorial sequence depicting a variety of peoples at work and play. It seemed that Suharto's state television, not his army, enforced Pancasila.

The most popular programs, judging by their frequency and variety, were the English-language lessons. I watched such a program just before my dinner date with Stan. It took the form of a skit involving two old flames, an unmarried British couple who met by chance in Singapore and spoke at cross-purposes about traveling together to Kuala Lumpur. The sketch was an amusing tale of alien courtship that softened the lesson's intellectual demands. She: "I didn't come to Singapore to see David, and I'm tired of all these personal questions!" He: "Why don't we go to Kuala Lumpur together?" The upshot was that the woman stood the man up at the airport, and the last scene showed her driving alone to the Malaysian capital. At the end of the program the English idioms used in the drama were reviewed by a benevolent, patronizing pair of instructors.

In any discussion of Indonesia's domestic problems, one topic inevitably came up: the plight of the ethnic Chinese, an oppressed minority all over the country. I asked Stan what he knew about them.

"If you're of Chinese descent, if you were born here and your parents were born here, you must carry a paper and produce it on demand to show you're okay," he said. "The attempted coup in sixty-five supported by Beijing was not that long ago. If a Chinese goes to a bank to make any transaction, he must produce that piece of paper. 'You have a Chinese name; you must show us the paper legitimizing you,' says the bank teller. This is done even if your people migrated to these parts two hundred years ago.

"But it's really an old story, going back long before sixty-five. You see, the Dutch brought the Chinese in as tax collectors, and they in turn became moneylenders, controlling the economy. Now they have their own banks, and the Indonesians resent it. The richest man in Indonesia is Chinese. He's called Liem Sieo Liong, and the Bank of Central Asia is his. Even though he's Chinese, he's an old chum of Suharto's. It's a shrewd arrangement. Suharto's kids are principal shareholders in that bank, and a lot of people resent such allegiance to that sort of wealth.

"There was a court case recently in Surabaya involving Javanese servants mistreated by their Chinese employers. All very hush-hush. Why? The government wanted it quiet because the locals would have run amok if they'd gotten wind of it.

"It's pretty futile to get exact numbers, because nobody wants to talk about it, particularly government officials. But my sources tell me that one half million Chinese were killed in the great sixties purge. A Chinese was a Communist and therefore subversive, so the logic went.

"Even so, the dynamics of Chinese-Malay relations today are

fascinating. Go to the Hotel Borobudur on Sunday afternoon. There's a swimming club there, and rich Chinese are the members. Exclusively. Watch them lording it over the Indonesian servants, demanding this and that—'I want this and I want it now' sort of thing. I have Indonesian friends who are well educated and know their views are not, as it were, politically correct, but they can't stand the Chinese."

Our driver waited, guarding the car, while Vera Lynn's plaintive voice trailed us to the street.

"Want to see some Jakarta nightlife?" Stan asked.

He directed the driver to take us to a disco he knew, a fifteen-minute drive.

The Tanamur was a smoke-filled discotheque with a hefty entrance fee to keep out the riffraff, but even so it was packed with couples gyrating to Western rock, many of them girls dancing together. "This is upscale, but not too far up," said Stan as we sought the bar. The patrons were mostly young Javanese women, with a handful of Western males, who, according to Stan, worked for oil companies.

Most of the women, I learned, were young mothers who had been deserted by their husbands. They had little if any legal recourse. They came to the Tanamur and other discos dressed in skintight sequined dresses that caught the kaleidoscopic lights when they danced. The idea was to be picked up by a man and taken to his quarters for the night.

It was considered bad form, Stan told me, for a man to proposition a girl with money. Such an overture would be met with silence and a demure downward casting of the eyes. An invitation to the girl to accompany the man was sufficient. By tacit code, after a night of sex the man would place his lady, who carried a change of clothes, in a taxi with a gift of thirty thousand rupiah— less than twenty dollars—out of which she would pay the taxi fare home or to work. Relatives or friends minded the children.

Most of the girls came here every night hoping to be selected, paying the door fee which guaranteed nothing beyond gaining entrance, and the pick of the lot were gone by midnight. In the late hours, however, fired by gin and tonic, to which they were unaccustomed, those unclaimed became as desperate and insistent as Tijuana bar girls and did not suffer rejection lightly.

These young women were not, strictly speaking, "butterflies," as prostitutes were known, and face was saved. By day they pursued other livelihoods before darkness saw them emerge from their chrysalises. They were waitresses, secretaries, shopworkers, seamstresses. Theoretically, a man could pick up a woman anywhere, but the rules of the game had interesting variations. Every reputable hotel, store, and restaurant employed its share of beautiful young Javanese women emitting scents that invited sexual collusion with customers, but for appearance's sake these establishments sent their female employees home by taxi. It was not the woman's reputation at stake but the establishment's, and failure to comply would result in certain dismissal. The weekly day or evening off relieved the establishment of potential shame on its doorstep while giving the woman a measure of freedom to call a telephone number discreetly given her and arrange an assignation. In any case, either party could back out of the proposed arrangement without loss of face, but with a single word: *belum.*

If any word is indispensable in the Indonesian lexicon, it is *belum,* a term that has different hues of meaning. It denotes "not yet," softening the pejorative edge of *tidak,* which means emphatically "no." But *belum* has a rainbow of other connotations, depending on the circumstances. Its essence is a cozy suggestion of hope, expectation, and, at the very least, possibility across a variety of fronts.

After a drink at another disco called Hot Men, we ended the evening at the Tambora Bar and Hotel in an area known as Bloc M on the south side of the city. There was no admission fee here, and the raunchiness was tangible, with a dance floor, a bar, and a pool table in three separate rooms under several floors of grim chambers for those wishing to consort with their dates on the premises. Oilmen, too, worked this terrain, but this was the city's steamy underside. Women were aggressive and not easily discouraged. When we entered, a girl grabbed my arm, entreating me to buy her a drink. She wore a shirt that consisted of a single panel in front like an apron, baring her satin-smooth back. Her tenacity was wearing; *"belum"* failed to discourage her, and a firmer negative brought forth a string of invectives as we departed.

Jakarta's nighttime underbelly was not limited to discos and bars and red-light districts. One evening I strolled up Jalan Thamrin for dinner at a Chinese restaurant, a fifteen-minute walk beyond the Hotel Indonesia. The way led past a scruffy park bounded on one side by a stinking canal. Streetwalkers posted themselves at odd intervals in the darkness and whispered their overtures as I passed, but it was when I reached the park that a Javanese girl of uncommon beauty stepped out of the shadows to accost me. She was small-boned, with a finely sculpted body and facial features, and her black hair billowed to her waist. Her loveliness seemed to mask a pathos that was oddly unsettling, prompting me to speak to her.

"You come with me there," she said, nodding toward the park. "What you pay, up to you." She flashed a smile of bright, even teeth.

Immediately we were joined by another girl no less lovely but who had dyed her hair blond. For an instant I expected trouble between them—but these weren't rival hookers at battle over turf, but companions in trade. The second girl seemed less furtive and spoke better English.

"We will take you there," she said in a low, throaty voice. "The park, but we must be careful about police."

I looked at the adjacent park. It was the tip of a triangle where a side street crossed the canal at a diagonal. Beyond, a group of boys played in the unlighted street.

I glanced back uneasily in the direction of my hotel, and the second girl misinterpreted the look.

"Oh, not hotel," she said. "Bad for us. Security there don't

like us. Beat us up. Very bad for us if we go there. You come
with us now," she said, sidling up to me. The first girl pulled me
into the shadows and began to caress me, while the second threw
her arms around my shoulders to kiss my neck.

I tried to pull away gently, but the grip she had on my shoulders
was like a vise. "*Belum,*" I said freeing myself. The scent of strong
perfume hung in the air.

"You come back, mister," the second girl said. It sounded less
like a come-on than a veiled threat.

After dinner I met them again, so I hurriedly crossed Jalan
Thamrin, only to be confronted by others. "You go with me to
park, mister." I flagged a cab to my hotel.

As I was being measured for shirts at my hotel the morning
after that encounter, I explained to the shirtmaker what had happened the evening before, having already guessed what she
told me.

"They were *bancis,*" she said matter-of-factly. "Women in the
bodies of men who in turn become women. They alone have that
portion of the city. They can be very dangerous," she continued,
"but not if you treat them right. But foreigners often make the
mistake of causing them trouble. More than one man has been
stabbed to death in that park. They look weak and feminine, but
they can be very strong."

I remembered the grip on my shoulders when I had tried to
free myself. That there had been no pimps cruising about on
motorcycles keeping watch over their charges should have alerted
me, but I had never before encountered so convincing a mas-
querade.

"Many men in Jakarta prefer them to women," the shirtmaker
continued, "and these are men who are not homosexual. A friend
of mine who quarreled with his wife would always go with the
bancis because he said the sex was much better than with women."

To be sure there is something of the epicene in Malay beauty,
which could account for the success of the imposture. The tradition

of the theater is deeply rooted in Javanese as in other Asian cultures, a factor that might have accounted for the elaborate transvestism. There were signals of self-parodying camp about the bancis. A yearly beauty pageant was held for them in Jakarta, with the winner crowned by the mayor.

Like any ancient capital and trade center, Jakarta had adapted itself to improvement through the time-honored rhythms of destruction and modernization, of change through loss. In daylight the vestiges of Dutch colonialism in the old city of Batavia seemed distant from the clamor and concerns of the present. Yellowed public buildings dating from the seventeenth century were either boarded up or converted into museums with little to distinguish their collections. The old opera house had found use as a theater for *wayang*, or puppet shows, an ancient Javanese art form, but in the main these buildings were scarcely more than skeletal ruins, belying any notion that Jakarta was intent on rediscovery of its Dutch heritage. That European legacy seemed an empty one, and Batavia's main square, where executions had taken place in colonial days, was filled with chuckholes and detritus.

Stan introduced me to a restaurant run by a retired Dutch merchant mariner who enjoyed telling stories. Old pictures and colonial memorabilia decorating the walls suggested a nostalgia that was largely confined to this eatery and the old man's own selective memory. "We were not like the British Raj in India," he admitted one evening over a Dutch pan-fried steak. "We were terrible colonizers. We bled the people and left them nothing."

Beyond petty governing, the occasional but bloody "pacification," and the gains achieved through trade, the Dutch colonial attitude toward the Malays was one of indifference, and after independence Malay ways supplanted those of the Dutch. The old Dutch drawbridge of Batavia became the Chicken Market Bridge, and remained so when I crossed it. At the ancient port of Sunda Kelapa, schooners lined the wharf, off-loading timber from Kalimantan and awaiting cargoes of sugar and flour. Wiry men suspended by rope slings patched hulls with new planking driven home with wooden pegs. Hawkers roamed the wharf selling contraband bottles of Christian Dior perfume and Johnnie Walker whisky, as well as different brands of black hair dye and a variety of creams to whiten the skin. Small wooden water-taxis ferried people between the trading vessels and the docks. But beyond the occasional Australian tourist, there were no Westerners to be seen.

I had my taxi driver stop at the Portuguese church dating from 1695 near the Kota railway station, and afterward at the All Saints Anglican Church, built in the 1820s not far from the great mosque. There was an old graveyard at each sanctuary, and the passage of so many years lent both structures a faded authority in their unlikely setting. The windows were made of hand-painted glass, the work of World War II British POWs interned at the Japanese camp near the port.

In Jakarta one legacy of the colonial experience was the flea market. Its current liveliness derived less from Dutch example than from the Malay's own inbred proclivity for trade. Scores of shops selling faux and genuine antiques and objets d'art lined one side of the street for nearly a mile on a long side street called Jalan Surabaya. I bargained for and bought an old Sumatran calendar, carved in Sanskrit on a piece of buffalo bone, as well as a wooden buffalo bell from Madura.

In the Malay Archipelago bargaining was a way of life. A transaction was, of course, the purpose of bargaining, but the process itself was no less important. It whiled away time, entertained participants and bystanders alike, and cemented relations. In my own negotiations for my purchases, I countered the original asking price with an offer so absurdly low that the merchant whooped with laughter and called his compeers to share the glee.

But despite the satisfaction gained from the elaborate gamesmanship, emotions were always close to the surface when you bargained. Later in my trip I would inadvertently cause a fistfight between two becak drivers because I broke off negotiations with one of them prematurely and accepted his rival's fare.

A strange thing happened as I prepared to leave the flea market. A commotion erupted across the street, and I walked over where a circle of onlookers had gathered. In its center was a live, coiled, twelve-foot python. One of the two handlers opened a plastic sack, and out slid a Sumatran black cobra, its hood spread. Fearful cries and near-panic ensued as the circle quickly dispersed. It was an unnerving sight, the agitated snake swaying back and forth as if to strike, but the reptiles were handled coolly and carefully by their keepers, for they were to be sold live for their skins and butchered on the spot.

In another section of town, birds were to be seen by the thousands at the bird market. Birds were loved by the Malays, who valued them for their plumage and song. The bird market was a hodgepodge of board and corrugated-tin huts where caged birds from all over the archipelago were for sale. One man tried to sell me a beautiful green, orange-beaked parrot from Irian Jaya; I had scarcely declined when the rare creature was bought by an old woman. There was a lively trade going. The air was filled with birdsong and feathers, and cats prowled. People lived here and were preparing meals, the smell of meat over a brazier crossed with the rancid air. It had been overcast all day, and the nauseous odors hung in the sullen humidity until a shower cleared the air.

My taxi driver on my return to the hotel was a loquacious English-speaker. "What do you think about Suharto? The news?" he said.

"What news is that?" I had read the morning papers but had seen nothing extraordinary.

"The corruption. He is a very bad man, like his predecessor," the driver said, pointing to the National Monument, which we were now circling, a towering monolith with a gilt flame at the top erected by Sukarno. Rumor had it that Sukarno had been a womanizer, and jokes about this four-hundred-foot phallus were legion. "You see that shopping center?" the taxi driver continued, pointing ahead. "It is owned by Suharto's son. And his wife? She owns everything."

The rapacity of Madame Tien Suharto and her children is well known. The first lady was known for years as Madame Tien Percent, though in recent years that title was supplanted by Madame Fifty-fifty. Development of the presidential family holdings in Jakarta proceeded with a vengeance, twenty-four hours a day, as though the city were preparing for a siege.

Royal vision could assume odd and immodest forms. While Imelda Marcos had built her opera house in Manila, Madame Tien Suharto's imagination and wealth led her to a more ambitious and nationalistic enterprise at Taman Mini Indonesia Indah.

Conceived in 1971 and opened in 1975 after the expulsion of thousands of families and construction costs of $26 million, this park southeast of the city was nothing less than a replica in miniature of the nation of Indonesia. Each of the twenty-seven provinces was represented by a traditional house, and museums featured handicrafts as well as life-sized mannequins wearing native dress. There were restaurants, cable cars, and other amusement-park accoutrements that enticed city families to spend a day in the country, including a miniature Borobudur, the great Buddhist temple of Central Java dating from the eighth century.

But the park was more than a Malay Disneyland. The most bizarre and revealing feature was a large lake containing miniature islands of the archipelago, done to scale. Here you could travel from Sumatra to Irian Jaya by rowboat, and, figuratively speaking, visit all the Malay Islands in an afternoon.

I struck up a conversation in English with a middle-aged family man, who wanted to know what islands I was to visit in the archipelago. I told him I was heading east across Java to Bali and then Nusa Tenggara, or the Southeastern Islands.

"I have been there," he said quite seriously, gesturing to the likenesses of Nusa Tenggara that seemed to float like giant, odd-shaped water lilies on the placid surface.

When I stood on the counterfeit Java, I decided it was time to leave the paradoxical lunacies of Jakarta.

Java and Bali:
West to East

*A*T 4:30 THE NEXT AFTERNOON, on the tenth day of Ramadan, the *Mutiara Utara*, or "Pearl of the North," buckled, then snaked out of Jakarta's Kota Station bound for Surabaya, the capital of East Java, five hundred miles across the island. I was assigned seat 3A near the window. An aisle seat next to me was missing. The wafting odor of mandarin oranges and the clove-scented cigarette smoke were nearly suffocating. The trash pail attached to the bulkhead at my feet overflowed with litter, and the catch on my red vinyl seat was broken, so that it bucked like a colt. The air-conditioning was on the blink, and the window wouldn't budge. The "Pearl of the North." I looked around and saw that I was the only one perspiring, the only Westerner.

Across the aisle two barefoot teenaged girls were eating fruit and spitting the seeds on the floor. One picked at her painted toenails. The woman in front of me smoked while reading a magazine article titled "SEXUM." A boy passed peddling Indonesian newspapers, followed by another selling unrefrigerated drinks. I selected a plastic bottle of "Golden Mississippi Mountain Spring Water" and passed up the tray of tea, coffee, and fried bananas.

Through the window I watched Jakarta's squalid fringes pass. A goat the size of a house cat foraged among heaps of garbage, while naked children played by the tracks. Nearly an hour passed before the endless mud and thatch huts with red tile roofs, punctuated by mosques, gave way to flat farmland, where scarecrows guarded irrigated rice fields portioned off by shallow, muddy waterways. Beyond were the mountains, but it was already too dark to see.

In the hot, full dining car I was seated with the only other Westerners on the *Mutiara Utara:* two Australian lesbians with outrageously red hair worn in the punk style and preposterous earrings, who were talking with a lovely Javanese girl in Bahasa Indonesia. These ladies had no ear for the intruder as they focused on the beauty beside me. A waiter served up a cold meal of soup, rice, and curried chicken, which I washed down with warm beer. Dessert was a can of Dole fruit cocktail opened by the waiter and poured into a beer mug containing dirty ice, which I declined.

I returned to my seat. Snubbed by the Aussie women, I resolved to practice my Bahasa Indonesia. It is a comparatively simple tongue with no tenses and an uncomplicated syntax. Sleep was out of the question with my seat shifting constantly back and forth like a rowing machine, so I made ready to spend the night with my phrase book and dictionary as we rocked through the Java darkness. As I studied, strange shadows flitted across the pages. I looked overhead to see moths with wings the size of both my hands shuddering around the neon tubing. What chimeric cocoon could they have emerged from?

The air-conditioning was now working, and it chilled my perspiring body. A boy had passed earlier offering blankets and pillows for rent, and I was happy to spend the few hundred rupiah for the small comfort. The call to evening prayers erupted over the public-address system and was met with both piety and indifference. Sarong-clad women placed their mats in the aisle facing the rear of the train, undeterred by the cigarette butts and spillage of soft drinks that littered the floor. Huge cockroaches appeared everywhere. A boy two rows ahead wore a headset and listened to rock music while the prostrate faithful prayed in the aisle. After prayers, when the worshipers returned to their seats, they fell asleep in a tangle of positions.

I stepped through the litter to visit the toilet at the head of the car. There was a sink with no running water, a commode that could not be flushed, and the stench of stale urine everywhere. The room was made for people smaller than I, which made aiming difficult and closing the door impossible, but an empty bladder was its own reward. Outside, between cars, the odor was even stronger, suggesting that unused exits were suitable for squatting as well. Wads of sodden pink toilet paper decorated the dark steps.

"Can you not sleep?" I looked up to see the boy with the headset. He was short and slight, and his dark face was only inches above my own.

"I'm practicing your language."

"My name is Rusmana. You are *belanda?*"

"No, I'm from America, not Holland."

"Ah, Amer-i-ka." His eyes took on a funny cast as if he were trying to imagine America. "Then you will play cards with me in the dining car. Dominoes? Marbles? How old are you? Guess how old I am."

I declined his invitations and answered each of his questions in turn. Satisfied, he vanished. The exchange couldn't have lasted more than a minute. Such benign confrontations, marked by bald curiosity and a convoluted logic dictated by the number of English phrases the conversant had mastered, would be commonplace on my trip.

Some of the stations the *Mutiara* rocketed past were so dimly lit as to seem like apparitions, their names exotic subtitles in an unreeling documentary of dreams: Karawang, Indramayu, Cirebon, Pemalang, Pekalongan. When we stopped, it was never for more than a few moments, but always long enough to allow station vendors to invade the cars. Even at Semarang, the large port city of Central Java, the frantic movement, loading and unloading amid the cries of merchants, lasted all of five minutes before the abrupt scream of the whistle and the lurch forward.

The *Mutiara Utara,* with its magnificently abundant filth, consigned romantic notions of trains to memory's quaint scrapbook. Yet, sipping scotch from my pocket flask as the hours ticked by, I finally was overcome by a perverse enjoyment of my circumstances. The train clacked along with its own jazzy drum-and-bugle-corps rhythm. We were well into East Java.

Orange-uniformed female attendants were now passing through the car, collecting rupiah for the snacks and drinks whose remnants littered the floor. If Indonesian Muslims fast during the day, they make up for it by feasting at night, especially just before sunup. I settled for a hard-boiled egg and strong coffee.

First light broke over the rice paddies just before five, and by half past workers treaded the dikes, looking like ghosts in the mist as they left their villages for the fields. The early-morning light had a feathery quality to it, unlike the harsh sun of day, and the lines of trees were reflected in the water as in an inverted Monet canvas. Everything was refracted through the mist. Six white herons rose over the water; they belonged on an ancient Chinese scroll. All of a sudden, after a long, sleepless night, the world seemed full of hope. Thirty minutes more and we would arrive at Surabaya.

Though I was far from Surabaya Johnny's waterfront, I tried to picture the city of Kurt Weill's song and imagined it a place of animal curiosity crossed with seething intrigue. Apart from the exotic ring of the name, I wondered whether Weill's collaborator, Bertolt Brecht, had appropriated Surabaya's mellifluous four syllables because it suited the mood of his music.

At the Joyoboyo bus terminal, as much an open-air bazaar as a station, I took an eastbound bus, and by 9:30, under a blazing sun, we rolled out of the station to reach open country. On both sides of the road, terraced rice fields shimmered in the light, many of them worked by men and women waist-deep in water and mud. Gunung Bromo, a volcano whose vast crater resembled a steaming lunar landscape, its peak shrouded in cloud and smoke, presided over a scene that provided a clue to Java's past.

Before recorded history, waves of people migrated from the Southeast Asian mainland to establish rice-growing communities on this island, whose exceptional fertility was nurtured by its many active volcanoes. Highly sophisticated systems of irrigation developed, requiring the cooperation of villages that eventually evolved into Hindu and Buddhist kingdoms, whose vestiges were the temples of the Dieng Highlands, Prambanan, and Borobudur of Central Java. By the fourteenth century one such kingdom, the Majapahit, had expanded its sphere of influence beyond Java to much of the archipelago. With the arrival of Islam in the fifteenth and sixteenth centuries came the subjugation of independent principalities and the rise of the Mataram kingdom in Central and Eastern Java. By the end of the eighteenth century the Dutch ruled nearly all the island, largely through the Javanese aristocracy, who were given a measure of autonomy as regents in the European administration. Today Java is one of the most densely populated places in the world, with one hundred million people in an area the size of Ireland.

"Are you going to Bali?" A dark, saturnine young man seated beside me spoke in halting English.

"I'll be passing through Bali on my way to points east."

"I do not go to Bali," he said. "The people there are Hindu-Buddhists. They eat pigs, which is forbidden because they are unclean animals. I am a Muslin. And you?"

"A Christian, but somewhat of a stray sheep."

He looked puzzled. "Catholic?"

"Anglican."

"Then you are English, not Dutch."

"American."

"Ah, Amer-i-kan." He seemed to seize on my nationality and took the idea of America with him when he got off in the next village. But something else struck me, a notion that I would see confirmed time and again. Indonesian Muslims, while they differ greatly in degrees of militancy across a broad spectrum of cultures and languages, are not proselytizers. "And what do your Christians in America think of our Muhammed?" That question, put to me months later in Banda Aceh on the western tip of Sumatra by a student, was prompted more by genuine curiosity than messianic zeal.

By contrast, in neighboring Malaysia, Islam commands that proselytizing is a sacred duty. Once when I visited a mosque in Georgetown on Penang Island, off the west coast of the Malaysian peninsula, a half dozen pious souls clad in white gowns and embroidered skullcaps tried to bring me into the Islamic fold. Among them were two students and the state executioner, a grizzled man with a stubble of beard who was performing his evening ablutions in preparation for his gruesome duty at the gallows the following morning. The condemned man was a convicted drug dealer. "Your laws in the West have no teeth in them," I was told. "They cannot implement justice."

The road first followed the coastline, which thrust south and then east, then the road turned from the north shore and plunged southward through a narrow part of Java to the inland city of Jember, where I would change buses. Despite its proximity to Surabaya and Bali, the country through which we passed seemed wonderfully remote. Its pristine cultivated fields and surrounding mountains set off by the diamond brilliance of the sun gave the landscape an overwhelming greenness, alternating with patches of blue sky reflected in the flooded paddies.

The vivid colors were lent a somber cast by the extraordinary number of mosques—two and often three in the smallest kampung. Though their roofs were tiled, the walls were often an ugly corrugated tin; the Islamic moon and star conjoined at the roof's apex, inevitably paired with the cones of loudspeakers, whose wires dangled like a wisp of chin hairs to a generator below.

The field workers wore sarongs and the conical straw hats typical in rural Southeast Asia. But in the villages and at the roadside, men and boys wore the traditional crisp black, brimless hat, the *kopiah*. One man in such a hat boarded and wordlessly shared my seat for the duration of his fifteen-minute ride. In his lap he caressed lovingly a fighting cock, which responded with an occasional soft cluck. Trussed goats and chickens were commonplace on the bus. The dress of the younger Javanese women passengers was fastidious: ankle-length sarongs, sashes, and bodices displaying their soft curves, and raven hair in buns highlighting dark, chiseled faces with a touch of elegance and peasant hauteur.

One diminutive young woman boarded with a basket of oranges and stood near my seat for her short ride. She was barefoot, her sarong and loose smock-like top were in tatters, and her hair was as wild as a gypsy's. She spoke to her companion, an older woman, resignedly and rapidly in a dialect that bore no resemblance to Bahasa Indonesia, pausing only to spit periodically on the floor of the bus.

Though Indonesian women were unconstrained by the purdah of the Middle East, they were nonetheless subservient to men. After one stop I saw the conductor order two women out of their seats so that a lone businessman could sit and open his briefcase. The command met with no resistance.

Our route through the fertile valleys took us across a network of streams and rivers, where women, often with their breasts bare, bathed and washed clothes. On Bali that rural picture would be as common as a postcard, but in East Java, with its reputation for Islamic zeal, this stripping for a bath in the open seemed a flouting of Muslim custom, if not law. For me, it was another reminder that the great faiths that had invaded the corners of Indonesia over the centuries were as opaque as the dark rivers in which these women bathed. The real currents were the contrary ones at work beneath the surface, which one never saw but sensed were there.

When we pulled into the depot at a place called Lumajang, it was noon. I got off for a stretch but decided not to stray far. It was to be a ten-minute stop but lasted more like thirty. Dust rose in the air. No one spoke English, though the curious but friendly onlookers followed me to a vendor, from whom I managed with my phrase book to buy a few mandarin oranges and bottled water. Thereafter, I was converged upon by hawkers attempting to sell me everything under the sun, from Indonesian newspapers I could not read to leaf-wrapped fried bananas I did not want. One boy even implored me to buy a paperback titled *How To Speak English Book.*

Conversation, such as I was able to manage in Bahasa Indonesia, revolved around entwined themes, with many recurring variations. Why, as a white man, was I not going to stay in Bali? All *orang barat* (Westerners) vacationed on Bali. Why not you, *tuan*? You don't like tourists? You don't like your own people? When I told the group that I was from "Amer-i-ka," there was an eruption of spontaneous applause. A horn blast announced the bus departure for Jember. A little girl touched my skin in wonderment. I boarded to find the conductor sprawled across my seat, saving it for me.

Jember was a city of a million Javanese and Madurese deep in the East Java heartland. With two hours to kill before my bus would leave for the ferry port of Banyuwangi on the eastern tip of the island, I took an orange *bemo,* one of many that plied the road between the bus terminal and town, a fifteen-minute ride. A bemo is an undersized van whose rear doors open like those on an ambulance to allow passengers to enter and face each other on wooden benches, knees interlocking. If my fellow passengers were flattered and amused at my attempted small talk in Bahasa Indonesia, they were hilarious over the rivulets of sweat that ran down my face.

"*Panas!*" said one toothless old man, pointing to my brow.

"*Panas,*" I agreed. Hot.

I turned to see what I could of the city we were entering. In the harsh light, the main avenue was wide, paved, and pockmarked, bisected by intermittent islands of scruffy grass that served as sterile bases for the grossly proportioned monuments in the style of Soviet socialist realism. The uncovered sidewalks were broken in places, and the buildings that faced them were rarely taller than two stories. The streets were busy with the traffic of push-bike becaks and pony-drawn *dokars*, small two-wheeled carts for hire.

I got out and walked through the blazing heat in the direction of the main square. Except for the vehicle-for-hire drivers, who dozed in the shade of trees and sidewalk awnings when they weren't hustling fares, most of the people remained indoors. Jember seemed more a town than a city. I would have guessed its population at most to be upwards of fifty thousand rather than a million, but Indonesians lived close together, and in big families. The government was waging a national campaign, largely unsuccessful, that stressed a maximum of two children per married couple.

It was not difficult to distinguish between the peoples of Java and Madura, the island that guarded Surabaya's harbor. The Madurese, numbering close to a half million in Jember alone, were darker and stronger and spoke their own dialect. The becak and dokar drivers were mostly Madurese, as were most of the manual laborers. I had heard that the Javanese scorned them as uncouth, while the darker tribe prided themselves on their devoutness as Muslims.

At one corner a group of young Javanese men were speaking in rapid dialect and in obvious hilarity, the butt of their japes a group of snoozing drivers sprawled together in a spot of shade across the street. Even my untrained ear could appreciate the singsong cadences, meaning conveyed through inflection, and the reliance upon repetition for emphasis.

"They're talking about the Madurese," said a male voice beside me, chuckling, "what lesser folk they are and how boorish and stupid they sound when they try to speak Javanese." I turned to see a scholarly-looking man at my elbow. He listened bemusedly, then gave me in English the sense behind the sound. From that I was able to concoct the following free translation of a rapid-fire, multi-voiced exercise in self-congratulation:

The Madurese are not so quick-witted as we;
No, to be sure they lack quickness of wit.
They are not so smart or clever;
Indeed they are not, and neither do they please their women;
Their women prefer us to their own savages.
Is it not so? And do the Madurese speak well?
Hah! They speak not well.
The Madurese do not speak good, nor do they bathe;
I do not lie to you: Their women prefer clean, manly men.
The Madurese women lie on their backs for a Javanese man;
Hah! They should be so lucky to be served with a real cock.
And the Madurese wear short pants, surely an affront to God;
And they grunt the sacred Koran like a pig.
What are we then to make of all this, my brothers?
The Madurese are stupid motherfuckers!

Though Jember was a provincial city, it offered a sampling of consumer chic. For every mosque I passed, there was a cinema that featured kung fu movies. Unisex hair parlors outnumbered markets, and each block featured several cassette tape shops blaring imitative country and western music bred with rock, sung in nymphet voices that were a weird amalgam of Madonna, Dolly Parton, and Diana Ross.

Jember was no place to linger. I passed an hour at a restaurant run by a wretched Chinese doyenne who was in a foul mood, braying orders to the Malay waitresses and two young handymen who were carrying successive loads of bricks into the kitchen. When she stepped out of the room the young men fell to arguing. After an exchange of insults, one seized a piece of wood, the other armed himself with a pole, and the duel would have commenced at my table had the waitresses not screamed. The Chinese woman rushed into the room and shot me a look of cold contempt as if I had started the row.

"Up yours, madam," I said as pleasantly as I could manage.

"U' Yosh," she responded, beaming.

Outside I hailed a bemo bound for the bus terminal.

The bus from Jember east to Banyuwangi tore along through the mountains, the road paralleling the rail line that circumvented the volcanoes Raung and Merapi. It was a jolting three-hour afternoon trip through a succession of market towns. Our driver negotiated hairpin turns with heedless aggression, passing on blind curves and inviting near-collisions.

Similar abandon caused at least one tragedy that I witnessed that afternoon. At the kampung of Sempai, we waited for an angry mob to move out of the right-of-way and saw a motorcycle in mid-road squashed flat as a soda can, its rider killed and his fellow villagers gone amok, screaming, smelling blood. The guilty truck driver was protected from the mob by armed police, who waved our vehicle past.

It was nearly dusk when the bus pulled into the station at Banyuwangi on Java's eastern tip. From there it was a few kilometers by bemo to the small port of Ketapang, where the ferry crossed the narrow strait to Gilimanuk on the western tip of Bali. The ferry accommodated vehicles as well as passengers and departed every twenty minutes, but this run resembled a ghost ship, transporting only a small truck and a handful of men, most of whom worked on the boat. In the canteen above deck the crew watched a blaring television featuring a wild crime melodrama of Japanese import, dubbed in English and subtitled in Bahasa Indonesia. I quenched my thirst with a half-chilled Sprite and walked onto the rear deck, where it was cool from the breezes funneling down the ribbon of sea.

As the ferry cut a southeasterly wake, I could see without benefit of moonlight a portion of both Java and Bali. Java was studded with village lights, and the wailing of evening prayers trailed the ferry to mid-channel, when the roar of the engine drowned out the cries. Bali loomed in darkness and mystery except for the dimly lit port we approached. Bali had once been a part of Java, but during the last glacial period the sea had risen, creating a strait two hundred feet deep and two miles across.

The Bali Strait was a truth confirmed for natives not by science but through countless retellings of myths. Many thousands of years ago, one legend went, a powerful Javanese priest sent his libertine son into exile in Bali, then connected to Eastern Java by a narrow isthmus. The distraught father then drew a line across the sands, causing the waters to meet and making the banishment absolute. That the father grieved over his loss—as David over Absalom—was given much weight in the story.

This curious reversal of the expulsion from the Garden of Eden—Adam and Eve were banished from the garden, but this dissolute young man was driven to it—was only the first paradox about an island as enriched by paradox as its cascading rice fields were enriched by volcanic ash.

A violent reversal of engines and churning of water announced that we were arriving in Gilimanuk. My plan was to catch the next bus to Denpasar, Bali's capital, in the south-central part of the island. It was at most a three-hour journey, and I would be rewarded at its termination by a late supper and a good night's sleep.

The scene, or lack of it, was strange. No local transportation greeted the ferry, and my few fellow passengers had disappeared in the darkness. It was disconcerting.

The moon had still not risen. In the darkness I began walking up the narrow, cobbled way toward the lighted houses. A boy passed me in a donkey-drawn dokar; I hailed him, paying a few cents for the short ride. The station was quiet without the usual belching of engines and hawking for fares. Bemos and minibuses were parked with no drivers attending them. I could see the lighted cigarettes before I saw the groups of men. They stood around or squatted in small circles, talking and spitting, and when they noticed me they converged.

"Where you want to go?"

"Denpasar."

"No minibus tonight, Mister."

"Why not?"

"Tomorrow."

"I want to go tonight."

"I take you for forty thousand rupiah," said one man clad in jeans and a T-shirt. It was an extortionate sum, twenty-five dollars.

"I'll pay you ten thousand."

"Haaaag." He snorted, spat, and walked away, obviously in no mood to bargain. An earnest young man then explained that the last scheduled minibus departed at six o'clock and the next would leave at six in the morning. I had unwittingly lost an hour because of a time change between the two ferry ports. Six o'clock on Bali was the hour just before sunset; the young man's logic suggested that as long as a journey commenced before darkness descended, all would be well. A journey after darkness could bring bad luck. That night would come almost immediately after getting under way seemed to have no place in the equation.

Spending the night in Gilimanuk was the last thing I wanted. The hotel a few yards away was a decrepit, noisy, and expensive bungalow. Beyond lay the village, consisting of smoking *warung*, or food stalls, a couple of restaurants, and a few *losmen*, or guest houses, where a bed and bath could be bought for the night.

The driver who had approached me earlier returned. "You no stay here. Expensive and dirty." He spat. "See minibus?" He pointed to a parked vehicle with two matronly women sitting in the rear. "When full ten people, minibus go to Denpasar. You pay twenty-five thousand rupiah, we go now. You pay one person, five thousand rupiah, minibus waits till full."

"How long will that be?"

He shrugged. "Maybe two hours, maybe morning."

I walked over to the vehicle and spoke to the two women in my mangled Indonesian, then returned.

"They paid two thousand rupiah apiece, and that's what I'll pay." I lifted my shoulder bags out of the dust and began walking toward the village, passing dokars in the darkness. Perhaps I could hitch a ride to Denpasar—but how could I if there was no traffic? The warungs and restaurants were fly-ridden and unappetizing, and the losmen were overpriced. Clearly, the whole point of Gilimanuk was to exploit people in my predicament.

I had fruit in my bag that I'd bought en route. It would serve for a light supper, even breakfast if I stayed the night. But first I would relax over a beer at the cleaner of the two restaurants. The place was empty, except for the two dark, lean young men who ran it. One spoke passable English. He explained that they were brothers from West Sumatra and ran not only the restaurant but the adjoining losmen, where they would rent me a room with an attached *mandi* for three thousand rupiah. I had lingered over two large beers and now was resigned to staying the night in Gilimanuk.

The windowless room was the size of a prison cell and was illuminated by a single light bulb that dangled ominously from the ceiling like a corpse from a gibbet. There were two rock-hard beds of unequal size, each covered by a single sheet. The sullen air was thick with mosquitoes, which gained entry through the high, open window in the mandi, the standard bathroom of sorts that you find all over Indonesia. The word means "wash," noun and verb; you pour water over yourself from a waist-high basin, using a bucket-like scoop. The water escapes through a floor drain. You flush the toilet, a porcelain-ringed opening in the floor that you either straddle or stand before, by washing away waste using the same scoop. Inevitably, the porcelain was crusted with the residue of the countless travelers who had preceded me. An infantryman's slit trench was grand by comparison. I had paid two dollars for a fifty-cent room, and it smelled like shit.

The towel handed me by one of the boys was filthy, so I dried myself with a pillowcase, which was not much cleaner. Outside, I padlocked the door, and at the shipping crate serving as a reception desk in the next room I completed the forms required by the police: name, nationality, passport number, date of birth, et cetera. Then

I went in search of beer to put me in better humor for the long night ahead.

In the road I was approached by a familiar figure on a motorcycle, the driver who had earlier tried to enlist me for his extortionate run to Denpasar. Gunning his motor, he drove around me in figure eights.

"Hey, Mister Walk-Walk, minibus full," he jeered, obviously thinking that I had reconsidered his offer and was returning to the station.

"Go to hell. I'm staying here." I *am* staying here, I told myself. People do not visit Bali to stay in Gilimanuk, and yet I was staying. The simple realization sent me into a perverse existential ecstasy: if this was my lot for the night, make the best of it. At a vendor's I bought large bottles of beer and a pack of the clove-scented cigarettes known as *kretek*. I had not smoked since the Marine Corps, but I was both curious to try this distinctly Indonesian product and, more practically, intent on repelling mosquitoes, whatever it took. The kreteks would become a mild addiction, and I would enjoy two or three of an evening for the rest of my trip.

At the losmen the boy gave me a mosquito coil, which I lit and placed at the foot of my bed. I had mosquito netting in my duffel and some cord, but the bare walls afforded no place to rig a protective tent. I stripped, covered myself with Muskol, dressed, and sprayed my clothes with the repellent. It was sweltering in my cell, but I ate some fruit, swallowed my week's ration of anti-malaria tablets, smoked, drank, and by the ominous light hanging high overhead read snatches of Conrad's *An Outcast of the Islands*, feeling outcast myself and strangely enjoying it as the malt took effect. Indonesia's patrimony from the Dutch was breweries.

Throughout the night people in the street hooted, shouted, gunned motorcycle engines, and played bastardized rock on ear-shattering radios. At four in the morning, Muslim prayers carried by loudspeakers wafted across the water from Java. At least on Hindu Bali I should be spared that.

A sleepless night, but I felt narcotized by the whining chants crossed with the buzzing of mosquitoes, followed by a feeling of weird exhilaration, as though my spirit were shedding its cocoon. The light overhead now seemed hypnotic rather than a presage of trouble. I knew this sort of lunatic epiphany would pass and my spirit would shrink back into its lair. Even so, from that moment I was no longer a reluctant traveler. The traveler takes it as it comes, banal but true, I repeated to myself.

Five o'clock was cockcrow. I rose, washed, made ready for the day. Shortly after six, I stood in the road and hailed a minibus bound for Denpasar, piloted by a grinning driver. The fare for the three-hour trip was a little less than a dollar, and I was squeezed into the shotgun seat beside the driver in deference to my long legs.

"Okay, Big Boss?" said the conductor.

"Okay."

"Big Boss Mister Walk-Walk?" His question recalled for me the taunting driver of the evening before.

"*Tuan Jalan-Jalan,*" I translated, and this amused him. "When do we reach Denpasar?"

He laughed and shrugged. "*Jam karet.*" This was another indispensable expression. Literally "rubber time,"it meant in this case that we would arrive when we arrived. We were off, and the motion began to make me drowsy. I slept.

A hand shook my shoulder gently, and I awoke with a start. The minibus had stopped, and I was the only passenger remaining.

"Okay, Big Boss Mister Walk-Walk. Denpasar bus."

I looked around. We were stopped in a town called Mendaya, and beside us was parked a larger bus. A group of women, their sarongs vividly colored, stood around preparing to board, with baskets of fruit and other produce balanced on their heads. It was clear what had happened. The minibus was accustomed to covering the stretch of road between here and Gilimanuk, and unless it had a full complement of passengers to make it worthwhile to continue on to Denpasar, it would begin the return run here. The arrangement was obviously routine, because the conductor on the larger bus motioned to me. I had not yet paid, and he would collect my fare when I got on. I checked my watch and glanced at my map. It was 7:30, and we were only a third of the way to Denpasar. The road ahead looked to be a fine one, free of settlements and following the gentle curve of the coastline before turning inland and eastward to the capital.

I was now awake and alert. *"Selamat jalan,"* I said in farewell to my former conductor, a cheerful fellow, and *"Selamat pagi,"* to greet my new one, a dour man, as I climbed the steps with my shoulder bags. There was an empty double seat over one of the rear wheels which I quickly claimed. *Selamat* has its origins in Arabic and is a blessing. When conjoined with other words, it can mean any number of things: in the first instance above, "May your journey be blessed," and in the second simply "Good morning," with strong connotations of the roles that fate and fortune are bound to play in the morning's outcome.

The bus coasted along the southwest shore, making infrequent stops during which I could hear as well as see the huge breakers plunging down on beaches unprotected by offshore reefs. Inland, terraced rice fields sculpted from a fertile valley created a patchwork of vivid greens that rose to meet the mountains. Such a scene, on the face of it, contradicted the skepticism I had brought to Bali on this trip. The reports from the Ministry of Tourism published in a Jakarta paper before I had left that city had proudly announced that by 1990 the number of hotel rooms on the island would have doubled. Bali had become Australia's playground, and its promotion as a cultural entity and tropical paradise was ludicrously disproportionate to the promotion of the rest of the Malay Archipelago.

Now, traversing Bali by bus, it was impossible not to have ambivalent feelings about the island. To appreciate its beauty in spite of the corruption that had arrived with Western European, Japanese, and Australian tourism required more than a determined suspension of disbelief. You went to Bali programmed to experience paradise on earth. Yet there was something theatrical, if not operatic, about the experience. I had once spent a month on Bali and knew that.

Every traditional Balinese story or song, especially when played out in ritual, served to enhance the island's exotic singularity. Its resplendency of natural beauty, history, myth, all were intricately interwoven into a culture like no other, or so tourist brochures claimed. In many but not all ways Bali was a honeyed charade, ingratiating itself with the aggressive taster of exotic sweets, fostering a forced enjoyment of the bogus.

When seen from the Bali Sea north of the island, the luminous-green, mountainous landscape, a profusion of clouds bathing its two volcanic peaks, suggested in its eternal summer a vast distance from the outside world. But to the islanders Bali *was* the world. One legend placed it at the center of a fixed universe, encircled by a malevolent sea of which the natives still remained fearful. It was a rare fisherman, working the lagoons at low tide in his sailboat, who could swim. Such keen respect for Indonesian waters was widespread and not merely superstition, for the remoter reaches of the archipelago harbored certain terrors: the lethal sea snake and the occasional but awesome saltwater crocodile, not to mention the ubiquitous shark. Indeed, the Balinese looked not seaward but landward and upward to gaze at the volcanic peak Gunung Agung, which they called "the navel of the world."

The bus ride was undeniably beautiful as it followed the coast road. As we drove under the midmorning sun, the land resembled a great, glimmering, rough-textured bolt of silk whose deeper folds were not yet illuminated. Ducks bathed and fed in flooded rice fields. Harvesters in the distance moved as if choreographed. This was country Cézanne would have painted.

It was ten o'clock when the bus pulled into the station at Denpasar, a noisy, busy metropolis landlocked in the middle of Bali's southern peninsula.

Kuta lay to the west. An infamous little seaside town, it boasted mighty waves revered among surfers, a celebrated sunset, and a lively nightlife; and young tourists, especially from Australia, flew there in droves.

I hailed a bemo. It was packed, mostly with women, but somehow the conductor squeezed me aboard. I was forced by the sheer weight of bodies pressed against mine, as well as the strain of having to balance my unwieldy shoulder bags, to gaze at a cleavage the color of creamed coffee four inches away. A trussed fowl hung from the handrail above me, forcing me to bend my head until my forehead nearly rested on the nape of the woman's neck. With every pothole, swerve, and jolt, the fleshy orbs of her breasts trembled. Sweating profusely, I raised my eyes to see her two female companions, who sat across from me, enjoying my discomfiture. When at last I was able to see the woman's face, fetchingly mature, she shot me a great bold look of amused sensuality, telling me that her appreciation of my embarrassment was keenest of the three. The two younger women might well have been her daughters. Lewd the woman was not, but her openness in acknowledging her assets, accentuated by the traditional low-cut bodice, spoke of a womanliness rarely encountered in the West.

Such facility with the silent language of sensuality would prevail on my travels all through the Malays, from Sumatra to Irian Jaya, from backwater villages to cities on the ancient trade routes that had evolved over a thousand years.

I breakfasted at a garden restaurant. Over carrot juice, yogurt with fruit, and strong coffee, I read a two-day-old *International Herald Tribune*. Nearby I rented a bungalow for the night.

Kuta was a rat's nest of a place. The sunsets were spectacular, as they inevitably are in this part of the world, but the beach was littered and dirty. Psychedelic mushrooms grown from cow droppings could be ordered in a lunch omelet at certain warungs. Brown women gave oily massages to pink bodies by day, but when the sun plummeted the ante was raised to include sexual service. After dark Kuta's streets smelled of sordidness, much like the Tijuana of 1959 after the bullfights, with that place's hawkers and hustlers.

You could see the gyrations of intercourse and fellatio performed warily, timed between police patrols.

Later that evening I returned to the restaurant for seafood. It was a lively place filled with Westerners and Japanese, all sunburned and high-spirited in the lantern light, determinedly happy in their paradise. On a bulletin board near the rest rooms was posted a score of miscellaneous messages, including advertisements in English for cremations, tooth filings, and native song and dance programs at various temples, all for a hefty entrance fee. Westerners paid, Balinese did not, and the atmosphere at such ceremonies inevitably turned courtesan.

After dinner I walked Kuta's streets passing gewgaw stalls, offerings of burning incense, and nightspots with names like Sand Bar, Rum Jungle, Bombay Rock, and Rogues. I was accosted on every corner by pimps. I went into a noisy discotheque, whose entrance fee included two drinks. It was mobbed with gays and straights alike, mostly Australian. The surfers wore tank tops and cutoff jeans. The young women were large and ungainly compared to their Malay counterparts, many of them wearing tattoos and indistinguishable from the men in the agitated light save by the heavily muscled arms of the latter. It was not an unfriendly place, and I leaned against the bar and ordered a beer.

"Hey, mate, how's it going?" I felt an arm on my shoulder and turned to face a huge bearded fellow, with naked, hairy arms and legs, looking like a strange beast from the sea. Two round holes were cut out of his shirt to expose a shaved chest. Over one shriveled nipple was tattooed "sweet," over the other "sour," in small blue letters. "Do you love it here, mate?"

"I love it here," I said.

"Don't see too many Americans."

"They'll catch on soon enough." We had to shout to be heard.

"You're a game old cock," he said. "I can tell that. You like ladies? Military man?"

"Yes and sometime back."

"Deck ape here, mate. Lots of queers here. Know what Churchill said? 'Rum, sodomy, and the lash.' You're a game old cock. Game as Ned Kelly.''

''Who's Ned Kelly?''

''Who's Ned Kelly?'' His tone took on an edge of mock belligerence. ''Australian outlaw and folk hero. Police blasted his shanty with gunshot and burned the place down back in eighteen-eighty. Inside was old Ned alive and kicking and dressed in an iron suit. They tried and strung him up on the deadly nevergreen.''

''I'll remember Ned Kelly,'' I said.

''Be careful where you stick it, mate. Don't stick it anywhere I wouldn't. Here or anyplace else.''

I agreed that I wouldn't.

''I've drunk myself motherless, mate, and I wouldn't admit this to anybody but you. I screwed a tart who refused to remove her blouse. I was drunk for a week, so I don't know where it was. But she had no tits, so what did I care if she left her blouse on, right?''

''Right, but if she had no tits, it must've not been here.''

''No argument there, mate. It must have been Hong Kong. I picked the ugliest whore I could find. What do you know she turned out to be the mama-san of the house. Half Japanese and half Taiwanese with a face that looked like some bloke had poured boiling oil on her. I mean it was scalded, cockie. Said her torso and arms were burned worse, so she wouldn't undress. Fantastic sex though, mate, the whole bleeding works. Afterwards, and this is the funny part, I couldn't resist having a look at the rest of her. I mean my curiosity got the best of me, only I wished that it hadn't.''

''What do you mean?''

''I mean I grabbed both wrists with one hand and rolled back a sleeve with the other. Her arm was scarred to be sure, but with needle punctures, not boiling oil. The bitch was a junkie, mate.''

His red eyes searched out mine with a thousand-yard stare, betraying an abiding nocturnal terror at once reinforced and abated by drink.

''When did this happen?''

"This trip. I'm working my way back to Australia from England and taking a year to do it."

"Even if she was a carrier . . ."

"I know, mate," he overrode me. "I should have the fucking test and be done with it."

"Then at least you'd know."

"That's just it, mate, I don't want to know. I'm terrified to know. So don't stick it anywhere I wouldn't. Get my meaning." He clutched my shoulders in both hands and then tried to grab onto my shirt collar, dropping his hands in embarrassment when I resisted.

"Sorry, mate. Don't usually go to the bad for the shadow of an ass. I didn't intend any rough stuff."

"No offense taken. Let me buy you a drink."

"Come to my funeral, you with Jamie Duff."

I ordered the second beer due me and gave it to him.

"Thanks, mate." He gulped it down. "You're a good Yank bloke, the first I've bloody fucking well seen out here, cockie."

"I won't be the last. Good luck and take care," I said and made my way through the crowd toward the exit. It was a twenty-minute walk back to the hotel.

(Notes from a Diary) But there is another Bali in the hills to the north far from the din of Kuta. Late in the afternoon the fading light lends a blue cast to the patchwork of hills and rice fields, and the air smells of mountain freshness and incense. My driver stops before the elaborate brick entranceway of an ancient palace in the royal city of Amlapura, where the descendants of the last king of Bali live. A servant allows me through a gate and leads me to the inner sanctum, where a great wooden door hinged upon old stone pillars opens.

"Welcome," says Mark, a burly, friendly American in his thirties, dressed in a sarong and wearing flip-flops. "I'm glad you called."

Mark is in the fabric-importing business and met his wife, the granddaughter of the last king of Bali, ten years earlier while on a buying trip. The couple spend six months every year in California and six in the family compound at the palace. A mutual friend in San Francisco had urged me to call Mark.

I remove my shoes and follow him through the house and out onto a terrace overlooking the city. Far beneath us is a brown river dividing Amlapura, and on its opposite bank sits a mosque. City sounds are distant and muffled.

"Until forty years ago my wife's family owned as far as the eye could see, but Sukarno ended all that."

"I'm a little surprised to see that mosque," I say.

"My father-in-law allowed Bugis settlers from Lombok to build it," he says. "It's really quite out of place on Hindu Bali. Neighbors still complain about the noise. Promoting a religion over loudspeakers runs counter to Balinese ways. That's what they don't like, but there's no trouble, really."

"So you are able to spend a lot of time here now?" I ask.

"We'll be here for nearly six months," he says. "But since the baby came, we're thinking of moving here permanently. Actually, as much of our fabric business is here as in California, so there's really no problem. Come meet my family."

We pass onto an adjoining terrace, where I meet his wife, Sirah, and the couple's infant daughter, surrounded by little girls attempting to coax a smile. I sense immediately Mark's ease with the family and their customs, and his fluency with Balinese. While he mixes drinks of rum and Coke, I hear music, sliding silver sounds carried on the wind.

"What's that chimelike music?" I ask.

"Look up," says Mark.

A flock of pigeons flies overhead, darting this way and that in unison like swallows.

"It's an old tradition of the royal family. They're raised on the premises and belled to chime as they fly forth from that dovecote on the roof, early morning and late afternoon," he says.

"It's lovely."

The music in the air seems to summon visitors of all ages, who arrive in great numbers.

"It's sort of a family laying on of hands," says Mark. "My wife's relatives have come from all over the island to see the baby." He laughs. "All we need to complete the scene from my standpoint is a rabbi, but that can wait."

I meet Mark's father-in-law, a slender man with a kind face. Mark's mother-in-law is a faded beauty. Most arresting is a cousin, a family priest. He's a gregarious old man with a ready smile showing rotted teeth, and a cackle for a laugh.

"He has fifteen children and smokes three packs of kreteks a day," says Mark as I shake the old man's hand. I feel something akin to an electric charge, and I mention this to Mark.

"He's a powerful man," he says, "sort of a witch doctor," while the old man cackles in agreement. The house is now filled with gregarious people of all ages, whom Mark greets and introduces to me.

"Let me show you the old palace while they see the baby," he says later. "Bring your drink."

He leads me out the way I entered, pausing for a moment before a wall of photographs.

"This is my wife's grandfather with three of his wives," he says, pointing to a small old man in bare feet and a ceremonial jacket with a chest full of medals, surrounded by three young women. "Two of them are sisters from Lombok. They bore him a lot of children. He wanted to ensure proper dissemination of his seed."

"How many wives did he have in all?" I ask.

"Fifteen. It's a huge family. It can trace its lineage back to the fifth century."

We cross the narrow way to enter the old palace grounds, an edifice five hundred years old. The main door is locked, so we remain outside, wandering among the communal baths beneath the arbors. Everything lies in disuse and disrepair, with weeds covering the walls and wildflowers growing out of the baths.

Nearby is a bathhouse with ancient murals depicting Sanskrit legends, with scenes of a sensual purgatory painted on the ceiling. Heavenward, the air sings with the bells of the pigeons.

"Ah, you must meet this lady," he says, adjusting his sarong.

An old woman is wandering alone in the garden, and when she sees us, she smiles.

"This is our aunt," says Mark, introducing us. "Would you believe her husband is one hundred eight years old?"

When darkness envelops the compound, Mark gives me a vigorous handshake at the gate, where my driver waits.

"So you're heading east tomorrow. Come back when you can stay longer," he says.

"You're a good host," I say, thanking him.

He smiles and gives me a fraternal wink as the car pulls away.

I leave with the feeling that Mark's pursuit of happiness has not disappointed him. Here is a Westerner who has found his princess and his Shangri-La at Amlapura, and how at home he is here! I am struck, too, with how suddenly the fortunes of the royal family were reversed, and how little bitterness its members seem to feel. Bitterness, in fact, seems alien here. It simply does not belong, and its absence shows in Mark. His seems the best of marriages because it fulfills promise on all sides. Times change, and the family sustains itself with new blood and new means. Mark seems dazzled with his Balinese princess, her family, their daughter, his business. It's a pleasure to envy him.

Nusa Tenggara: Steaming to Sumbawa

*F*OR THE SHORT MIDDAY FLIGHT from Denpasar to Mataram on Lombok, across the deep blue river of the Lombok Strait, the pilot maintained an altitude only a few hundred feet over the white-capped water. In contrast to the shallow strait that separates Bali from Java, the Lombok Strait, also known as the Wallace Line, is over a thousand feet deep. The famous naturalist Alfred Russel Wallace wrote in 1856, "The strait is here fifteen miles wide, so that we may pass in two hours from one great division of the earth to another, differing as essentially in their animal life as Europe does from America." Indeed, parts of Lombok, as well as other parts of Nusa Tenggara, were as dry and hostile as Bali was lush and alluring.

The Lombok Strait was significant in its depth, for it bisected national ideology and marked the boundary between Asia and Oceania. The Balinese had a saying about their island's eastern-most extremity: "Here the tigers end."

Wallace owed his penetrating observations about the strait to circumstances as common in this part of the world today as they were in June of 1856: uncertain shipping schedules. "It was after having spent two years in Borneo, Malacca and Singapore, that I made a somewhat involuntary visit to these islands on my way to Macassar," he wrote. "Had I been able to obtain a passage direct to that place from Singapore, I should probably never have gone near them, and should have missed some of the most important discoveries of my whole expedition to the East."

He noted the hazardous Lombok tides. "This violent surf is probably in some way dependent on the swell of the great southern ocean, and the violent currents that flow through the Straits of Lombock. These are so uncertain that vessels preparing to anchor in the bay are sometimes suddenly swept away into the straits, and are not able to get back again for a fortnight! What seamen call the 'ripples' are also very violent in the straits, the sea appearing to boil and foam and dance like the rapids below a cataract; vessels are swept about helpless, and small ones are occasionally swamped in the finest weather and under the brightest skies."

The contrariness of the waters dividing Bali and Lombok suggested to Wallace "one great division of the earth to another," and one hundred twenty years after the publication of *The Malay Archipelago*, scientists have plumbed the implications of what Wallace discovered.

Today one widely accepted theory is that hundreds of millions of years ago the earth had only one landmass, now called Pangaea, which in time separated into the supercontinents of Gondwanaland and Laurasia, the former including what would become Africa, South America, Australia, and Antarctica, and the latter Asia, Europe, and North America. The movement of landmasses over the many eons is mind-boggling in its implications about the interchange, and lack of interchange, of animal and vegetable life throughout different parts of the world.

The extension of Southeast Asia, including Sumatra, Borneo, Java, and Bali, resides on Asia's Sunda Shelf, while Lombok and its eastern neighbors, stretching to New Guinea and Australia, cling to the Sahul Shelf. But the eerie ring of science fiction veils a truth. Australia collided with Asia some fifteen million years ago, and the deep blue trench that my aircraft was now flying over divided not only Asia and Oceania but the ancient supercontinents Gondwanaland and Laurasia as well. And it was from these last mentioned that the newer continents evolved, according to this theory.

Since the early years of the seventeenth century, when the Balinese crossed the Wallace Line to invade Lombok's Sasak people, the island had assimilated much of its Western neighbor's culture and religion. Besides Balinese Hinduism, however, there were Islam, practiced with varying degrees of militancy, and the curious *Wektu Telu*, a religion unique to Lombok that offered doses of other faiths and meshed with the ancient, indigenous animism of Lombok's hill people.

As we approached Lombok's west coast, the aircraft began to climb and bank. To the south the landscape was flat and scrubby, outback country in sharp relief against a barren peninsula of rugged mountains. This was the cape that vainly beckoned westward toward Bali, stopping abruptly at the invisible trench. The light was harsh, unmuted, lending a starker hue to the red tile village roofs as well as the rice fields, which yield only a single crop a year, and sometimes not even that. Unlike Bali, which is roughly Lombok's size, Lombok has known droughts, and as recently as the mid-1960s a famine claimed fifty thousand lives.

Today, however, Lombok faced a different threat: an epidemic of dengue. Carried by mosquitoes, it raged in five-year cycles after the wet season; and as this was the appointed year, the time for it was ripe. My reading for the short flight was the *Indonesian Times*, and the paper featured an alarming story on the number of fatalities, while emphasizing the scores of emergency clinics that had opened to cope with this crisis in the nation's health.

The airport was a single building, deserted except for a brown man in Arab dress sweeping the floor with a long brush broom. I hailed a boy driving a dokar to take me the few kilometers into the settlement of Ampenan, and dozed in the heat to the creaking motion of the two-wheeled cart and the clopping of hooves. I found a hotel, a run-down place filled with cats and flies, on Lombok's only west–east road. The manager, a wheezing fellow with a broken front tooth who collected empty liquor bottles, advised me to pass the night there and flag a pre-dawn minibus to Labuhan Lombok across the island for the early-morning ferry to Sumbawa, the next island to the east.

Whether it was the real danger of dengue or my imagination that cast a pall over Lombok I did not know. But in the absence of hard evidence, the signs as I read them told that Lombok held a touch of menace. When I went to prowl around, the streets were littered and dusty. The community had no center but was a nexus of stores and houses strung endlessly along the road. Walking west, I crossed a bridge over a river no cleaner than a sewer, where naked children bathed among the detritus. I chartered a bemo to visit nearby ruins and temples, but the day turned sullen, with a squall that shorted out the bemo's horn and rendered the windshield wipers useless.

When the weather cleared, I walked to a nearby beach facing the Wallace Line to watch the sunset over Bali, only to be confronted by a wild-eyed man in rags who tried to sell me a contraption to crush betel nut and abused me loudly when I declined. Stung, I stopped in a small *toko*, or store, and bought a liter of "Extra Special Old Scotch Whisky from Golden Mountain Wine Factory," which advertised itself as "The Finest Tasting Whisky from Surabaya," but the two-dollar bargain turned out to be cloyingly flavored tea that had me gagging.

I turned in early, and awoke later with a start and switched on the light. On the pillow inches from my face was a spider the size of my hand, a great hairy creature with clawlike legs. I brushed it onto the floor and smashed it with my shoe. I checked my watch. It was after two, and I knew sleep was done.

At 4:30 I flagged a minibus in front of the hotel for my journey across the island. It was an hour before sunrise; the vehicle was lighted inside and out like a Mexican bus at Navidad, and the driver's tape deck played a deafening succession of Indonesian hit tunes rendered by the inevitable nymphet voice, backed by the odd East-West amalgamation beat. The minibus was nearly empty when I got on, but it stopped frequently and soon was full. I dozed off, only to be awakened when a slumbering Sasak boy's head fell against my shoulder. We were far beyond where my excursion had taken me the day before, and my fellow passengers were timid country people. They stole glances at me, interspersed with an occasional bold look, but no one spoke.

At first light the full moon hung like a jack-o'-lantern over the unseen horizon. Suddenly the music was shut off, mercifully, I thought, in deference to Ramadan. The lights as well were out, but it was impossible in the sweltering humidity to see out the befogged windows. The respite from the music was short-lived, lasting only long enough for the Muslim faithful to murmur prayers. I wiped moisture from the window with my sleeve, and the flat countryside appeared frost-ridden under a hard freeze, though this appearance was an illusion.

When we pulled into the station at Labuhan Lombok, it was only a hundred-yard walk to the rusted ferry under a seven-o'clock sun that burned like a wad of flaming gauze. The view eastward was blinding and the one west and north serene and majestic; this was the best time of day to see Gunung Rinjani. It rose in the north, bathed serenely in clouds, at eight thousand feet the second highest mountain in Indonesia outside Irian Jaya. It dominated the island as a giant statue of Buddha commanded a temple.

Hundreds of people were waiting to board the ferry, strung out in long lines to buy tickets at three wooden sheds, and I was the only foreigner. Expecting harassment, I was surprised that even the hawkers selling foodstuffs and soft drinks were satisfied to regard me from afar. Beggars, mostly cripples, worked the crowd, including a pitiful man clad in shorts that revealed twisted, shriveled legs. Wearing the traditional black kopiah on his head, he dragged himself with his hands through the litter.

A uniformed officer approached and took me by the hand to a window, where he bought my ticket for the dollar fare. In exchange he asked for my home address, which I wrote on a piece of notebook paper and handed to him.

"Amer-i-kan, ahhh. Stevie Wonder, Ronald Reagan, and George Bush."

We laughed. "How long does the ferry take to cross over to Sumbawa?" I said.

"To Labuhan Alas. Maybe three hours, maybe six. You board now."

As the sole Westerner I was allowed to precede the others and choose my place. I made my way over the rusted hull of a derelict ferry, to which the operative ferry was tethered by thick hemp ropes stained the color of seaweed. My choice was a simple one: above decks or below. The sun was ferocious, and because I burn easily, I decided to station myself below near a porthole where I could see out as well as keep my belongings safe.

I took a final look at Labuhan Lombok. The port had a worn charm of its own, already with a flavor of the outer islands. I saw the thatched huts typical of the island, but something else as well. A small village rested on stilts above the water, a sign of the enterprising Bugis tribesmen from South Sulawesi, who as intrepid seamen and notorious pirates of centuries past had claimed the entire archipelago as their own.

I bought a bottle of "Golden Mississippi Mountain Spring Water" from a boy, went below to find a seat against a bulkhead vibrating from the engine, and waited. In my smaller shoulder bag I fondled a piece of coral that happened to be phallic in shape I had taken from the beach the day before. It was my only souvenir of Lombok and would make a nifty paperweight and conversation piece, I had told myself. But now, in a part of the world where ferries routinely foundered, drowning hundreds of people, it had become a talisman.

It seemed a signal. Once I disappeared from the sight of the native passengers still on the embankment, the ferry bound for Labuhan Alas on Sumbawa was boarded in a mad rush and scramble. Among the passengers were the hawkers with their singsong calls exhorting customers to buy rice cakes wrapped in banana leaves, sodas, candies, cigarettes, and whatever else; and the beggars, who made their solicitations in silence. One boy of about twelve carried on his back a child perhaps the same age, who suffered from a nervous disorder that had rendered him paralyzed. His eyes were unfocused, his emaciated body wrapped around his carrier like a coat. When they stopped before me and I met the doleful stare of the healthy boy, I fished in my pocket for money, and wordlessly they moved on. I watched the other passengers shake them off.

It was nearly eight o'clock when the diesel engine started. The cacophony of driving piston against cylinder wall was deafening, and the bulkheads of corroded steel plate over rotten timbers shivered with baleful vibrations. The crew outside the port opening swung along the hull like a tribe of spider monkeys, and when they slipped the moorings, we were driven out of the harbor, ungainly, crablike, and surreal, as though Times Square Station at rush hour were being towed to sea.

Uncertainty was a major theme on this voyage. The bulkhead nearest me hosted a patchwork of odd signs, including one in English, an incongruity that stood out: "Almost everything serious is difficult, and everything is serious." My seat was on the port side, and there were so many of us huddled together that movement was virtually impossible. The ferry listed to starboard, and it was clear why. Most of the rows of wooden benches stood inexplicably to the right of the keel, as did the covered and uncovered deck spaces, and not a square foot was unoccupied. The list was so great that from where I sat, no horizon was visible in any direction. On my side of the vessel there was only sky, and on the other the brown, oil-slicked water of the harbor gave way to shallow green and then deeper blue as we got under way.

Some of the people looked apprehensive, others merely resigned to a familiar run. This was inter-island travel at its cheapest. Ferries and cargo boats, scheduled and unscheduled alike, plied Indonesian waters, and the journeys were measured in hours, even though they often stretched into days: four hours, sixteen, thirty-six, ninety-six. Rendezvous with a ship in the Malay Archipelago was more often than not a matter of happenstance. You waited in whatever port you found yourself in for a vessel's arrival; determined its destination; negotiated a fare with the skipper that was at most a few dollars; boarded with food and water to claim a space on deck; suffered through angry squall and unrelenting sun or paid a crew member for a relatively dry, louse-infested bunk; gratefully accepted a plate of rice from the ship's cook, which you ate with the fingers of your right hand; reluctantly visited the unspeakable single head, a shack at the stern with a hole in the deck more often missed than scored; and washed nowhere.

I had counted on passing the few hours aboard the ferry to Sumbawa taking in the stunning seascapes: the numerous sail-driven outrigger fishing boats coasting among the coral heads and sculpted, cone-shaped, barren rock islands, defunct volcanoes upheaved eons ago. Consigned as I was to a narrow, cramped space, I was forced to crane my head to get snatches of such views when they presented themselves. When they didn't, I dozed off for minutes at a time. Awake, I practiced my Bahasa Indonesia on my fellow passengers, all of us bound by a common plight: that of reprieved rats on a condemned ship.

A stocky soldier dressed in a camouflaged uniform stood near the ladderway puffing kreteks. A young, pretty, ocher-skinned woman in Javanese dress nursed her baby, under the protective gaze of her solemn Muslim father, or brother, or husband. The woman sitting next to me, barefoot with a filthy sarong and a face like a pig, continually dug her elbow into my ribs, presented her palm for money, and spat on the floor between us like a spitting cobra when I shook my head.

"Where do you go, tuan?" The speaker was in his late teens. He was sitting in front of me and had turned to practice his English. He measured his words carefully.

"Wherever this ferry takes me," I said. "Are you a student?"

"Yes, from Bima." Bima was a port on the eastern end of the island. "Is tuan a tourist?"

"No, I am a traveler," I said. "A wanderer who takes notes."
The last I managed in Indonesian.

The boy's face brightened. "Then need a *gweeday*."

"A what?"

"A gweeday, sire. You know what means gweeday? An English
word surely. If you need a gweeday, I be your gweeday."

"I do not know that word. Please write it here." I handed him
my notebook and pen, and he carefully printed "GUIDE." I cor-
rected his pronunciation, and he said the word several times to
get it right.

"You are kind," I said, "but I must travel alone and meet places
and people as they come, as I met you on this boat."

"Are you *belanda*, Mister?"

"A-mer-i-kan."

"Ah, from London or New York?"

"London is in England. I once lived in New York and have
visited London, but I now live in San Francisco, which is in
California."

"Then you are very far from home, tuan."

"And you are not so far from home. Once we disembark will
you travel to Bima by bus?"

"Yes, but even it is a long journey, over three hundred kilometers from Labuhan Alas. There will be many buses meeting
the ferry. And you? Do not stay in Labuhan Alas. A bus to
Sumbawa Besar is only two hours. Rest there, and then continue."

He had quite a good ear, and the more we spoke, the more
precise his English became. Better, he had given me a destination.
By now, a curious group had gathered around us, and the boy
translated each of our exchanges to approving murmurs, save for
the woman next to me who hawked and spat.

The boy read disgust in my face. "She cannot help it, sire. She
is crazy."

"I believe it, but please do not speak that in Bahasa Indonesia."

"I like American music," he said suddenly. "Rock music."

"Then you must like Stevie Wonder. He is coming to Jakarta. You must go and see him."

His face brightened for an instant. "He is a dark man, and . . ." He pointed to his eyes. "But I cannot go to Jakarta. It is far, and I am only a student. I have been only to Lombok. But I love Stevie Wonder and other American music." By chance as we spoke, a cassette was heard over the din playing Stevie Wonder's "I Just Called to Say I Love You." It was a recording I heard all over Indonesia, more than any other American song.

"Why do you like Stevie Wonder and American music?"

"Because it is happy music."

"And sometimes sad."

"Sometimes sad, but happy sad. It makes me feel good." He turned to explain all this to our audience, and they all agreed. American music and Stevie Wonder were very good, America was good, and I was good.

By now the sun had risen to the point where the fierce rays blasted my corner. I glanced around to catch the eye of the young Javanese mother, who regarded me with an unsmiling, relentless curiosity. I smiled and she looked away, but her baby grinned, and others seeing the trade-off were amused. Around her women were grooming each other, combing hair and picking out lice. Beyond, on the starboard rail, a group of men perched like a row of blackbirds on a telephone line while they smoked kreteks.

"Excuse me, sire. I go meet friends," said the boy, and he was gone. Such an abrupt departure after an encounter I now knew to be commonplace. For my part, I was finding the heat stifling; and seated between a searing bulkhead and a crazy woman, I felt claustrophobic. It was clear that we were approaching Sumbawa, for people began to collect their things. I checked my watch: 10:40. A path to the ladderway opened, so I shouldered my bags to go topside.

The aft deck, like the one below, was covered with orange peels, mango seeds, paper wrappings, and spittle, but I was caught up in a moving herd of passengers anxious to disembark. I was drenched with sweat, and an across-the-bow breeze was cooling. Sumbawa lay a mile or so off to starboard as we steamed dead ahead for Labuhan Alas, though the sun made me squint to make out the port. Behind it Sumbawa, larger than Bali and Lombok together, was a long, bizarrely shaped island with deep inlets guarded by long, thrusting peninsulas. East of it in a wider strait lay Komodo Island, home of the giant, flesh-eating Komodo dragons, and beyond it the large island of Flores.

Low rain clouds hovered around Sumbawa's green mountains, obscuring the peaks. A Bugis village on stilts reached far out into the harbor. Any number of boats rode at anchor, and as many were active: thatched houseboats, long boats driven by automobile engines, Bugis schooners. There was a clang of bells, and the engines began grinding in reverse, churning up brown harbor water as we glided toward the pier, the crewmen ready with their ropes.

The Sumbawans were more aggressive and insistent than their Lombok neighbors. At least a score of buses greeted the ferry, and the drivers were highly competitive. As I made my way through the dust and throngs to inquire about a bus to Sumbawa Besar, I was accosted several times by men hawking tickets. The color of the ticket determined which bus line you selected, and as they were all the same to me, I took whatever was handed over. It was not yet a matter of money; the conductor on the bus would collect the fares, so I ignored the screaming entreaties and walked over to what seemed the newest and cleanest vehicle of the lot, where an officious man snatched my blue ticket and ordered me aboard. A boy took my larger duffel and tossed it up to his compeer on the roof to be tied down. There was no room on the bus for it, he said. It was sweltering and the bus had no air-conditioning.

Several minutes passed before another officious man boarded and asked for my blue ticket, which had already been collected. When he saw that I had red and yellow tickets instead, he brusquely motioned me off. I tried to explain, but communication was hopeless. The original ticket collector ordered me back aboard, while the other barred my way; they got into a row. Anger boiled up in my guts. When a fellow passenger snatched away my phrase book to leaf through it, I snatched it back. What was this sideshow? My luggage was out of sight, and I feared it might be stolen.

"I'm getting my goddamned bag and taking another goddamned bus," I said, seeking hand- and footholds, and began climbing the side to retrieve my duffel. It had been battened down under canvas along with boxes and crates of all sizes, colors, and shapes, but I caught a glimpse of it. At least it was secure. But the bus crewmen resented my invasion and angrily told me to get down.

"*Pam-pam bis! Pam-pam orang bis!*" I shouted. It was the only insult I could manage, and even then it was only a jury-rigged approximation to vent my spleen rather than draw blood. Using strange words in a foreign language you're trying to learn in such circumstances is like handling wild horses. Blood I didn't draw, but mirth I did. The group suddenly exploded in laughter, doubling over, shrieking, pounding each other; repeating what I had said and countless variations upon it.

"Fuck this bus and the men of it!" was what I had said, or tried to. How it translated I had no idea, but to them it was very funny indeed.

"Mister okay, okay. Into, Mister, into." The men waved me down, and I descended with the confidence of a dragonslayer. "Okay, okay, okay, Mister, into, into." I must claim my seat, for the bus would soon be leaving. But their maniacal laughter continued, and the joke spread beyond our bus to the others in a chorus of hootings and jabberings. It was a happier man who steamed in this midday sauna for another twenty minutes before the bus with its share of passengers swayed behind the grinding train of other vehicles, gearing down to climb the precipitous dirt road that met the single paved one crossing the island.

The road turned inland through steep, green, eroded volcanic country before swinging north to trace the twisting coastline, affording stunning views of the sea and islets to the north and of the winding ridges of ancient lava flows to the south.

Sumbawa's history is complex. Ancient stone tablets told that Javanese traders based themselves here as a stepping-stone to the Moluccas and introduced wet rice cultivation, while the Balinese aristocracy extended its reach past Lombok to the western part of the islands. Before the seventeenth century, and even after it, Islam, brought in by the invading Bugis and Macassarese from Celebes, was pocketed in the petty kingdoms of the coast, while animist cults thrived in the interior. In April of 1815 the now silent volcano Gunung Tambora erupted with sufficient fury to kill ten thousand natives, followed by disease and starvation that killed three times that number, before another wave of immigration from other islands occurred. The Dutch East Indies Company managed Sumbawa from afar, for with its warring factions and dearth of commercial promise, it held little interest for the white colonialists.

The bus crew suggested a place to stay in Sumbawa Besar, the island's largest town, and detoured from their route to drop me there. With good humor they retrieved my duffel from overhead, and were still laughing and waving at "the man who screwed buses" when they turned back onto the road to Bima and disappeared from sight.

The hotel appeared to be in the middle of nowhere, and in Sumbawa Besar it was; but if nowhere, a legitimate traveler's destination, was crossed with a spot of charm, it was a good place to be. Situated on a dirt road near where it crossed another, the hotel had a quaintly run-down Mediterranean air about it. The rooms faced onto the same garden that the thatch-roofed, open-sided restaurant at one end overlooked, and the office at the other end was presided over by a pretty young woman who rented me a room for three dollars. It had a ceiling fan, a nice-sized bed, and a mandi of dubious cleanliness, but a tap-water basin in the room itself with a mirror and fresh towels and soap.

It was lunchtime, and I was both tired and dehydrated. I had a large beer in the restaurant before my fried rice was served me by a barefoot girl while recorded gamelan music played. Where I sat I faced a bar of woven bamboo with stools that featured a singular attraction and as singular an oddity. The attraction was a half-empty liter of Johnnie Walker Red Label, the one and only, the genuine article. There was a group of Japanese staying at the hotel, and I resolved to get to the scotch that evening before them.

The oddity that stood guard before the bar was a life-sized figure carved from wood of a naked black man sporting a huge erection, perhaps twenty inches long. The painted face bore the exaggerated, red-lipped grin of a 1930s minstrel-show end man.

I set out on foot to see something of this provincial capital. Lining the streets were the thatch-roofed bungalows with walls of woven matting, familiar to these islands, as well as small stone homes and clusters of stores.

The sultan's palace stood in large fenced-in grounds of packed sand and scabby patches of weed, next to a large mosque. The decrepitly ornate wooden palace, its exterior lifelessly restored, resembled an Iowa livestock barn on stilts. Groups of children played nearby. I gained entrance by a steep wooden staircase, at the top of which a guide dressed in a white robe and skullcap waited while I removed my shoes and then led me into the spacious audience chamber near the main door. The windows were shuttered, and each of the rooms he led me to was illuminated by light bulbs of such low wattage that what there was to see appeared in a thick gray haze like an enormous spiderweb. The objects in the throne room, the covered sedan chairs, the spectral carvings on the ceiling beams, even the warped, uneven, splinter-ridden floorboards seemed at once indifferent, melancholic, and Dickensian-sinister.

Throughout my tour of the palace my guide, an ingratiating gay with anguished eyes, ignored my Bahasa Indonesia and insisted on speaking in an inscrutable English, misconstruing my questions and providing incomprehensible answers. The only hard facts I heard was that the last sultan had been dead for ten years, and the palace had been built 103 years before. I already knew that the sultans had been stripped of traditional office by the government and as a sop had been given petty administrative posts in the towns and settlements they had once ruled. At the door the guide had me sign a guest book and pay a modest fee for "restoration." The name above my own in the book was that of a Javanese from Surabaya, and the corresponding date was ten days earlier. I declined the guide's invitation for tea at his house.

It was dusk when I arrived at the hotel. I bathed and washed out my rank cotton clothes and hung them to be dried by the overhead fan. Around the small circular neon light on the ceiling, a lizard stalked insects.

At the bar the girl who had rented me my room was keeping accounts in a ledger. She had changed into familiar native evening dress, a flowered sarong, matching bodice, and a white orchid adorning her hair. The place was empty, and the level in the bottle of scotch had not dropped, a reassuring sight.

"Would you like a drink?" she asked in good English. She retrieved the bottle, placed it before me, and went to fetch ice. Taped to the bottle was a small note, "1250 rp per measured drink." At seventy-five cents a shot, I could manage it. She returned with a bowl of ice and a tumbler and encouraged me to pour my own. She was an attentive hostess, quick to smile while making polite conversation.

"Oh, no. I'm not the owner, just the manager. The owners are not here."

"You are not Sumbawanese?"

"No, I am from Bali, though I live here with my family."

Her family had lived here for some time, though she often returned to Bali to visit other relatives. She had also traveled east to Flores to see the three volcanic lakes of Keli Mutu and warned me about poisonous snakes there, especially the green ones that could not be seen until they struck. Bali, Sumbawa, Flores: that was the extent of her world. I wondered if she were descended from the Balinese aristocracy who had gained a hold on western Sumbawa so long ago.

"Can you satisfy my curiosity about something?" I said.

"Of course."

"What is that statue there?" I pointed to the silent guardian of the bar who held not a spear but an oversized male member.

She laughed. "Oh, that! It is called a *kukul*, and it is from central Bali."

"What is it for?"

"I shall show you." She left her station from behind the bar to approach the grinning black man, and I turned to watch her seize its donkey-proportioned penis, lift it from the lifeless crotch, and beat out a tattoo on the wooden figure's body, eliciting a variety of tones that depended on where she struck it, keeping perfect rhythm to the seductive sounds of the taped gamelan playing in the bar.

"Very nice indeed," I said, walking over.

"Oh, yes, it is very nice. Now you try."

"I'd rather watch you."

"Please."

I took the long wooden cock from her hand and tapped this curious figure from toe to head, accompanied by her sparkling laughter and the wooden man's silent, exaggerated grin.

"The rhythms of the gamelan are too complicated for me," I said. Smiling, she took back the instrument and beat out the recorded rhythm while I sipped my drink.

"Please pour another," she said, and I happily obliged, while watching her over the next several minutes accompanying the gamelan as though she were in a trance, until the end of the tape.

"Did you like it?" she asked.

"Oh, very much. Where do you find such a kukul?"

"Oh, I'm afraid only in Bali's central highlands. They are placed before houses."

"I see. So it is a fertility symbol. Good for rice crops, good to make a large family."

Her eyelids raised inquisitively, and her smile was genuine but uncomprehending. "It's a drum!" she said.

"Yes, a drum," I repeated.

I finished my drink at the table. The barefoot girl lit a mosquito coil at my feet. After a few minutes she brought my order of curried prawns and vegetables with a large beer. Over dinner I struck up a conversation with a Japanese businessman who had taken an adjacent table with a small group of his countrymen.

"You're crazy if you stay here, man. Crazy, crazy!" he said. He had spent some time in Los Angeles and laced his English with outdated slang. "Dengue fever, it's here, right on. One of our guys has it. Fever, rash, inflamed joints. Our business is here, right? Tourism, right? We're supposed to stay a week, right? But are we staying another night here? Wrong! We're off to Bali. Special flight tomorrow."

"I've just come from Bali," I said.

"Then you'd better go back, man. Our flight's full, but Merpati has another, right? Fully booked. Best to stand by, right on. Don't stay here. You can die from dengue fever. You don't fly tomorrow, you don't leave for a week, or maybe if you get sick you don't leave at all."

"That sounds pretty ominous," I said, "but I'll take my chances." I rose to retire to my room.

"Man, it's your funeral."

I walked back to my room, passing others in the party of Japanese who sat in chairs before their rooms, smoking and talking, their lighted cigarette butts drawing fiery arcs as they were tossed into the garden.

Along with the men's voices, a strange malady visited me that night, not so much invading my sleep as bracketing it. When I readied myself for bed, a burning presumed to drop in like an unwelcome relative, inflaming my joints and inducing a cold sweat. I slept, but the pain receded only to stand by, the men's voices outside lending my nightmare a flesh-and-blood vividness. I dreamed of hooded creatures and predatory birds lurking near my bedstead.

Over a breakfast of banana pancake and strong, sweet black

coffee, my discomfort faded, then returned with a will of its own. I pondered my next move while the group of Japanese readied themselves for departure. Be realistic, I told myself. Why should you believe yourself immune to the dengue plague? Hadn't it struck one of the Japanese? I examined the mosquito bites on my ankles and arms. Face up to the possibility that you may be on the verge of a grave illness. Get help. See a doctor.

Suppose my trouble subsided and I proceeded east and backward in time as far as the Solor and Alor archipelagos, to the island of Lembata, say, where men hunted whales in small boats? Or to isolated Alor, whose natives had taken the heads of rival tribesmen until a few years ago and still worshiped the *mokos*, mysterious bronze gongs they had found buried and thought to be gifts from the gods? If my trouble were to return, what treatment would I receive at the hands of a witch doctor?

Prudence took the day. I would go back to Denpasar on the morning flight from Sumbawa Besar for examination and treatment, if necessary. If my symptoms were a false alarm, at least I could continue my travels with an easy mind. But the Japanese had told me over dinner last evening that the flight was fully booked.

The open sores on the donkey's withers distracted me from my own discomfort during the short, jolting dokar ride to the airport, and I wondered whether I could bribe Merpati for a seat. At nine I arrived at the airport, a concrete-block building beside a single weathered asphalt strip on the edge of town. A herd of goats grazed in front. Inside the terminal I approached an agent dispensing tickets for cash to passengers at a makeshift table near some scales. Occasionally the agent paused to scream into the static of a two-way radio, which screamed back at him.

"Impossible today. Both planes full," he cried. He was working with two manifests. The troop of Japanese were preparing to board their chartered seventeen-seater.

"Hey, man, you wised up, right on!" cried the man of the evening before, who was near the head of the line. I saw a figure on a makeshift stretcher being borne ahead of the other passengers toward the airplane. "Don't take no for an answer. Dengue fever makes you crazy before you die."

"Standby," the agent said curtly. "Today full. One week maybe." He jotted his name and address on a piece of paper and handed it to me. At the bottom he had printed, "I LIKE USA FLAG." He asked, "You will send to me?"

"I will send to you if you get me on this flight."

"Today full!"

I looked at his manifests and pondered the importance of documents in such a country. A reservation was worthless if it was never transposed to a tattered, scribbled-on list of the sort this man held, and inevitably much was lost in translation. "One week maybe." On the other hand, one week maybe not. "Dengue fever makes you crazy before you die." In a week I might suffer death from lunacy.

"Can I help you?" I turned to find a slim, uniformed man about my own age wearing tinted glasses and an ironic half-smile that suggested an unruffled malevolence. He had the lighter skin of a Javanese, and that with a calm, intimidating manner distinguished him.

I explained that I wasn't well and wanted very much to take one of the two planes. The first flight had already boarded the Japanese and was out of the question. That left the scheduled flight at eleven.

"You look well. Don't you like Sumbawa Besar? Where do you come from?"

Oh, I was an American who liked Sumbawa Besar very much, I said. But I needed to see a specialist in Denpasar. This bland explanation seemed to satisfy him. His English was as good as the boy's on the ferry, and we now had the attention of many people in the room. If anybody could help me, this was the man.

But he echoed the younger man with the lists who liked American flags. "Why are you in Indonesia?" he said. He was going through the motions of cleaning his pistol.

Writers were regarded with great suspicion. This prejudice was rooted in foreign coverage of the Communist uprising of the mid-sixties, as well as the Indonesian government's annexation of Portuguese Timor a decade later, when five Australian journalists had been killed by the military. The notion of a free, uncensored press, or television for that matter, was unthinkable here. In Jakarta dissident writers were either under house arrest or in prison, and their books, lauded by PEN chapters, were banned. A provincial bureaucrat or a police or army official with borrowed authority and a mean spirit could have me expelled from the country.

But this officer's spirit suddenly seemed one of accommodation, his manner guardedly friendly. Whatever his position and whoever he served, he was clearly the boss at Sumbawa Besar's airport.

I replied that I was writing a travel book, that any assistance would be appreciated, and so forth. I added that while Australians knew parts of Indonesia by virtue of their proximity, most Americans did not, and I finished with a platitude: that my work would be good for both countries. I produced a letter from my publisher. Dengue was now the last thing on my mind. I'd begun with the hope that the letter might give me a measure of credibility, if not an airplane seat. Now I prayed it would not get me booted out of the country.

The officer looked at me thoughtfully, and the stylized attitude of attention he displayed soon had a cadre of a dozen onlookers surrounding us. The ironic half-smile never left his face, even when he spoke.

"Why don't you stay at Tirtasari? It is only one kilometer away, and it is on the beach. There you can swim, take a ride in a small boat, have a nice girl. There's a picture of it there."

On the wall at the far end of the building was a poster, so I walked over to inspect it. It colorfully advertised a hotel with beach bungalows, and it looked totally unspoiled and was reasonably priced. Had I known such an idyllic place existed, I would have had the bus drop me there yesterday.

"It is fifteen thousand rupiah a night at most. I think you can afford it, tuan Char-les." Did *tuan* as he used the title have a barb to it? My status now was so uncertain that I sweated profusely.

"Are you married, Mister Char-les?"

I produced a colored snapshot that I kept in my passport, showing me in black tie with a friend in an evening dress. The relaxed formality in the picture was always so incongruous with the situations in which I showed it that it never failed to impress the viewer.

"A fine couple, and you're alone?"

"For the time being."

"Then you're alone."

"I am alone."

"It is not so good to be alone, Mister Char-les." For an Indonesian I knew this was especially so.

This officer did not cast a short shadow. I feared dengue less than antagonizing someone who could either help me or see me deported.

"How do I get to this hotel?" I said.

"The hotel will come for you. I shall call them. Then you can swim, ride in small boat, have girl, a nice girl if you wish. I shall visit you this afternoon to see how you are. Why do you not stay longer in Sumbawa? Bali is a city of evil and crime cursed by the presence of Australians. Sumbawa is quiet and peaceful."

I repeated my earlier litany, and he gently shook his head.

"You will like the Hotel Tirtasari," he said with great conviction. "It is new."

I had no doubts that I would like the place. The pictures on the poster were appealing and couldn't be too misleading. I envisioned white beach, grilled seafood, and Eliot's "silken girls bringing sherbet"—a Muslim's earthly paradise before I succumbed to the hell of dengue.

"So you want to leave today?" he said.

"I beg your pardon?" The sudden drop to ground took me unprepared.

"You want to leave now?" The sun filling the terminal caught his glasses and made me squint. He had not mentioned money and I had offered him none, as if by tacit agreement the exercising of his whim were payment enough. It was plain to me that he thought so.

I hedged, explaining that while I wanted to stay, I thought it best to have a checkup. If a seat had suddenly become available, I would be proud to occupy it. I would return another day to enjoy the pleasures of Hotel Tirtasari.

He now took a seat in a row of chairs at mid-room, as though every move had been blocked out for him by a stage director. "Your bags, Mister Char-les. Take them there." He pointed to the baggage scale adjacent to the counter, where a boy awaited me. An hour earlier I had been ignored, but now all eyes were on me. Dutifully I padded over with my shoulder bags.

"Place your cabin bags on the scale as well. Then go buy your ticket there," said the voice behind me, "but you must tell me how much you weigh."

"One-eighty. Pounds," I added.

"Kilos? I think perhaps one hundred kilos," he said.

At the flag-lover's post I peeled off a sheaf of bills: forty-five thousand rupiah, about twenty-five dollars, while hearing his even voice behind me.

"You have no guns, knives, heroin?" There was no X-ray machine.

"I have my utility knife," I said quickly, and I reached in my jeans to show it, but he brushed it off. The agent handed me a ticket.

"Mister Char-les, let me see how much you paid for your ticket." The officer motioned for me not by crooking his index finger, which Malays regard as a rudeness, but by a gentle, swimming wave of the hand, the identical gesture favored by refined Spaniards and Latin Americans. I assumed that the practice had been brought by the conquistadors to the Philippines in Philip II's day and had made its way along with spices, foodstuffs, weavings, and other stocks-in-trade down that archipelago to the Malays.

By now every eye in the place was on me.

"Is this correct? The right price, I mean?" I said.

He smiled, nodding. "You have your boarding pass here," he said, placing the card in my shirt pocket, "and here is your baggage check. Now you may put your ticket in your bag, a souvenir."

He smiled and shook his head, a sympathetic schoolmaster before a dull child, while the ticket agent whooped. "You send me USA flag, please, Mister, okay?"

"Okay!"

"Now, Mister Char-les," spoke the seated figure, "I'm going to give you my name and address, and you must return and call me, and we shall enjoy the pleasures of Tirtasari together when you return, do you understand?"

"I understand."

Taking his own pen and flashing his identification tag on his uniform shirt, he wrote in clear block letters his name and address. When he inked the last letter, a great siren wailed, driving the ubiquitous pariah dogs from their shady places, howling mad. When the siren finished, the drone of engines replaced it, and within moments the incoming flight touched down, taxied to the loading zone, and cut its propellers.

"Please satisfy my curiosity about one thing," I said. "The ticket agent had told me that today's flight was fully booked, and that it would be impossible to leave before tomorrow. You yourself said so as well. How did I get on?"

The officer expanded his lips in a beatific smile and said, "They are afraid of me."

He offered his hand, after which a behatted Muslim who had admired my watch followed suit.

Shouldering my bags, I turned to see the officer walking hand in hand with a young uniformed agent to inspect the loading of cargo into the aircraft's hold. For a Malay, a person or thing doesn't exist unless it's touched, I thought. I followed the remaining passengers to the plane and took the only remaining seat, and shortly after eleven we were airborne. My ticket identified me as "Ch Crow," but at least this crow was flying.

Back on Bali I sensed immediately the old contempt that familiarity breeds. At the airport English-speaking hustlers were everywhere, and the sullen boy at the hotel's desk behaved as though he were my benefactor when I asked for a room. "We're always full. You very lucky," he said, handing me a key.

The hell I was lucky. This was the last place I wanted to be. I made a couple of telephone calls, got the name of a reliable doctor trained in the West, and visited him that afternoon to learn that my symptoms, while intermittently painful, were benign. It was simple dehydration that had set my system afire. The prescription was to drink plenty of good water and to pack a surplus of the plastic-bottled stuff on future boat and bus trips.

In Kuta's streets, surrounded by legions of pink Australians and red-kneed West Germans dressed in shorts and tank tops and wearing earrings and tattoos and punk hairdos, I resented being one of a herd of coddled, reviled Westerners. By paradox, in Nusa Tenggara the color of my skin had conferred on me an anonymity that suited me far better. I was a loner, and as I traveled, so was I met. The officer's gentle persecution and final reprieve at Sumbawa Besar's airport was proof enough of that.

At the hotel, after consulting my maps, I called Merpati and booked a seat on the next day's flight to Waingapu, on the island of Sumba south of Sumbawa and Flores. No outbreaks of dengue on Sumba had been reported. From there I would proceed to Timor and the eastern extremity of Nusa Tenggara, with the blind hope that somehow I might connect with a boat for the long return.

Nusa Tenggara:
The Capture of
Charles Bronson

IT WAS LATE AFTERNOON when I stood before Mr. Hassan's bungalow, situated on a hill at the edge of town and guarded by a long-tailed monkey tethered to a post. Waingapu, Sumba's capital and main port on the eastern side of the island, is a flat, arid settlement of houses raised on stilts and made of woven bamboo with thatched roofs. Mounds of dyed yarn dry in the dust around each house. Horses, goats, and geese have the run of the place, and black pigs forage in the garbage beneath the houses. With no town center, you either walk in the heat to your destination or take advantage of the lively dokar service, or, if you want to see the countryside, negotiate with Mr. Hassan for the hire of his van. I had been here only a few hours but had learned this much.

Sumba is two hundred miles long by seventy-five wide, and it hovers alone in the Indian Ocean south of the chain of islands that comprise most of Nusa Tenggara. The Sumbanese are dark Malays with varying strains of Melanesian. While women wear ankle-length skirts, the men array themselves in turbans and short, bright ikat sarongs with loincloths, and sport wooden-sheathed knives in their waistbands.

For centuries native petty rulers, whose tenuous claims to legitimacy were their legendary ancestors renowned for exploits in battle, had their clans fighting among each other. The heads of victims were taken until the early twentieth century, when the Dutch established a military command here. To the trained eye the designs of the ikat fabrics found on Sumba tell of such exploits. But there is a more vital holdover from this heroic past. On the lush western part of the island the *pasola* rite, an annual mock battle involving opposing armies of several hundred horsemen armed with spears, is reenacted with sufficient enthusiasm that fatalities are not uncommon.

A lovely young Malay woman holding a baby opened Mr. Hassan's door. Behind her was a smiling older woman, perhaps the young one's mother, with garish red lips, stained with betel nut, which allegedly strengthens the teeth. The dimly lit front room, separated from the rest of the house by a drawn curtain, was furnished with maroon overstuffed furniture and dark mahogany tables on which stood colored-glass figurines of the five-and-dime-store variety. Solemn tinted photographs of relatives hung on one wall surrounding Suharto's official portrait, which was no larger than the framed photograph of Charles Bronson on the opposite wall.

The women disappeared, and after a suitable interval Mr. Hassan, barefoot and dressed in white shorts and a green polo shirt, parted the curtain and entered the room. A slender, bespectacled man of middle years, he wore a Cheshire-cat grin and extended a hand with fingernails fully an inch long. I declined his offer of a cigarette as well as tea and coffee.

He spoke to one of the women beyond the curtain, and in a few moments the young woman I took to be his wife entered with a tray holding two glasses of orange liquid. This was a typical Indonesian soft drink: the store-bought bottled syrup was available in a variety of fruit flavors, and it was mixed with water to make a cloyingly sweet drink. My host inserted a cigarette into a holder and fired it with a propane lighter, while a group of townspeople watched us through the window.

"Mister Char-les," he began. "What I propose is that you charter my car tomorrow. I will be your guide, and we will be able to see much of this side of the island. I will tell you much of the island's history, and there is a nice beach where we can relax. The fee for the day's excursion is fifty thousand rupiah."

That was nearly thirty dollars, an extortionate sum. I told him so.

Mr. Hassan, however, courteously but adamantly refused to lower his fee. Twenty percent for the driver. Oil and gas. Wear and tear on the car. This was a standard rate. It would be the same at my hotel, if I inquired.

I had taken a room at one of Waingapu's two hotels, each owned by a Chinese family who regarded the other as a bitter rival. My hotel was a scab on a small mangy field a block off the main road, and was so pounded by the sun that it appeared to flatten and cower behind the scrub that guarded it. For the remainder of my visit that afternoon, Mr. Hassan, an advocate of the other hotel, tried to convince me that I had erred in my choice. As he spoke, his outline fleshed out. He was an operator, a Sumbanese Snopes, who shrewdly intercepted my quick study of him.

"I work for Merpati," he said. "But I do other things."

Merpati flew into Waingapu only two days out of seven. For the rest of the week Mr. Hassan used the Merpati van in his own enterprises. Though Sumba, by virtue of its isolation, saw few travelers, all travelers to Sumba inevitably saw Mr. Hassan.

"And one of the things I can do is to arrange a cheaper outing for you tomorrow, by motorcycle."

"But I do not know how to drive a motorcycle."

"Do not worry. I will arrange something."

I agreed to meet him at eight in the morning and returned to my hotel in the dark.

The hotel's owners were an elderly couple who spoke no English but grinned at me with gold teeth and screeched orders at their Malay staff. Their pregnant daughter, her hair always in curlers, kept the accounts; her husband spoke some English and kept me company when I dined.

Throughout dinner, he spoke in hushed tones, distracting me

with a nervous tic that was punctuated by a sniffling hiss, and watching me closely with the beady eyes of a predatory lizard. Judging from the drift of his conversation, I sensed that he feared I might forsake this hotel for the other. As he considered each of my answers to his questions, his tongue flicked between his lips before he translated into Chinese for his in-laws, sitting nearby. Finally satisfied that I would not be lost to the competition, he left me alone, saying as he rose, "You must forgive the old people if they stare. We have not seen an American before."

I arrived for my morning meeting at the other hotel after a kilometer's walk and found relief from the heat in the dark lobby. The cross-shaped room was furnished with rattan sofas and chairs, and in the dank air swarms of mosquitoes buzzed. Hawkers lounged about, but when they rose to greet me, I waved them off. A large painting of a seductively posed Chinese lady lent the place an atmosphere of seedy sensuality. I covered myself with Muskol and waited.

When Mr. Hassan arrived, I saw why he championed this place. Near the entrance was a Merpati counter that advertised Mr. Hassan, from his tours to his textiles. He placed his briefcase on the counter and came to take a seat opposite me in the lobby. Dressed in a Ralph Lauren shirt and neatly creased cotton slacks, he removed his sandals to reveal cracked and torn toenails. He was a picture of fastidiousness rooted in dirt.

Scarcely had he sat down when he waved a greeting across the room. "Mister Char-les," he said, rising, "come meet Johnny."

Johnny was a Chinese in his forties pushing a motorcycle through the fly curtain into the lobby. He adjusted the kickstand and walked over wearing a snaggle-toothed smile and combing his slicked-back hair. He placed the comb in the pocket of his white shirt and extended his hand.

"Me Johnny, what your name?"

I told him.

"Ah, George. I had a brother George, but he died."

"No, Char-les."

"Char-les! My brother Char-les dead, too. But my sister alive"—he pointed to the smiling wife of the hotel owner—"I'm alive, and you're alive."

"And next week Johnny will sing at a family wedding," said Mr. Hassan. "He sings like Elvis Presley."

"He looks like him, too," I said. It was weird but true, and Johnny cackled at the compliment.

We negotiated a day's rate of twenty-five thousand rupiah, which was fair—half that proposed by the unctuous Mr. Hassan for his car and driver—and Johnny dropped me at my hotel, promising to return for me in an hour, after filling his gas tank and his belly for the expedition. "You wait for me, okay?"

At 10:30 Johnny entered the hotel grounds, gunning his two-wheeler and drawing a wide circle before he stopped, allowing the engine to idle while I mounted behind him. Wetting an index finger, he held it aloft. "Headwind," he said and spoke to one of the hotel boys, who ran inside and returned with a newspaper, which Johnny placed inside his shirt as a shield against insects and other airborne hazards. He wore a white helmet and had a yellow one for me. It fit me like an undersized football helmet. When I pulled it down, it pinned my ears sufficiently to fashion two natural ear trumpets, which caught the explosions of exhaust, making conversation—already difficult under the circumstances—nearly impossible. When I tried to remove it, the thing tore at my scalp like an adhesive bandage, so I left it in place.

Our destination was Rende, a native village known for its monolithic tombs and ikat-weaving techniques. We roared out of the hotel grounds and swung onto the hardtop that passed the airport. We hadn't motored fifty yards, gearing up to speed, when wind and torque lifted Johnny's helmet, spinning it like a Frisbee, then dropping it in the middle of the road behind us, where it shattered like an eggshell. Johnny slowed and circled back to inspect the remains.

"Aha-ha-ha-ha! Aha-ha-ha-ha-ha-ha!" He exploded in the

staccato of laughter that characterized his speech. "Give me helmet. Driver must. You next."

I tore mine off and was happy to be rid of it, but a half mile uproad, just beyond Waingapu, he stopped in front of a small store and hailed the woman inside in a rapid-fire interrogatory. She brought another helmet out to us, mine for the day and a better fit.

"I have many friends," he said as we sped off into the countryside. Johnny was an incessant talker, and though we had to shout to hear each other except when we made the occasional stop, we conversed for the entire trip. "I know all holes in road," he said. He maintained a cruising speed between 85 and 100 kph, slowing only for the jolting bridges that spanned a network of rivers flattening out at the coast.

Johnny was an attentive guide. We crossed the Kambaniru River near the airport first, where families bathed and three men worked at burning out a log to make a dugout canoe. Two canoes floated placidly in the green water, as ancient and seasoned as large crocodiles. I asked Johnny if the reptiles inhabited the island's rivers, posing a threat to bathers.

"In Sumba crocodiles there are no more of except maybe a few," he said.

Beyond the airport, with the sea to our left, the road took us through open country like no other that I saw in Indonesia. This was range land, broad, undulating savannas portioned off by stands of palm. For centuries sandalwood forests had covered these spaces, for the sweet-smelling timber that was processed to perfume soaps and religious incense had been prized from Europe to China. But in more recent times the land had been systematically cleared of trees, leaving grasslands to enable another natural resource to thrive. Here the noble Sandalwood horses were bred and raised. These animals resembled the palominos of the American Southwest, and though broader of withers and shorter of leg, they were stocky beauties nonetheless, with a constitution suited to the tropics. Sumba has been world-famous for these horses, which were coveted by the British Raj for the cavalries of India and South Africa. Herds of white Brahman cattle also grazed in this glistening, fenceless country. Johnny referred to the boys who tended them as "cattlers," a coined term so appropriate that it rang with authenticity.

We motored on, passing through wide salt flats before the road turned inland and began a gentle but steady rise. A motorcycle appeared a few hundred yards on, traveling in the same direction we were. We closed the gap and passed it, receiving a horn blast from the driver as a rebuke. Several miles up the road he overtook us, but Johnny urged his machine forward, making a race out of it. The other driver, however, gave us no road, and we were no more than two lengths behind when Johnny's speedometer read 100 kph. The road now was paved only intermittently, and I feared for my life, but just before I cried out, our fellow racer slowed for a turnoff, and Johnny sounded his horn, waving as we passed. "Aha-ha-ha-ha-ha!"

The bridges we crossed en route to Rende were especially grueling; when we hit the steel-framed structures with beds of unevenly spaced railroad ties, the bumps jolted the spine and produced a clattering like erratic machine-gun fire.

"That wedding next week where you're going to sing," I said when we stopped for a stretch. "Is it to be a traditional Sumbanese ceremony? Is it Muslim?"

"Christian," he said, lighting a cigarette. Johnny was a chain-smoker and a constant belcher.

"Are you a Christian?" I said.

"Pentecostal," he said. "Most people on Sumba Christian."

I assumed that Johnny meant the "civilized" Sumbanese. In my research for the trip, I had read that only twenty percent of Sumba's population had been converted to Christianity, and that Islam, imported by Arab horse traders, had scarcely gained a foothold. "And Mister Hassan?" I said. "Is he not a Muslim?"

"Hassan Pentecostal, too. Aha-ha-ha-ha-ha!"

I found myself liking Johnny, who was an original, and preferred him to Mr. Hassan, whose oiliness underlined the huckster in him. Johnny was only half Chinese, I learned, for his mother was from Sulawesi. This dual heritage was a source of pride for him, for he spoke with contempt of the "pure Chinese" who ran my hotel. It was another reminder of the uneasy truce between Malays and Chinese in these islands. He was married to a Sumbanese woman and had a daughter called Sabrina, named after the Audrey Hepburn character in that movie of the mid-fifties which also starred William Holden and Humphrey Bogart. When he learned that I knew such trivia, he became my friend as well as a paid guide.

Johnny had learned English when he worked in Surabaya and Jakarta singing in nightclubs, and I tried to picture the neon-lit, smoky dives, the nocturnal hangouts of sailors, prostitutes, and other lowlifes, where this self-styled Elvis imitator had been king. He played guitar and piano by ear, he told me. He could not read music.

"Do you know a song, 'Surabaya Johnny,' by Kurt Weill?" I said at one point.

He had me repeat the song and composer several times, even hum it, but his knowledge of Western music did not include the idiomatic cynicism and despair of 1930s Berlin cabarets. He was taken, however, by the song's title.

"Now, you call me 'Sumba Johnny,' " he said, cackling his infectious laugh. And so I did.

Our talk turned to politics. He wondered why Ronald Reagan, a name that rolled mellifluously off Malay tongues, could not have continued to be president. When I explained that a president was prohibited from seeking a third consecutive term, he was perplexed.

"And Suharto?" I said.

"Aha-ha-ha-ha-ha-ha. Suharto! Aha-ha-ha-ha. Suharto be president when he dead. Aha!"

I wondered whether Malays were anarchists at heart: loyal to family and village custom, religion, and law, but distrustful of the central government so remote from local affairs. Lip service was paid to Pancasila, with its five principles stressing unity in a country where unity was virtually impossible. To be sure, Suharto's nearly twenty-five-year rule, the cohesiveness he gave his nation of islands and disparate peoples, was a remarkable political feat. But while Pancasila was formally embraced by "civilized" Indonesians, stories of government corruption from the top down were impossible to dissociate from the official meliorism.

As we approached Rende the road became more tortured, both by the seasonal rains and the unrelenting sun, which now baked the white ruts harder than asphalt. Johnny explained the traditional Sumbanese religion of *marapu*, which could be seen in various chameleon guises throughout the archipelago. Marapu taught that the invisible world beyond our own ruled the visible world and its inhabitants. While death would claim us all, what happened after was less democratic, and a family was required, on pain of retribution by its ancestors, to send its deceased well prepared for the long journey to the invisible kingdom. Hence the sacrifice of animals and the flaunting of wealth in ikat and jewelry at burial ceremonies, not to mention the erection of gigantic tombstones. Such a sendoff would ensure that the spirit of the deceased would find the invisible ladder at the island's Cape Sasar and ascend to the spiritual world, rather than remain earthbound as a shade to haunt living souls.

The village itself stood on a barren hill covered with goat droppings and consisted of wooden buildings as old as two hundred years, with steeply sloping thatched roofs now covered with corrugated tin and walls decorated with buffalo skulls. Fewer than a hundred people now lived here, and most were tending crops in the fields. Outside the central house Johnny introduced me to the chief, an old man who clutched a stubble of unlit cigar in his stained teeth. His body was covered with tribal tattoos.

Rende was a devitalized shell of a place. The veneer of ancient tradition remained, but the young men of the tribe had trickled away, sometimes taking their women with them, often not, to seek livelihoods elsewhere, in Waingapu and the hamlets around it. In the absence of people I was greeted at every building by snarling, mangy dogs who instinctively allied themselves into a growling, moving circle. When I reached down, pretending to pick up a rock, they slunk away. In some of the buildings women sat on woven mats, engaged in the various stages of ikat production, weaving and dying, using such plants as the indigo leaf, but their work seemed pitifully resigned.

The oddest sight was a red 1960 Buick sedan parked behind the chief's house. According to Johnny the automobile had belonged to the last tribal king, whose role the Indonesian government had disallowed by way of breaking up rival petty kingdoms that had waged war over land claims. As he was now the elected chief, the car had passed to him, and it decorated his premises like a great steel idol.

Accepting a cigarette, the chief invited me to inspect the village's tombstones, mammoth stone pillars supporting rectangular slabs with elaborate carvings, which protected the graves of aristocrats.

They stood at mid-village in a line, marking the burial ground. Though some were as old as the village, bearing weathered carved monkeys and other sphinxlike beasts, others were quite recent. The chief explained that it took as many as a hundred men to plunder the mountain, using axes, to cut free the huge slabs of stones—some weighing as much as twenty tons—and then drag them with ropes made of bark fibers back to the village. He pointed to such a rope; it was thicker than my leg.

Rende remained a half-forgotten monument, enticing only the traveler like me, forced to make the best of the decision that had brought him here in the first place. The heat was stifling, and I was relieved when Sumba Johnny suggested we start back to Waingapu.

Once we stopped in a settlement for a drink. The tiny café was a filthy hole in the wall. Outside, the ground was covered with excrement, and the stench of fish drying on racks fouled the air. The scene was presided over by a hunchbacked dwarf who asked us for cigarettes. Inside, rude wooden tables were mired in a dirt floor, where cats and dogs and naked children crawled among the betel-nut stains. The place was run by a native Roman Catholic, who had pictures of a blue-eyed Christ in various roles, the healer, mystic, and martyr, on the mat-covered wall. We sat at a table and ordered bottled water, but the proprietor had none, so we settled for warm Sprites. Outside, the dwarf begged for more cigarettes as we mounted the motorcycle.

"When you leave?" said Sumba Johnny suddenly over his shoulder.

"Tomorrow, for Kupang," I said, "if I can get a seat on the Merpati flight."

"I no blame. There's nothing here," he said, exhaling a great blast of cigarette smoke. For once he didn't laugh, and he had the look of a man who had seen something of the world, but not enough, before the fates cast him up on Sumba.

Timor hovers like a disembodied finger some three hundred miles from the northwestern face of Australia. The island, the largest in Nusa Tenggara, is three hundred miles long and sixty miles wide, and Kupang, the island's capital, is the southernmost city in the Malay Archipelago.

I flew into Kupang with the hope of obtaining a *surat jalan*, an official travel permit, which would enable me to visit the politically troubled eastern part of the island, at this time off-limits to foreigners. But that would not be so easy, for the *Fretilin* (the Revolutionary Front for an Independent East Timor) still prosecuted its interests with a vengeance, and the Indonesian military routinely forbade foreigners to travel there. The Fretilin has mounted guerrilla operations against Indonesian forces for over fifteen years, since the Portuguese dictator Salazar's ouster by the Portuguese military in 1974, the new government's abandonment of its luckless colony in 1975 (like its abandonment of Angola in Southern Africa, which spawned a lengthy civil war), and Indonesia's annexation of East Timor in 1976. Annexation was achieved despite a United Nations resolution that urged self-determination for East Timor's bewildered citizens, caught in a political vacuum turned battlefield.

On Pearl Harbor Day in 1975, Indonesian forces invaded East Timor with an assault on the port city of Dili. For a couple of years the Fretilin guerrillas proved their mettle as fighters, before they were worn down and diminished into scattered bands. The world beyond seemed little interested and learned almost nothing of this civil war. That, as the Indonesian government saw it, was all to the better, as proved by the army's killing of five Australian journalists covering the war.

I learned firsthand that the Indonesian military does not appreciate a foreigner's curiosity about this history. My application for a permit was flatly denied by the commandant at the Kupang Military Command. The post was on the outskirts of the city hard by the governor's mansion, a bizarre chartreuse fortress heralded by a row of Doric columns painted British racing green.

"You may not hope to go to the east under any circumstances," a flamboyant colonel curtly told me in English, after I had presented him with a copy of my letter of introduction. "Do you realize that I could have you expelled from the country for possessing such a letter as this? Your letter speaks of conducting research. What sort of research? You must have a document from the High Military Command in Jakarta to conduct any research."

The germination of the current separatist struggle can be found in Timor's colonial history. Like many of the islands of Nusa Tenggara before European colonization, Timor was divided into small kingdoms, in this case of Atoni and Tetum peoples, who waged war among themselves and took the heads of their enemies. But the Portuguese arrived in the sixteenth century to seize the sandalwood trade; they were followed a hundred years later by the Dutch, who began a protracted nudging of the Portuguese into the eastern side of the island before a formal boundary was defined in the last century.

Control of Timor by the two European powers was largely nominal and benign, for the mysterious hinterland remained largely unknown to Westerners, while Kupang on the western tip of the island idled and thrived at the hands of the Dutch until Indonesia's independence in 1945. That the Europeans had invested little in the island beyond the sandalwood trade is crucial in understanding East Timor's separatist movement. The Fretilin's position might be summed up as follows: if the Portuguese presence was little more than vestigial and natives of the former colony wanted self-determination after its abandonment, then the Indonesian invasion of East Timor was criminal and its annexation anathema.

The joining of mountains and sea around Kupang composes a picture that belies any trouble in the interior. A long, bent arm of peninsula, a ridge of saw-toothed peaks, gathers the bay in and seemingly portions out the sea beyond as if to its liking. The beauty of the natural harbor is sharpened by a sense of remoteness. American whaling ships of Melville's day called here, but the island has seen few Americans, or any outsiders, since. Kupang is closer to Darwin in Australia's Northern Territory than it is to Bali. In 1857 Alfred Russel Wallace saw a population of Malays, Chinese, and Dutch, with a large native population more closely allied in physique and skin color to the Papuans of New Guinea than to the other islanders of Nusa Tenggara. Today only the Dutch are no longer present, and there has been the inevitable intermingling of races.

The city of Kupang is highly charged, with an active street life, especially in the mornings and late afternoons, before and after the fierce blasts of heat, when the storefronts are open. Along the busy Jalan Suderman pass barefoot, sarong-clad hawkers and peddlers wearing the traditional pyramidal hats of straw, carrying their wares in baskets at either end of a wooden pole. Many carry strings of fish, and they all walk slowly but with purpose, unperturbed by the din of horns and Western rock music that announces the passing of bemos.

I had found on my arrival a small hotel with a garden on this busy avenue. In the lobby, cooling fans whirred overhead, recalling

Somerset Maugham and an earlier day. It was a charming oasis with a faithful and colorful clientele of assorted expatriates and natives. My satisfaction in staying here was double: I was surrounded with the cozy familiarity of English-speakers, who were not tourists but lived and often worked in the archipelago and regarded the hotel as a home away from home.

There was Peter, a Dutch-born, bearded, pipe-smoking missionary who had taken the room across the garden from mine. He was returning from a church conference to his home in the interior, where he had lived for years with his family. Nick, a large, affable man, was a Canadian engineer based in Jakarta who was involved in projects all over the archipelago. He had lived in Indonesia for years, was married to a Balinese woman, and spoke Bahasa Indonesia fluently.

Clarence was a hard-drinking retired hotelier from Australia, and Logan was a punch-drunk, mercurial middleweight gone to seed, with a bleached face so swollen with scar tissue that he resembled a figure from a wax museum. Clarence and Logan, both in their sixties, lived at the hotel; independently and together, they paid court to Diana, a Timorese with carnal eyes and crooked teeth who dressed smartly and constantly combed out her Afro. Diana had two children and a husband in Darwin. She was keenly aware of the scent she threw off which crazed the two older men. Johan was a young married Timorese who managed the hotel and dreamed of quitting to find work in Australia. We were an odd lot when we assembled by chance in the hotel's small bar and restaurant.

On my first evening after dinner, when the others had left, Peter underscored the remoteness of Timor's hill people.

"Recently, I made a visit to a village in West Timor whose inhabitants hadn't seen a white man since the agitation for independence forty years ago," he said. "Though the villagers knew the struggle against the Dutch was over, they wanted the peace confirmed and formalized for them in ritual that would be noted in village records. Thereupon the elders proposed that I accept a gift of village handiwork, but only on the condition that I accept it on behalf of the Dutch government. An elaborate ceremony was held, attended by the solemn villagers, and the gift was accepted by me in the name of peace and the sanctity of the human bond. Can you imagine that?''

"What became of the handiwork?" I asked.

"Why, the fabric's on the wall of my own house. What else was I to do with it? Send it to The Hague? The Dutch had little use for Timor beyond the sandalwood trade, and they've been gone for forty years."

"Except for you."

"Except for me," he agreed, laughing and exhaling smoke. "It's rather a nice story, a gift bridging a forty-year schism. There's a lot to be said for ritual."

"Especially when it succeeds," I said. "My ritual to acquire a permit for East Timor came to naught this morning at the Kupang Military Command."

"What happened?"

"I was told that authorization to visit the east had to come from the High Military Command in Jakarta."

"That must mean Suharto himself," said Peter, half joking.

"If I could produce such an official document, then he would issue me a permit."

"Why do you want to visit East Timor?"

"If no foreigners have been allowed there for years, there must be a story in it," I said.

"I wouldn't try it," Peter said flatly. "There could be trouble. Best to forget about it."

Late the next morning I ran into Nick, the engineer, in the lobby and told him of my failure to get a permit. His driver, standing nearby, listened attentively.

"The post seemed a rather laid-back outfit," I said. "Not so spit-and-polish."

"Though they can be," said Nick. "In some of the outer reaches these fellows wear their pistols strapped to their legs when they go out on the town in civilian clothes and put on quite a show to impress the locals."

Suddenly the driver began speaking with some agitation. Nick listened, then explained.

"Neither can he go to East Timor. He has an ID card placing him here. The military in Indonesia likes to know where everybody is. But let's say he has family beyond the border, is refused a permit, but decides to risk the trip anyway because he hasn't seen his family in years. So he boards a bus and crosses the island. At a checkpoint, sentries board to inspect passengers and their documents, and they discover he has no bona fides. They haul him away and think nothing of roughing him up more than a bit. What with confinement and torture, they make a sterling example of him.

"You'd be spared at least that. You could simply go, or try to, and see what happens. You can always claim ignorance, and perhaps the worst that could happen is that they'd send you back. The worst from the military, that is. Far worse would be to fall into the hands of the Fretilin terrorists, but I'd say that's a long shot. The Merpati agents won't sell you a ticket unless you have a permit, so you can forget about flying. This is not a suggestion, but you could just get on an eastbound bus and see what happens. If you're caught, plead ignorance."

Nick departed with his driver to attend to business, but he left me with the tantalizing notion of sneaking a visit to East Timor. As expected, the Merpati officials in the office next to the hotel refused to sell me a ticket to Dili without a permit, so I decided to try the buses, whose conductors would be more interested in a fare than a destination. I prepared a small bag and planned to leave that night.

The darkness, I reasoned, would make me less conspicuous to officials at checkpoints. I studied a map. A single road traversed the length of the island, passing through such towns as Camplong, Soe, Niki-Niki, Kefamenanu, and Atambua and the port of Atapupa, both near the old border. If I established Atapupa as an intermediate destination, I could reach it by morning and then take another bus into Dili, the capital in the east whose harbor was lined with sunken Japanese vessels from the Second World War. Dili was supposed to have a Portuguese charm, though Wallace in the 1850s had found it "a most miserable place compared with even the poorest of the Dutch towns."

Dili also had a more recent distinction. In the fall of 1989, Pope John Paul II traveled to Indonesia and became the first world leader to visit East Timor since Indonesia invaded the territory. In Dili he celebrated Mass on a barren plain that had been a killing field for government troops during the annexation, when 200,000 East Timorese out of a total population of 650,000 had been slaughtered by the Indonesian army. Though the Pope insisted that his visit to this rare Catholic stronghold in the archipelago was pastoral rather than political, he delivered a shrewd homily on human rights that was translated into the local Tetum dialect.

In his sermon he denounced "destruction and death as a result of conflict" and addressed his 100,000 listeners as "victims of hatred and struggle." As the Mass began, he knelt to kiss a crucifix placed on a cushion on the ground; that brought forth cheers. The widespread perception was that this papal kiss, reserved for countries visited for the first time, conferred upon East Timor a tacit acknowledgment of autonomy. After the celebration, as the Pope departed for the airport, the still smoldering passions resulting from a decade and a half of Indonesian rule erupted into a melee between East Timorese separatists and the military police.

Kupang's bus terminal was in the old city near the waterfront. I carried my own food and water and wasted little time in buying a ticket and boarding, and soon after seven the bus pulled out of the terminal and wound its way through the city toward the highlands. Though we stopped frequently for passengers, the bus was never full, and the highlanders with their sacks of papaya, cassava, and other staples were sober and quiet.

It was barely light when we reached Atambua at the border.

Only a few kilometers from here was the old cattle port of Atapupa, dating from the sixteenth century, where the mountains plunged down to the sea. It would be a good place to stop for a morning's swim before continuing to Dili along the road, which turned toward the mountains from the coast and then back at a ninety-degree angle to the East Timor port. With any luck, I would sleep that night in Dili.

But as I was searching out a bemo to take me to Atapupa, a uniformed man hailed me and ordered me into a corrugated-tin hut just off the terminal's grounds, where an army officer and two enlisted men were stationed.

The young officer, speaking English, demanded to see my permit, and when I said that I had none, he asked for my passport. From behind his sunglasses, he looked at me the way a cat might a goldfish.

"You are Mister Char-les?"

I gave him my full name, which was already spelled out in the passport.

"Not Char-les Bronson?" He laughed and so did the other men, flashing menacing gold teeth in the early-morning sun. "I think I shall call you Mister Char-les Bronson because Char-les Bronson is very strong and very brave, and he is an American like yourself."

Drawing an official rebuke, even a raving one, and an order to return to Kupang was to be expected. But I hadn't counted on being taunted.

"I admire Char-les Bronson very much," I said. "I am proud that you have given me his name. I only wish that he were with me now."

That prompted another bray of laughter. "Char-les Bronson, superstar," said the officer. "Now, Mister Char-les Bronson, why are you where you are not supposed to be?" He flipped through my passport, smiling as though it were a comic book.

I told the officer that I didn't know I was not supposed to be here, that I was not interested in politics, that I wanted to see the other side of the island, et cetera, and then produced the official-

looking, benign letter of introduction from my publisher. Indonesians, I found, coveted documents, which were tactile and as
such conferred a degree of status upon the bearer. Many times
throughout my trip, I was asked for a business or calling card. A
workable compromise, if a bit unwieldy, was Xeroxes of my letter,
which I prudently dispensed. The letter, as I saw it, was a subtle
method of self-confirmation: I was tuan, Big Boss, Important Man.
It was capable of opening doors or slamming them in my face.

"So Mister Char-les Bronson, you wish to go to East Timor.
And what will you do there? It is no place now for tourists or
even a traveler, as you like to call yourself. Even if you had a
permit, I would strongly urge you to turn back. Now I must insist
on it. Think of the trouble you might cause both our countries if
the Fretilin were to take you. If you were lucky, you would be a
hostage. If not so lucky, you would be killed in an unpleasant
fashion. They would hack off your hands and feet, cut off your
private parts, stuff them in your mouth, and sew it shut with tree-
bark fibers for thread and a wooden needle. We, of course, could
not report such an incident, and you would never be heard from
again."

"Where did you learn to speak English so fluently?" I asked
with genuine curiosity. Part of me believed his grim forecast of
politicized terrorists gone amok.

"At the military academy, and then I was trained by the U.S.
Army Rangers."

"So was I." It was true. As a Marine Corps reconnaissance
officer, I had passed through the Ranger course years before. It
was preposterous, these studly, ersatz claims of fraternity in a
wretched tin hut hard beside a border in central Timor.

He stood and returned my passport, then offered his hand. "I
must warn you, do not try to come back, my captain." He gestured
to the policeman. "My friend will show you to the bus."

I turned to leave, but heard the officer behind me. "One final
thing, Mister Char-les Bronson. May I have your autograph?"

I was tired and both angry and ashamed at being caught so far off the bag, sufficiently so that I had difficulty appreciating the extraordinary scenery on the daylong return to Kupang. Later, of course, it became funny, and I had few doubts that the young officer would produce the slip of paper with "Charles Bronson" scrawled on it for his compatriots and convince them that the movie star had actually passed through his hut. He had a document as proof.

But the incident had given me a new arrow for my quiver. Uncountable times for the rest of my journey, I would work the Char-les Bronson gag to my benefit. The actor had the most famous American name in Indonesia, with Stevie Wonder a close second, and I provoked laughter and made friends easily when I passed myself off as Bronson. If our State Department were to send Charles Bronson on a goodwill tour of Indonesia, he would be mobbed like a rock musician, and relations between our peoples, if not our governments, would be forever and happily cemented. Later in Kupang I asked an ardent fan if Clint Eastwood was accorded equal standing.

"Absolutely not," I was told.

"Why not?"

"Because he went into politics!" was the derisive answer.

An hour out of Kupang, the bus wound along a ridge that commanded intermittent vistas of the sea, and I gazed through the foothills to the coast where the Japanese launched their invasion of the island in 1942, enveloping a large contingent of Australian troops that had massed in Kupang to block Japan's invasion of their continent.

The Australian troops who eluded capture engaged the invaders with guerrilla tactics, aided by the Timorese. The latter paid dearly for their collaboration, both at the hands of the Japanese, who destroyed whole villages, and later at the hands of Allied bombers, whose strikes were undiscriminating once the Australians were evacuated in January 1943. Famine ensued, and by war's end sixty thousand Timorese had perished.

Twenty miles out of Kupang, the bus stopped at a market village whose only concessions to modernity were a few overgrown Dutch ruins and a small whitewashed palace fringed by poinsettia and bougainvillea, as well as two sandalwood trees giving off the faint sweet aroma of soap. Ikat was woven and sold in this small palace, on whose living-room walls hung photographs. One, taken outdoors a half century ago, was of Buan's last king, young and starched as a cricket player in white drill shirt and trousers, and barefoot. Another was a parlor portrait of two princesses: one seated, the other standing, both in the stylish Western dress of that earlier day and high-heeled pumps.

The market was only a short walk away. A kid, its legs bound, bleated in terror as it was carried toward a compound several hundred yards in circumference, where similarly trussed squealing shoats and chickens were displayed. Young cattle were tethered to trees outside the market, while within, men and women were seated on ground stained red with betel-nut spittle and smelling strongly of livestock droppings. In three different dialects, by my count, they were hawking wares from tiny dried shrimp and other foodstuffs to long utility knives fashioned from hard, pliable steel, weapons evolved over centuries of headhunting.

Beyond were several crowded thatched warungs, the open windows curtained off by hangings of raw and cooked pork, and behind them a footpath led downhill to a two-room *ruang*, or house, where the *kepala kampung*, or village chief, lived with his wife. The chief was a gregarious fellow, and he invited me inside. I expected the place to be filthy, but it was as spotless as it was simple. Its walls told that they were a Christian couple, for pictures of the Protestant Jesus were everywhere. The chief's lips and chin were smeared blood-crimson from betel nut, while his wife, a busty woman wrapped in a sarong and seated on the floor, clearly avoided the habit.

The betel-nut crimson on the lips of these peasant women highlighted their natural sensuality. One woman selling vegetables

had blond hair and gray eyes, though her skin was no lighter than
the others', and when I tried to converse with her in Bahasa
Indonesia, she answered in a tribal dialect.

"Her father . . . sailor," said a woman, rising from an adjacent
stall. "You sailor, tuan?" She cackled and elbowed me in the ribs,
a pointed reminder of the fictional Surabaya Johnny's legacy in
these islands.

At the bus the police had boarded to check for livestock stolen
from the market. The delay seemed interminable, so I began walking toward Kupang. After two kilometers I heard female voices
in the jungle and turned off through a grove of sweet-smelling
sandalwood trees to find a small group of young women bathing
in a pool fed by a spring, surrounded by centuries-old rain trees.
Some torsos were covered and as many were not, the dark areolae
of their nipples shriveled from the chilly bath.

The smell of deep, fresh water in such abundance was nearly
overpowering. Believing myself an interloper who had stumbled
upon a forbidden sight in the Garden of Eden, I turned to leave,
but the boldest of the girls laughed and invited me to join them,
and her brazenness steeled the others. "I love you, I love you,"
they chirped. I habitually wore a pair of swim trunks under my
trousers for the occasional chance dip. When I placed my shoulder
bag on the ground and began removing my shirt, the covey
squealed in embarrassment and glee and rushed from the water
to hide. When I started back toward the road to flag a bus, their
voices trailed me in an uneven chorus of teasing siren-song. "I
love you, I love you."

Though few Westerners have heard of Kupang and fewer still
can locate it on a map, this backwater port was the termination
of one of the most remarkable feats of seamanship ever recorded.
In 1789 Kupang was Captain William Bligh's landfall after the
Bounty mutineers, led by Fletcher Christian, set him and his eighteen loyalists adrift in a twenty-three-foot open longboat with a
beam of six feet, nine inches for a voyage of thirty-six hundred

miles from the Tonga group in the South Pacific. I would find no native of Kupang who had ever heard of Captain Bligh, though the remains of some of his crew lie under weathered stones in the old Dutch cemetery.

Late one morning, Nick, the Canadian engineer, hailed me in the hotel and invited me for lunch. We had beer and shrimp at an old place in the original harbor, overlooking the surf. Naked children played in the water, and men were beaching an outrigger dugout where Captain Bligh's prow had grated sand two centuries ago. When we had paid and were about to leave, the waitress cleared our table by tossing beer bottles, paper napkins, and food scraps out the window for the incoming tide to claim.

We went in search of the final resting place of Captain Bligh's crew. Nick had bantered with the girl who served us lunch, and as we walked I remarked on the essential Indonesian character, which the waitress seemed to personify.

"Whatever else, there's a sweetness about these islanders," I said.

"I'll tell you a story," he said, nodding. "A few years ago I was administrative head of a project up in Central Sulawesi. The chief engineer on the job was a Ukrainian chap who had no family. He was both a perfectionist and a prima donna and could be very difficult. The chief of the work force was a Sumatran, and one day he ran afoul of the Ukrainian, who in a fit of anger ordered the man out of his presence.

"Now if there's one thing you never do with an Indonesian, it is to lose your temper. Very bad form. Very bad form indeed. So here I was with this quarrel dividing the engineer and the laborers and a government contract on my hands to get on with the work.

"I went to the Ukrainian and explained that he ought to apologize for his rage, and he absolutely refused. You can imagine the bind this put me in, but it gave me an idea.

"So I went to the Sumatran and told him, 'The engineer is so ashamed of his actions that he cannot face you. He has sent me to apologize for him. Please accept it. You perhaps do not know that he is absolutely alone in the world. His father is dead and his old mother is in the Ukraine, but he is not allowed to go back there again, ever. His only brother was killed in an automobile accident. He has no wife and no children. He is absolutely alone. Isn't that a pathetic condition?'

"This was all true, of course. Not invented by me except for the subterfuge about the apology. But the reaction of the Sumatran was astounding. 'Absolutely alone,' he mumbled over and over in disbelief. Tears welled up in his eyes. Now by chance, the Ukrainian was passing by outside the quarters where we were talking, and when the Sumatran saw this he rushed outside, threw himself upon the startled engineer, and embraced him long and hard like a lost brother now found."

We looked in vain among the rain-worn stones for members of Bligh's crew who had survived the ordeal only to die here; the years of weathering had made it impossible to identify the oldest markers. The plots were unkempt, and at one place between two graves there was a garbage heap. The ground was rock-hard, and we wondered how it could be broken to accept a coffin or shrouded body. A lone goat foraged among the ground cover of briars and wildflowers worked over by swarms of bees. At the cliff's edge were two thatched huts, with large fishing nets drying in the sun. It was eerily quiet except for the undulations of waves below and the occasional cock crowing and goat bleating: a place banished from time.

That evening Nick and I took a bemo blaring raucous rock music back to the waterfront, this time to Teddy's, a self-styled barbecue place with a dirt floor, run by a Timorese married to an Australian woman. Kupang's bemos bear such names as "Flying Fortress," "Chelsy," "Madonna," "Mick Jagger," "James Bond," "Menhetten," "Bellini," "Americana," "Liberty," and "Fata Morgana"; and these are not simply hip whimsy but indicate the names and destinations of the lines. We boarded "James Bond" and paid our fare to a conductor who admitted to nine years of age. At the restaurant our lobsters were cooked on an open fire in an oil drum. Over dinner Nick elaborated upon the sanctity of family he'd touched on earlier.

"We're entering the final week of Ramadan in a few days, and it's the holiest time of year for Indonesian Muslims. Do you know that at this time upwards of one million people leave Jakarta for their native villages, whether on Sumatra, in Nusa Tenggara, Kalimantan, Sulawesi, wherever? One million! They go home to beg forgiveness of their sins from their parents, and this is a tradition that runs far deeper than Islam.

"The Balinese and other Hindu-Buddhist sects believe in ancestor worship as well as reincarnation. My wife is typical. She firmly believes that her grandparents are up there watching over her. For a Balinese your antecedents may come back as your children, and that accounts in part for the tremendous love for children in this country. You're not one person but countless people. It's all deeply spiritual, and the human bond is all the stronger. You know, it's funny. My wife actually feels sorry for me. Not in any sanctimonious way, but she knows she's happy in a way I can never understand."

"Small wonder they feel sorry for us," I said.

"A happy people," said Nick. "Indonesians feel good about themselves. No wonder villagers are suspicious of outsiders who arrive armed with Freud, feminism, confused social notions, not to mention an unhealthy dose of spiritual poverty."

Nick left the next morning, and I arranged passage on a ship returning to Java. That evening, my last in Kupang, I joined Clarence, Logan, Johan, and Diana at the place that served the best native fare in town. The expansive Australians swelled the ranks at our large table with unattached girls, one of whom slid into the empty chair beside me and took my hand. "My name Lena, I like you, I no bullshit," she said, and the others laughed.

"She's from the island of Roti, mate, and she's only nineteen. But what a nineteen," said Clarence.

Clarence and Logan positioned Diana between them and presided over a liter of Johnnie Walker Black Label, which the men cut with warm Coca-Cola. Logan pontificated on the joys of drink, while I sipped my scotch neat.

"So I drink but never on the job," he said, happily downing the sweet mixture.

"Yes, of course you don't drink on the job," rejoined Clarence. "You're not a desk-drawer drinker because you have no desk and no job. So of course you don't drink on the job, Logan. Chuck, you've got the sweats. Are you hot, mate? Lena, what are you doing to our Yank, girl?"

I was perspiring not only from the heat but from the spicy smoked meats and seafood served up. Switching from whisky to warm beer failed to extinguish the fire.

"Look at Johan," said Logan. "He never sweats. 'Course, Diana gives him no reason to."

Johan had worked in Darwin and spoke English with an Australian accent. He wanted to secure papers to emigrate with his family to Australia as keenly as Clarence and Logan had wanted to escape it. But he bristled at Logan, who clearly was a mean drunk.

"We Malays are used to the heat," he said.

But Logan, who talked in fits and starts, wasn't convinced. "Brown people simply don't sweat," he said, "though I must say that sweating here is a lot healthier than sweating in Melbourne. I think it does more good for your skin, cleans it better than the priciest creams, and then the breezes come up and cool you off. But niggers simply are different. You know the pygmies of Africa live in forests where there's no breeze, as if they're in a sauna or a greenhouse, but the bleeding savages of darkest Africa don't perspire the way a white man does."

"We're used to it," said Johan flatly, showing more than a hint of irritation.

"Don't mind old Logan, Johan," said Clarence. "You mean well, don't you, Logan, you sudsy bastard. Your hair hurt, mate?"

"My hair don't hurt. I mean well. Sure I do. Of course I mean well. Who says I don't mean well?" said Logan as another round of drinks was poured. "What are you trying to make me out to be? Don't fucking patronize me, you son of a bitch," he said, half rising from his chair. "You've imbibed some giggle water yourself!"

"Now, Logan, we got a proper guest. Act like a civilized man, if you think you can manage."

"Yeh, let's have a civilized discussion for a change," said Johan.

"Johan speaks to me of civilization," said Logan. "Do you hear that, mates? Suppose you tell Chuck here the story of how you negotiated a successful dowry for your bride, who was seven months pregnant when you married her in a Christian ceremony."

"Piss off, Logan," said Johan, while Logan snorted a loud laugh.

I excused myself to leave but outside was accosted by each Australian in turn. Each spoke with the desperation of a drowning man.

"Good luck, mate," said Logan. "Sorry about in there, but I could kick him in the trophies for the way he rides me. Clarence is a bloody superior snot. But what I wanted to ask you, Chuck, is, say, could you spare a fellow white man a few thousand rupiah notes? There's a good bloke. You like the girl from Roti? Lena? She's yours. I'll send her to your room. Clarence fancies her, too. But she's yours if I tell her so."

"Thanks just the same," I said and offered my hand.

"Don't mind Logan, mate. Safe journey, Chuck," said Clarence, closing my taxi door. "I've got a bad heart, you know. Never know when the ax is going to fall, so I'm finishing my run here. But if I've got a bad heart, that poor devil has a bad head, the old poltroon."

"How does he get along?"

"Better than you might think. Somebody sends him a little money. Not much but enough for the time he's got, and that's not a lot, but it makes him rich as a Fugger in Kupang. Then he hits up me, you, whoever. You know I'm sixty-seven. Poor Lo-

gan's sixty-two, and he's losing it fast. Why the hell Johan wants
to find work in Australia is beyond me. The grass is greener, I
suppose. Why would anyone want to ever leave here for Rotten
Row in Darwin? I don't admit to sounding Podsnappery, but Kupang's as tidy a place as any to ring in the changes."

I was leaving tomorrow.

Notes from a Diary: Sailing the *Keli Mutu*

*F*ROM A GODOWN at Kupang's stench-ridden port, the *Keli Mutu* appears as white and glimmering and inaccessible as a glacier. Outside in the foul heat, I wait to board the ship with a thousand other human bodies. The security guards seem to relish the crowd's discomfiture, for they take their time about queuing the huddled masses to allow passage through a makeshift wooden gate, where we will show our tickets before mounting the gangway.

Though sea travel is cheap in these latitudes, stowaways are legion, and officials inspect every ticket. But the gate hasn't opened, and so we stand, an immobilized, expectant, passive mob, while the ship takes on cargo in the sullen late afternoon. Finally the gate opens, and passivity becomes active confusion, anarchy, a mess, as we move helplessly in a forward surge of humanity, funneling through the narrow way. An hour later I stand at the rail, and I notice that my clothes are drenched in sweat. I want to smoke, but the pack of kreteks in my pocket is soaked.

The *Keli Mutu* is a passenger ship, not a cruise ship, and it will be my home for seven days on the return to Java from Timor through the islands of Nusa Tenggara, with the odd run to South Sulawesi and South Kalimantan. A first-class passage, consisting of a shared cabin with three meals a day and afternoon tea, costs a mere hundred dollars. Afternoon and evening meals consist of such island fare as buffalo innards and dried fish. Rice porridge is served for breakfast. Economy class, where the majority of Indonesians as well as Western "budget" travelers are billeted, is a steerage of nearly nine hundred hard bunks welded together, entrance gained from the foot. Here below decks in the evening, the lights burn as bright as in a Manhattan precinct station while fully clothed men, women, and children try to sleep and others play cards.

I have been on many ships, but this is the strangest. The *Keli Mutu* has a bar that serves no alcoholic beverages, a dance floor where dancing is prohibited, a library with no books. In the evening for prayers, Muslims dutifully prostrate themselves on the floor of the mosque, the largest cabin on the ship, with the women behind the men and wrapped in burnooses and caftans from head to toe, their dress resembling brightly colored floral nuns' habits, as is customary in the outer islands. Protestant services are held in the bar, the small congregation singing "What a Friend We Have in Jesus." Outside, the fantail is covered with litter discarded by raucous Malays, many of whom have earlier worked the crowd outside the godown as pickpockets. They wear ear and nose rings and gather in groups to drink beer and listen to American country and western over the loudspeakers.

Days at sea are diverse in their uniformity. Schools of flying fish skip across the azure water; billows of cumulus clouds gather on the horizon, portending the occasional squall in the dry season and rendering the sea and sky one. Often the light is strange and bleakly surreal: days are often overcast, but inconsistently so, kaleidoscopic. What is typically tropical one instant is cast in what looks like slanted northern light the next. At such times, if not for the heat, we might be in the polar region, for the cloud on the sea surface suggests a vast, stained ice cap illuminated by a subdued, gauzy remote sunlight.

In a country of countless islands, I anticipate constant land sightings but discover that this is not the case. The thrust of the Malay Archipelago is essentially west to east, but our zigzag route westward to Java crosses the Flores and Java seas on the north to reach Sulawesi and Borneo, and crosses the Savu Sea on the south to approach the remoter southern rim of the chain.

Islands become visible the way all mountainous islands work their magic at sea: a sudden apparition that seems at first more ephemeral and insubstantial than a cloud, an illusory, massive gray outline as though sketched and shaded by an artist's pencil. It simply wasn't there when you last looked, and now it materializes like a slowly developing photographic print. Rising out of the sea with great green and purple folds and its peak lost in supernal cloud, the island is a sight that lifts up hearts, an exhilarating vision from the crow's nest in more perilous days of Bugis pirate vessels and European square-riggers.

Indigo water gives way to shallow green as we make port. During hours at portside, we witness the loading of sugar and other foodstuffs into the forward hold and the exchange of passengers before we are under way again, pushing away from lush coastline ringed by white beach on a northwest course through the fiercely rolling seas of the Sumba Strait, or southeast across the placid Bali Sea.

There are ten ports of call in the week, so passengers cannot complain of boredom, and each port and its inhabitants differ markedly from the last. History has seen to that. When the great faiths of the Indian and Arab and European colonizers invaded the archipelago as the handmaidens of trade, they collided with ancient animist beliefs. The islanders of the archipelago surround themselves with familiar island spirits and customs as well as the constant, more oppressive strictures of Mecca and Rome, managing to reconcile any outward contradictions. The play of opposites in these backwater ports, with the opposites assuming different guises from one port to the next, lends these cities diversity, color, and verve.

Before dawn on the second day, the seeming absence of motion tells that we have crossed the Savu Sea and glided into the half-moon harbor of Ende on Flores, a Roman Catholic stronghold. Moments later the fierce grinding of anchor chains announces our arrival. In the still darkness men in longboats filled with mandarin oranges, bananas, avocados, and other produce hover around the ship, exchanging their foodstuffs for money through portholes within reach from water level. It is five in the morning, and when dawn streaks over Flores, the market boats take on the graded hues of their cargo: bright greens, oranges, and yellows that contrast sharply with the brown, red, and russet ikat sarongs worn by the women.

Flores and the islands to its east—the Solor and Alor group—are nominally Catholic, with the Pentecostal spirit varying in intensity from island to island. A portion of Magellan's fleet traversed the strait separating Lembata from Alor in 1522, and Portuguese settled in these islands a few years later, purportedly to Christianize the natives. But the old ways were slow to change, and headhunting continued on the remoter islands until thirty years ago.

I descend the gangway to climb into one of the wooden boats circling in the water like a school of carp. The rising sun's glare whitens out much of Ende, rendering it as indistinct as though it were spun in permanent haze. Ten active volcanoes slumber on a central ridge of the island, bordered by tropical forests and lakes of varied hues. Flores, named for its beauty by Portuguese traders who colonized and used it as a staging area for exploiting the Moluccas, or Spice Islands, is arguably the most beautiful island in Nusa Tenggara.

The boat, carrying a dozen or more people, is propelled toward the waterfront by a single oarsman who stands in the stern working the figure-eight technique of Venice's gondoliers. The boy's

T-shirt is emblazoned with "Make me late for breakfast." The boat cannot be completely beached, so we wade ashore in knee-deep water to find hundreds of curious townspeople awaiting this weekly link to the outside world. In the early 1930s Sukarno was banished here by the Dutch and lived under house arrest, scorned by the locals as a leprous rabble-rouser from afar. He remained in Ende until he was freed by the Japanese to foster goodwill for their occupation during World War II.

Beyond the market and its displays of fly-covered prawns and vividly plumaged trussed hens is a large church I take to be the cathedral. The front door is locked, but I enter unchallenged through a side passage at the transept. The empty sanctuary is a curious hybrid of Eastern and Mediterranean, with a lofty ceiling, a high, deep altar, and stained-glass windows, some broken, that depict Portuguese missionaries as well as an island Madonna and Child before a Flores hut. Soon I hear the echo of footsteps, and turn to see a black-robed young man holding a missal approaching me.

In the conversation in English that follows, he explains that he is a seminarian but confesses to having second thoughts about his life's work. The subject of matrimony is much on his mind, an alternative to celibacy that he is considering. With no one else in the sanctuary, he speaks openly, punctuating his speech with exclamations.

"In Indonesia when you marry, you must give to your mother-in-law and to your father-in-law cows, buffalo, perhaps a motor-cycle, and some gold."

"Even though you are a Catholic, you must pay such a dowry?" I ask.

"Oh, yes," he says. "It is the custom in Maumere, my home, and the rest of Indonesia, and it is a pity! And about marriage, what is the custom in America?"

"In America you do not have to give such a dowry. Parents are usually happy to be rid of a daughter, though they pretend otherwise."

"Ha, ha! That is a very good custom! A very good custom! If I do not become a priest, I would like to go to America and marry an American girl, but I think that she would not like me because I am an Indonesian and as an Indonesian, as you can see, I am a dark man. But I cannot go to America because I have no money, and that is a pity!"

"If you are from Maumere, then you must have seen the Pope."

"The Holy Father," he cries. "For me, the chance of a lifetime. Imagine! The Holy Father here at Maumere on Flores. What a miracle!"

En route to Timor in the fall of 1989, Pope John Paul II stopped at the port of Maumere on the north side of the island, where he delivered his sermon from a thatch-roofed altar and spoke of the plight of Indonesian Catholics. They comprise a mere three percent of the country's 180 million people and believe themselves discriminated against in a land that is overwhelmingly Muslim. Even so, the roots of Catholicism in Indonesia, while narrowly constrained, run deep. In 1546, Francis Xavier, the missionary who was one of the six founders of the Society of Jesus, the Jesuits, traveled the Spice Islands and wrote that his arm had become lame from pouring the baptismal waters so many thousands of times.

Undoubtedly aware of his zealous predecessor, the Pope addressed the country's need for "better education and training, more jobs and just wages, and more equitable distribution of the advantages of economic and cultural development." In a nation where the per capita income is $450 a year, his homily did not fall on deaf ears.

"Do Catholics in Indonesia have a bad time of it?" I ask.

The young man, whose name is Simon, ponders a moment before responding. "Not so bad, because all Indonesian people are very religious," he tells me. "All," he adds emphatically. "Even those who are not Catholic. And in America?"

I recite a standard litany of separation of church and state and explain that religion in a secular state is largely a matter of individual training and conscience. But as I do so, I appreciate the elliptical diplomacy of his remark about religion in Indonesia, an echo of Suharto's party line in the Pancasila. It seems to be much on his mind, for he returns to it.

"There is one God," he says, "but in Indonesia many ways of worshiping Him. The Holy Father recognized this when he spoke at Maumere, that Catholics are few and Muslims many."

"You come often to Ende?"

"Oh, no. This is the first time. What a fine city!"

Maumere is a day's ride by bus across the central mountain range that bisects the island. This young man has studied theology, English, and Latin, but his world is at once circumscribed by the parochial and extended by the papal visit.

A blast of the ship's horn summons the passengers, and I extend my hand.

"I hope that I will see you again," he says, "but I do not know whether it will be as husband or priest."

I leave him with his two opposing notions of what might become his life.

The third day. Bima, a dusty Muslim port on the northeastern coast of Sumbawa, seems a world apart from Ende. Ende's Roman Catholic veneer is subtler than the vivid Muslim overlay at Bima. The women here wear not ikat sarongs but ankle-length caftans and floral headdresses that make colorful trains as they speed about on motorcycles. Bright red-and-gold pony-drawn dokars work the dusty streets, and chickens and goats wander at the roadside. One hears the squealing of pigs in Ende, but not here. From a small map I judge the town to be about a mile from the harbor, so I set off.

This day and the next are holidays marking the end of Ramadan. Prayers have just let out, and men and boys file down the road from the mosque under a searing eight-o'clock sun. I pass two cinemas: at the Jung Theater *Disciples of Shao Lin Temple* is playing, while the Surabaya Theater features *Rage of Honor*. Roadside warungs are offering holiday fare, and rock music blasts from loudspeakers. There are small mosques here and there as in any Muslim city, but the largest for this celebratory occasion is the soccer field, where thousands of newspapers, prayer rugs for the devout, have been scattered by the wind. Not far from it is the sultan's palace, from which the kingdom of Bima was once ruled.

The palace is a rambling building of yellow stucco and green eaves, guarded by two gatehouses flanked by five cannons gone to rust. Outside I spot an Australian traveler called Barry from the ship, a bespectacled fellow with a caustic wit and an air of talkative irresolution. We enter together.

Once we are inside the building, the caretaker, a dark, lean man nearing sixty years, with darting eyes, immediately seizes a ceremonial spear and shield from a wall and begins affecting a prancing ceremonial dance, with wild gesticulations, culminating in his unraveling of the sultan's banner. It is a moth-eaten hodgepodge of Dutch and Portuguese flag colors, the Islamic moon and star, and inscrutable lettering suggesting a family motto, and bearing the date 1790.

"Take picture, take picture," says the caretaker's assistant, appearing from nowhere. This seems to be the only English the man knows. A high school student happens along to practice his English and act as a guide.

"I'm damned if I'll take that old bugger's picture. Chuck, mate, please snap me there on the sultan's throne," Barry says, handing me his camera. There is a huge wooden toilet in a large room off the empty one where we stand, and Barry drops his trousers to half-mast and mounts it in regal fashion. When the flash goes off, the three Bimanese look at us as if we are lunatics. "Who is this caretaker fellow?" says Barry, buckling his belt, to the student.

"He sultan cousin. Live in bell tower." Outside at the corner of the property is a high, run-down structure that might house a bell. The caretaker is leading us from room to empty room while performing his screwball arabesques. When we reach winding steps that lead to the cellar, the "translator" stops, as does the student, while the caretaker motions us to follow him below.

"*Jin! Jin!*" cries the translator with a look of terror on his face. We look at the student, who explains, "He no go down. Spirit in form of snake. He say best you not go down either. If snake bite, you die."

This arouses our curiosity, so we follow the sultan's kinsman, while hearing the repetitive, fearful mutterings of the translator above. "Jin, jin, jin, jin . . ." I have not heard that word before or since and cannot find it in my dictionary. But Bahasa Indonesia is a language supple enough to accept localisms. The boy follows us tentatively but remains on the stairs, his fear palpable. The cellar is a small room filled with dusty faux-leather furniture of the sort I remember, with a medicinal smell, from my doctor father's waiting room. I try the sofa and it hisses and wheezes, eliciting a great wail of terror from above.

"Where is the snake?" demands Barry.

"There in corner." We look to where the boy points and see nothing except a paint can and some rags. Then the boy, wide-eyed and solemn, translates the caretaker's words. The sultan when he died went first to heaven and then returned to earth and transformed himself into a snake. Only Abdubahim, the caretaker, sultan's kinsman, and legitimate prince of the kingdom of Bima, is allowed to see this serpent. To everyone else it is invisible.

"Prince Abdubahim has two children, but his wife dead. Her spirit alive here in house," the boy explains as we ascend the steep steps. "Wife looks like visitor to house. Prince Abdubahim say wife looks like you," he tells Barry.

"You mean I look like his wife?" says Barry.

Prince Abdubahim intercepts the question, nodding with great conviction. A group of townspeople have gathered and look at us in speechless horror as though we were ascending from Hell. "Jin, jin, jin . . ." they mutter.

At Prince Abdubahim's urging, we take a dokar to find the

sultan's tomb, reputedly the most spectacular sight in Bima, and take the boy as our guide, traversing roads rutted and baked harder than stone.

The tomb, situated in an oasis in the middle of a scraggly field, is an eighteen-by-six-foot piece of what appears to be stonework under a thatched hut; closer inspection reveals it to be mortar over brick. The carved inscription reads, "Raja-Raja Bima Tolubali—1931," and there is Arabic script on the partially exposed inner vault. A herd of farting goats has conscripted the place, nibbling at tufts of grass atop the tomb as well as trash beside it. It soon becomes apparent that this is two graves, not one.

"His wife?" asks Barry.

"Friend," says our guide.

"Girlfriend?"

"No, man friend."

"Probably why the dynasty ceased," says Barry. We leave while patriarchs chant their prayers at nearby family plots.

Bima lacks charm, but it has two thousand dokars, and all are gathered at the harbor with passengers for the *Keli Mutu* and loved ones to see them off. Women in their varicolored caftans hold large black umbrellas to protect them from the sun as they cry their farewells on this next-to-last day of Ramadan. It has been a long month, and this is a happy time for happy people on this day called *Idilfitri,* the holiest day in the Islamic calendar.

Making his way through the crowd at the godown is Prince Abdubahim. He approaches us frantically flashing a dog-eared snapshot of a short, flaccid man in dirty robes and bare feet who overflows his chair and glares petulantly at the camera.

"Sultan of Bima, my cousin. You buy!"

But we decline.

On the fifth day we make Java. Surabaya, with a population of at least three million, is marked by a sinister worldliness. At the waterfront I wander about its seamen's bars, where the heedless adventurer of the night might discover at dawn that his drink had been drugged and his person robbed. I try with little success to see such parts of Indonesia's largest city after Jakarta as imagined by Brecht and Weill, but this section is seedy, unkempt, charmless. The Surabaya of the song was a figment of Brecht and Weill's imagination, which like a balloon on a string could stray only so far from the dissonance of Berlin's cabarets of the 1920s and 1930s. Even at midday prostitutes beckon from the shadows of doorways and behind partially shuttered windows. I enter a dingy place two steps down from the street and order a beer. Two dark Madurese girls sit at the bar waiting for a pickup, and in the back is a bandstand. I suddenly remember Sumba Johnny and wonder if he ever worked his Elvis number here.

Invariably dinner conversation aboard ship revolves around the peculiar circumstances of Australia, a Western nation adrift in an Asian ocean. Ironically, these Australians claim Indonesia, especially Bali, as their field of play, while they harbor palpable fears that Indonesia might one day expand its boundaries into Australia, a continent the size of the United States with a population of nearly seventeen million. An Australian can take a package vacation in Bali more cheaply than he can take one at home, though with interesting risks. When the Australian press makes its periodic attacks on the Indonesian government, its target is corruption, especially that of the first lady and her children. Invariably the comparison is made with the Marcos government of the Philippines, and Jakarta responds nastily by preventing planeloads of Australian tourists from entering Bali.

Talk turns to Indonesia's president.

"Suharto is very, very shrewd, and his Pancasila was a bold stroke," says Jan, an autocratic missionary from Holland who has lived in Indonesia for ten years. "Islamic factions wanted and still want for Indonesia to become a Muslim state, but Suharto knew that would be the end of Indonesia. The implied compromise is that all Indonesians must believe in one God. He's an extraordinary man, Suharto is. No, Islam did not inform this conviction.

But his Javanese mysticism did. Too many people have made the mistake of underestimating Suharto, on pain of their ruin."

After dinner I fall in with Barry, my cabin mate, Donny, and their Australian friends. Donny is a lantern-jawed first-timer at sea who suffers nightmares and suffers them vocally. He eschews native food and eats alone in the cabin whatever approximations of Western junk food he can find in the markets of each port: wafers, chocolate, canned sodas, Nescafé, and powdered milk. Like many Australians who travel in Indonesia and home in on Bali, Donny has no spiritual affinity for the archipelago but comes here because he is between jobs in Perth, and it is cheap.

He is not unique, as I learn over card games. Gabriel and Alice have been traveling in the Middle and Far East for years. Through a typical evening and into the early-morning hours, interrupted by a steady stream of visitors, we play a variety of games that are new to me, a hopelessly maladroit novice. When I initially try to excuse myself on grounds of ineptitude, they patiently explain the rules and allow me a few practice hands to get the hang of such games as Contract 500, Oh Shit, and Queen of Spades, otherwise known as Black Bitch.

I soon learn how resourceful the Aussies are as travelers, their enterprise proportional to the simple purpose they impose on travel: a cheap and rootless way of life. Ashore, unless they share Donny's culinary prejudices, they eat at warungs and sleep in the cheapest losmens. When they find a place they like, they stay: a week becomes a month becomes a year. When they hear about a better and cheaper place confirmed by a fellow Aussie's seal of approval, they move on.

Such information is habitually exchanged among strangers over a card game. Our group on such an evening smokes kreteks and consumes a liter of Johnnie Walker Black Label, the Aussies mixing the whisky with Coca-Cola. In their conversation they seem a throwback to the sixties. There is talk of having nearly been conscripted in the waning days of the Vietnam War and of the ensuing demonstrations in which they marched. When they are dealt a good hand, the invariable response for luck is "All the way with LBJ." They spin exotic tales of camel safaris, water slides, rock climbs, and sport parachuting, and mundane ones about work papers and odd jobs wherever they fetch up to earn money for further travel.

They are from working-class backgrounds. This binds them in their quest for the open road, though beyond that the quest is vagueness itself. A card game becomes an artful definition of themselves and others. It passes time and expands the fraternity of travelers. A deck of cards is as vital to an Australian as his passport and money belt.

It is late, but no one wants to go to bed. For Barry, sleep is out of the question.

"Those fucking Christians in the cabin next to mine," he says, "will start singing Protestant hymns at four a.m."

It is nearly dawn when we visit the rail to see a heavenly alignment that is the identical configuration of the Islamic moon and star suspended over the deep black ribbon of the Wallace Line. The water is eerily still and beautiful, like a mirror, and the wake our ship cuts through its stillness and through the holy reflection seems a lovely profanation. The Malay passengers take it as a sign from God of peace and goodwill, a benediction on our voyage. At dawn there is a mingling of water and sky at the indistinct horizon. Then the constantly shifting patterns of Java's great green folds, the terraced rice fields against a rise of mountains tantalized by sun and shadow alike, and on the Java Sea we steam toward Semarang, our destination on the north coast in the central part of the island.

From Semarang I'll ship north to Borneo.

Kalimantan (Borneo): Rivers at the Equator

*T*HE *Melolo*, a freighter out of Semarang, cut its speed a few knots in deference to submerged tree stumps and other hazards borne to the sea from the vast hinterland of Borneo. The muddy, fecund Barito River was five miles wide here at its mouth, and freighters rode monotonously at anchor until high tide would clear the channel. Our ship had a draft of four meters, while the channel at its shallowest was five meters deep. On past voyages the *Melolo's* keel had plowed bottom, so today's arrival was carefully timed to coincide with a high incoming tide. Likewise, from our destination, the port of Banjarmasin twenty miles upstream, the freighter would wait for the midday ebb tide to ride on departure.

Soon the shallow-drafted *Melolo* would not be so uniquely privileged. The Japanese had contracted with the Indonesian government to dredge a deeper channel in the Barito for access to Banjarmasin so that Japan could gain a monopoly on Borneo's plywood trade, which accounted for eighty percent of the world's total.

As we steamed toward the navigable passage, I stood at the rail and watched the flotsam, tangles of vegetation, pieces of trees, churn by. This part of Borneo, the province of South Kalimantan, is meandering delta country. There are no conical volcanoes on the horizon, but forests and vast jungles, stretching endlessly.

Soon the broad reach of river mouth gave way to a channel a half mile wide, cutting through dense swamp. On the west bank a few hundred yards away was a small village on stilts, its mosque adorned with curled corner eaves and a silver cupola. Beyond it lay hundreds of miles of cypress swamp. The east bank was different, less dense, with banks of palmetto and palm giving way to jungle that climbed to the small, worn finger of the Muratus Mountains, a thousand meters high in the distance, which defined this southernmost Borneo promontory.

Fishermen naked to the waist worked the river in canoes they propelled with double-bladed paddles of the sort one associates with kayaks to avoid the rush of huge patches of vegetation floating downriver. Bugis schooners, riding low, plied the waters en route to Java. A tugboat pulling a barge loaded with timber rounded a bend under a blanket of fierce white factory smoke.

The towering chimneys told that we were approaching Banjarmasin. They did not belong to oil refineries, which proliferate on Borneo, but belched smoke from timber mills, one after the other, where mammoth logs were loaded onto barges to be transported downriver. The city soon loomed on both sides of us, and brightly colored water taxis ferried people from one bank of the Barito to the other.

Banjarmasin literally rises and falls with the tide. This city on stilts bestriding a Borneo river comes at you in a rush, assaulting the senses with its dark, teeming smells and visual contradictions. Though Banjarmasin is notorious as a stronghold of militant Islam, there are scores of brothels in this river city of wooden houses on floats surrounded by swamps. Most of the people here are Banjar, or Malay coastal people, physically larger than their Dayak counterparts of the country upriver, though there are Chinese and tattooed natives as well, and disenfranchised beggars from the interior who work the markets.

In 1887 when he served aboard the *Vidar*, a three-hundred-ton steamer out of Singapore that made regular runs hauling coal and resin between Borneo and Celebes, Joseph Conrad knew the discordant flux of this port. Though Banjarmasin was an important settlement as early as 1698, it has today an atmosphere of boom-town: an inevitability, given Borneo's vastness as the world's third largest island after Greenland and New Guinea, its abundance of natural resources, and the Indonesian government's determination to realize those resources' potential. The island's timber, gold, oil, and diamonds here in the south near Matapura are only beginning to be tapped, but they are being exploited in haste.

One of the world's largest forest fires raged over a two-year period in 1982 and 1983 here in Kalimantan and destroyed an area the size of Holland. Indonesian authorities blamed the Dayak tribes practicing slash-and-burn cultivation along the rivers, but the tim-ber industry had ravaged much of Kalimantan, and the inferno was exacerbated by furious logging practices unchecked by the government.

While the crew tied up fore and aft at the godown, Avis Lubis joined me at the rail. He was a thin-faced, chain-smoking Javanese who had been educated in the United States and now was a middle-level government functionary attached to the Ministry of Popu-lation and the Environment. I asked him about the inevitable collision course between environmentalists and developers.

"Conservation is a rich country's pose, but the truth lies else-where," he said. "Unless the rainforests are developed, not totally developed, but modestly developed to accommodate our swelling population . . ." He paused and spat in the river. "Without some development, the rainforests will die. Look at the hypocrisy of the West. The West bans importation of forest products. If you ban them, that keeps us in poverty. If you keep us in poverty, we will prey on the forests. So it is a global affair to be sure, but your editorialists confuse the dynamics involved."

Mr. Lubis explained that the Indonesian government's intention is to see fifty million acres of devastated lands (such as that claimed by the fire of 1982–83) reforested, but the annual budget of $300 million will not allow completion of the project for another sixty-five years.

"Sixty-five years! Imagine that!" he cried. "You want to know how to help us, your friends in New York, Washington, D.C., and California? Sixty-five years won't sit well with your friends in California. Your people march in the streets to save the whales and fur-bearing animals. Some kind of posturing, huh? If Californians wish to save the tropical forests, they should follow the example of your own Johnny Appleseed. Help us plant trees. That is not as glamorous as sitting-in protests and marching in parades, but it would speed things up." He glanced at his watch. "Excuse me, I must go pray and then to business."

It took a half day for the *Melolo* to be unloaded of its cargo of sugar and flour and take on a partial load of plywood before riding the ebb tide downriver. At the mouth the river suddenly fanned out, the main channel now marked by a series of buoys seemingly anchored in a sea of green, for the clumps of entangled vegetation and whole trunks of trees that slowed our voyage upriver now stretched to the horizon. As the ship left the coast, the floating islands separated, giving the rippleless surface the appearance of broad mudflats alternating with tufts of vegetation, with the ships at anchor resembling odd-shaped buildings marooned on shifting sands.

Miles from the coast, eons of silt deposits and the resultant shallowness of the sea told of the Barito's presence, even when Borneo was invisible. The freighter steamed westward through the Java Sea for the port of Pontianak at the equator.

Pontianak, the equatorial capital of West Kalimantan, lies inland from Borneo's west coast, at a confluence of rivers several miles upstream from the open sea. Unique among Indonesian cities, it was settled in the eighteenth century by northern Chinese traders, gold miners, and farmers, and today their descendants form the majority of the city's polyglot population. As it has been a major trading center for two centuries, Bugis from South Sulawesi and Malay people from other islands have migrated here over the years. In recent times nearby transmigration camps carved out of the jungle have brought in still other islanders, including large groups of Madurese.

As Pontianak bestrides the equator, you can—theoretically at least—walk a few steps from the Southern Hemisphere into the Northern and from fall into spring. But the four seasons in the Torrid Zone are blurred into the wet and the dry, and the conventional seasonal distinctions are meaningless.

Pontianak, with a population of a half million, is isolated and sees few Westerners. The only road from the city goes north along the coast, though an offshoot turns due eastward through the swamps before it is lost, after 120 miles, at a small village in the middle of the rainforest. In fact, few of Kalimantan's urban centers are connected by road, except in the east, where a north-south highway links the villages and ports like beads on a string. But to get from Pontianak to, say, Banjarmasin, you have to travel by ship or airplane. Rivers are Borneo's highways, and the Kapuas, whose headwaters are in the Kapuas range at the center of the island, is the longest in Indonesia.

(Notes from a Diary) "How far upriver are you going, sir?" asks the young Chinese backpacker, who has introduced himself as Michael Hong from Singapore. He is about thirty, wears glasses, is fastidious of manner and speech, and carries a paperback edition of *Paradise Lost.*

"Putussibau, and you?"

"The same, if I can manage it. Depends on the sun, the rain, the leeches, and mosquitoes. . . ." He trails off with singsong irony.

"You won't have to worry about leeches until you're in the jungle," retorts the woman. "You're not going to find the Garden of Eden where we're going."

"How do you know?" says Michael pleasantly, and this clearly irritates the woman. Her name is Janice; she is a white South African dressed in a loose-fitting blouse and khaki shorts that hug her tan thighs. Older than Michael, perhaps in her middle to late thirties, she verges on being attractive, in a full-figured but tom-boyish way. She fiddles with her blond hair constantly, pinning it up and taking it down, and when she removes her sunglasses reveals an odd cast to one eye.

Our boat, known locally as a *klotok*, chugs along against the black current, a quarter mile from an uncertain shore of green swamp on either side. Hours earlier, in a rat hole of an office at Pontianak's waterfront, we paid twelve dollars apiece for a fare on a river bus, our destination the center of the island. Breakfast and two meals of rice are included, but precious little else. The accom-modations are a spot claimed by spreading a sarong on the deck beneath a shelter; quarters are close. There must be upwards of a hundred people on board, and except for us all are Malays.

These boats, with shallow drafts especially designed for river travel, depart daily and generally take five days for the five-hundred-mile voyage to Putussibau at the foot of the Kapuas Range. But there are uneven currents and seasonal floods to con-tend with, not to mention the hazards of floating debris, hidden mudbanks, and the occasional rapids. If things go awry, the trip can take two weeks or even a month. But this is the dry season, and the captain is sanguine about the five days. I study the map and see that the river snakes back on itself repeatedly in great coils.

Michael and Janice are an odd couple whom travel has united, but not in matrimony. He is a civil servant on a two-month leave, and she is a free-spirited backpacker determined to see every square inch of every country in Asia if it takes her a lifetime to do it. They met in Pontianak and agreed to voyage upriver together to Putussibau, from where they plan to ascend the Kapuas to its source, then cross the Muller Range to the headwaters of the Mahakam, and descend that river to the east coast. It's an insane scheme for the inexperienced. The hundred-mile overland journey between the rivers will take six weeks, for there are nearly im-penetrable jungle and mountains to contend with. And there are the Dayaks.

The Dayaks, a generic name for the two hundred hill and river tribes of the interior, inhabit sunless pockets of hilly jungle far up the twisted Kapuas River. Their ancestors, the original settlers of the island, migrated thousands of years ago from Mongolia down through Southeast Asia and were displaced from the coast to the mountains by the later-arriving Malays. Some tribes live in *lamin,* or longhouses, while others are nomadic hunters, and their most distinguishing features are their tribal tattoos and pierced earlobes, elongated by the weight of heavy brass and gold jewelry.

In most places in the world people speak of the old days and how times have changed, but not here. Times *have* changed, to be sure, but the river is as indifferent to change as a great, shifting, unappeasable god. During the rainy season the Kapuas rises fifty feet or more, filling the entire basin, bringing floodwater and often crocodiles into the stilt villages. But when the river pushes over its banks, it sweetens as well as troubles this land it has made, for the deep red-brown water carries the soil that colors it, depositing annual layers of silt across the wide, flat alluvial stretches. In the dry season the river is a great highway, and the riverboats travel the channel, caught in the river's coils and twisting and turning upriver or down.

Winding into the heartland riding one of nature's great forces is exhilarating. The day is divided by meals, the rice served up by the Bugis captain's wife, who cooks over a charcoal fire. I remain in the shade of the shelter, for the sun is scalding.

I cover myself with Muskol when the shadows lengthen, and go forward to stand in the bow as the river suddenly closes in. The klotok passes the thick undergrowth of the banks with its giant orchids and mangrove flowers, and overhead I see the occasional python. Tualang trees with trunks as gray and smooth as gunmetal rise to great heights without fork or branch to a magnificent dome of foliage, beneath which I see scores of poisonous sacks, wild bee nests. Rhino birds and kingfishers hunt in the shallows, where crocodiles lurk beneath the murky surface, and through the choking humidity the steam rises from the stinking mudbanks. I think of one of history's quirks: that two thousand years ago Indian merchants brought Roman beads to Borneo. No doubt they sailed this very river.

Evenings are pleasant. Malays sing songs over the engine and accompany themselves on rude instruments I've not seen before, strings and pipes and gourds and drums. Muskol keeps insects at bay, and the running lights of the occasional other boat reflect like carnival lanterns in the water alongside the stars. How does the captain avoid the mudbanks and tree stumps in the dark? I don't know, but he does, and his young son, learning the pilot's trade, never leaves his side.

Now I know why large eyes are painted just above the waterline at the bow. A man in his riverboat needs all the help he can get, and if the boat has eyes, all the better. That's sound Malay logic. Sometimes we tie up, but not often. Stops are brief, though once we pass most of a night at a kampung. We guard our belongings in the dark when passengers get on and off. When we're under way the engine grinds relentlessly, and sleep is a sometime thing. We bathe with buckets of river water at dawn, before breakfast and the start of another day.

The only roads out here are cart tracks connecting some of the villages. The real highway is the river, and all life centers here. The klotoks furnish transportation and information to villages, but these river people for the most part are not Dayaks. Long ago when the late-arriving Malays pushed the Dayaks far into the watershed highlands, most of them remained there, and some tribes have lived undisturbed for centuries.

These people of the Kapuas are fishermen and traders, and they greet our boat with a severe air of business before the crew poles our way to deep water and our voyage upriver continues. We pass villages whose provincial names roll off the tongue: Sanggau, Semunai, Sungaikaid, Sungaiaya, Sepauk, Sintang, Silat, Semitau,

Suhaid, Selimbau, each initial letter mimicking the softly drawn
S-curves of the river.

I hitched a ride back to Pontianak on a missionary aircraft and
at the pilot's suggestion rented a room in a Chinese hotel on the
river adjacent to a green park. It was a friendly place. A wedding
party was in progress when I arrived, and a band played festive
Chinese songs. At sunset families picnicked on the green and
watched the river traffic: Bugis schooners, longboats, water taxis,
ferries, canoes, transport barges. When darkness fell, smoke from
the warungs in the alleyways turned the air blue.

Two blocks away was the "Riviera Ice Cream and Steak House,"
which became my preferred restaurant in the city. It was a small,
air-conditioned, neon-lit place with cozy booths and rolls of toilet
paper on the tables in plastic containers, providing napkins of sorts.
The eatery was owned by a Mr. Lee, a bespectacled, mannerly
Chinese in his forties whose forebears had come to Pontianak when
the city was founded over two hundred years ago. A loquacious
man, Mr. Lee spoke no English and eschewed Bahasa Indonesia
out of ethnic pride, so we both relied on his teenaged daughter,
Marina, on vacation from school in Singapore, as interpreter.

The Lees adopted me for my stay in the city and told me a great
deal about the ethnic Chinese in Kalimantan. The Chinese and
Dayaks had intersected at a crucial juncture in Indonesia's history,
and the Western missionaries were recent invaders in a land whose
history could be regarded as a microcosm of the world's.

There was a dark chapter in recent Dayak history, and it concerned the Chinese living on the island. Tribes in the lower hills
had been mobilized by the Indonesian military in the mid-sixties
to murder many thousands of Chinese in the wake of the Beijing-
sponsored coup. Marina told me that many of these tribesmen
now lived on the outskirts of Pontianak in houses and villages
once owned by the Chinese they had slaughtered.

"You know," the girl said, "my father had already planned to take me on an excursion tomorrow from Pontianak before I return to school in Singapore. Would you like to join us?"

I met them in the morning at the restaurant. Mr. Lee called for his car, a spiffy Toyota sedan, and Madurese driver. I had the back seat with Marina, and the two men sat in front. Marina at sixteen was more girl than woman, and she wore jeans with a white blouse decorated by colorful, squiggly drawings of elephants and birds with words in script, the stuff of a nursery.

The entire afternoon, Mr. Lee discoursed in Chinese for Marina to translate into English for my ears alone, excluding the driver. Though desultory at first, the conversation eventually dwelled on Chinese-Malay relations, characterized by ethnic and class conflict.

We stopped on the edge of town for fuel, and a surly Madurese filled our tank while he japed contemptuously in dialect with a fellow attendant. Mr. Lee listened for a moment and spoke to Marina.

"They are ridiculing us," she said. "My father says that the Madurese are a coarse, violent race, and that they habitually ridicule those who are better off such as ourselves, the butts of their jokes."

Heading north, we crossed the equator at a traffic circle and, once in the country, passed through thick swampland and the occasional village, where women sold fresh and dried fish from roadside stands beside the fetid canals. We were close enough to the natural waterways to see odd assortments of boats floating in the slime-green water. According to Mr. Lee, these were owned by Chinese and rented to Malays, and the profits realized from fishing or other enterprises were shared.

"My father says," continued Marina, "that Malays are shiftless and lazy. If assigned a task, they insist on payment first. They need constant supervision, and if you turn your back, they stop working and spend the money you advanced them."

Our route took us through a series of rubber and pepper plantations, and afterward the road began a gentle climb into the hills. The settlements here were sparser, but we had left the Malays at sea level and were entering country now claimed by the Dayaks. We passed through a village of wooden houses, two-storied with covered porches and passageways. I learned that this had been an old Chinese village, settled two centuries ago, but since the blood-bath of 1965, it had been inhabited by Dayaks.

"No one really knows why the Dayaks killed so many Chinese," said Marina, translating for her father. "Perhaps they were iden-tified with the Communists, but that would have meant nothing to Dayaks. But the government put the Dayaks up to killing Communists, and so the Dayaks killed Chinese. No one really knows why."

The Lees spoke of the mass slayings of two decades before matter-of-factly, though in hushed tones as though it were a for-bidden topic, even in so ancient a diaspora as theirs. Had this been a casual encounter, I would have guessed they were talking about a race alien to their own. But the killings were obviously very much on the mind of Mr. Lee. Several days later he had Marina explain to me that nothing he had told me was based on "official" evidence. He had no proof of numbers of Chinese killed, and so forth. His amendments served to underline that inflammatory statements were under government interdict. I never asked Mr. Lee, who must have been in his late teens in 1965, how he had managed to escape the pogrom.

Marina explained that the villagers were "modernized" Dayaks who worked the plantations, but today they were idling on their porches and in their houses. They looked more Chinese than Ma-lay, with squat builds and light skin evolved over centuries of life under the rainforest canopy. The younger ones wore jeans and T-shirts, while their elders were wrapped in sarongs and were naked from the waist up, with tribal tattoos.

"After they killed the Chinese," continued Marina, "the gov-ernment allowed the Dayaks to occupy the houses of this Chinese village and many others like it because it moved them out of the mountains and made it easier for the military to control them."

"Why is the town so quiet?" I asked.

"It's Sunday. But even if it weren't . . ." She hesitated.

At this point, Mr. Lee cut in and spoke at length.

"My father says that the Dayaks have their own laws. If a crime is committed, restitution in the form of pigs is made to the victim. In the mountains upriver the government stays out of things, but around here it wants a hand in. But it can do nothing about laziness."

One scene of historical tragedy had been followed by another. Mandor had been the site of a Japanese work camp during World War II, and in recent times, according to the Lees, the Japanese had erected a memorial in apology to the Indonesian people for the atrocities visited upon Malay natives during the occupation, when the Japanese had wrested much of the East Indies from the Dutch.

The memorial was a large cast-iron frieze in an open field over mass graves. A mosque stood nearby. The frieze depicted Japanese soldiers torturing, bayoneting, and shooting the helpless workers. It was hard to believe the Japanese would have admitted to such cruelty. But Japan now was busily engaged in exploiting Indonesia in other ways, and I supposed that the monument was mollification with an ulterior motive of trade and tourism.

"There were Dutch and Chinese victims, too, but no one knows how many died," said Marina. Uncertainty, it seemed, was safe ground to tread. "But it was many, many thousands," she said in a whisper.

"The plantations and gold mines around here were once rich," she continued. "But now they are fallow and have been ever since the Chinese were driven out."

We drove into the late-afternoon sun on our return to Pontianak.

"My father would like to know whether you are going to Sumatra," said Marina.

I said that I was.

"My father says that it is not so civilized as here. It is very backward. There are not so many Chinese on Sumatra."

This simple exchange illuminated the crux of the Chinese attitude in the archipelago. Malays, in their view, were brutish people, a servant class, and Indonesia was a nation of plebeians. Counter to this strongly held view was the Malay conviction that the Chinese were a rapaciously bad lot. There could be neither friendship nor understanding between the two sides, and the void was filled with a mutual hostility.

The Indonesian government had in fact institutionalized the Malay resentment of Chinese. The law forbade the teaching of Chinese in any school, as well as the importation of any printed matter in Chinese characters. There had been talk in Jakarta of improved relations with Beijing after a nearly twenty-five-year hiatus, but these prohibitions were still in effect.

The sun had not yet set, and Mr. Lee negotiated the hire of a longboat so that we could explore Pontianak by river and the network of canals. We set out from a pier of rotted timbers, the boat parting the flotsam as we cruised into mid-channel.

The half-mile width of river floated heavy traffic: large freighters hauling rubber and timber bound for Singapore to the northwest shared the water with the ubiquitous Bugis schooners making for island ports, and the local motorized sampans. A procession of smaller boats moved upriver with cargoes of rice, and others returned loaded with brown sugar, coffee, and pepper. These were some of the oddest boats I'd ever seen: barges with houses constructed above decks, and they were even slower than the river buses and could take weeks to reach the interior.

We motored upstream past the royal mosque of the old sultanate, which stood a hundred yards from the palace, and turned in to the city on the opposite bank by way of the canals. Marina explained that this side of the river had no tap water, as we watched women gathering buckets of river water for cooking and coffee and tea in the warungs. The houses on the canals rose and fell with the nudge of the tide, and this was the time of day when entire families descended wooden steps from their bungalows to wash themselves.

The river was the habitual recipient of baser urges as well. One comely young woman was washing her hair not fifteen feet downstream of a boy squatting on the spaced boards outside his bungalow to defecate in the water, the splash of his excrement of no concern to the girl, to her brother, brushing his teeth, or to anyone else. The Lees pointed this out with some glee, for it was obvious that they held these urban river people in low esteem.

"These are not friendly people," said Marina as we cruised the narrow canals, passing under wooden walkways, inviting silent, contemptuous stares.

Farther upriver we encountered the strangest sight of all: an elaborate floating Chinese temple. As the original immigrants from China had been largely impoverished, illiterate people, they had been equally unsophisticated about the nuances of the three religions they had brought with them and consequently mixed them like ingredients in a stew. Here the traditional Buddhism, Taoism, and Confucianism evolved into an amalgamation called the *Tri Darma*, or Three Ethics, a curious unification unique to Indonesia. This hybrid of the three faiths showed in the architecture and decorations of the temples. On the elaborately carved roof, two dragons fought over the pearl of wisdom, while two tigers were frozen in combat alongside two phoenixes vying for a peony. The longboat turned in a wide arc and headed downriver into the flames of sunset.

It was nearly dark when we arrived at the Lees' house, where we removed our shoes at the door. The living room was comfortably but sparsely furnished, but the house was obviously the residence of a man who had met with success in his various enterprises. Off the room was a garden. I opened the door to inspect it, but, prompted by her father, Marina seized me by the arm. "Do not enter the garden," she said. "Our houseboy saw a cobra this morning."

Mr. Lee's wife entered, a beautiful woman carrying a male

infant. Refreshments were brought out, while all eyes rested ador-
ingly upon the little boy. After a short visit I left this Chinese
family, so content in its insularity, and returned to the hotel.

The next morning I struck up a conversation with an elderly
Chinese man staying at the hotel. He was from Singapore and
was visiting family here. When I told him where I lived, he guf-
fawed. "San Francisco is a beautiful city. What on earth are you
doing here in Pontianak? It's a dreadful place."

But I liked this estuarine city with its cultural crossfires. If the
mutual hostility of the Chinese and Malays created a schism that
neither was inclined to bridge, my own status as a Westerner
awarded me ipso facto an unofficial visa, allowing me to pass back
and forth between the two communities. Whatever resentment
either race harbored toward the other, it did not extend to me.

That evening an American missionary I'd met at Mr. Lee's
restaurant dropped by the hotel, eager to talk to a countryman.
He knocked on my door before dinner. Doyle was a tall, narrow-
faced native of Oklahoma, but he had been a missionary out here
for thirteen years. His son had been born in the Borneo interior
and knew nothing of the United States, where the family was
going on home leave. Doyle's home in Kalimantan was a Dayak
village two days upriver from Putussibau. He was intense, did not
smile readily, and showed a flush of anger when I asked him about
Westerners who trekked across Borneo and stopped in his village.

"We get a lot of these clowns coming through, these trekkers,"
he said. "I really shouldn't say that, but they cause a lot of trouble.
We get West Germans, Scandinavians, Austrians, British, Aussies,
some who know what they're doing and others who've never set
foot in a rainforest and don't have the foggiest. The problem for
me is that they need guides, and the only one who can negotiate
for them is me. I get caught in the middle, and my natives get
'nigger rich,' as we used to say in Oklahoma. They've never seen
so much money, and they spend it as fast as they make it."

"I'm afraid you're going to get more and more trekkers," I said.

He smiled as he rolled his eyes. "I don't doubt it, and I shouldn't complain," he said. "Besides, who can stop it? Anyway, my wife and I love it out here, and of course our son knows no other life. In a way I dread going back to the States. We'll be with my wife's folks in Ohio."

I was not entirely comfortable with the role missionaries had proclaimed for themselves in the Third World. While I admired their courage and fervor, their insistence on promoting a theology at odds with traditional tribal beliefs had seemed to me ingenuous in its stance of moral superiority. But to argue against their presence was a specious denial of the past. Countless waves of migrations bringing strange gods had been the manner of the archipelago's history for thousands of years. Missionaries had always come here. Hindu-Buddhism, which had once proliferated across Java, evidenced by such stunning ruins in the central part of the island as Borobudur and Prambanan, had been nudged by Islam into Bali and Lombok. Arab traders had brought not only commerce but Islam's Koran and sword as well. With the Portuguese had come the Jesuits. The Christian missionary armies of today were suspect anomalies to me because they were bland Johnny-come-latelys.

The next morning the Mission Aviation Fellowship office held out some hope for a flight to the interior, though my seat could not be confirmed until the arrival of the aircraft. The MAF, an interdominational Protestant organization, was headquartered in Redlands, California, and had been active in Borneo and Irian Jaya, though there were other missionary groups as well and a lot of them. I took a taxi to the airport and the small blue building that was the MAF terminal. The two Malays manning the office weighed me on baggage scales and had me sit in a small waiting room with a large map of Kalimantan on the wall and littered with old magazines, mostly religious publications. Shortly, the roar of an engine announced the airplane taxiing up to the building.

This outward run was hauling little cargo, so I took the copilot's seat and one of the Malays from the terminal sat in the rear. Dan, the large, raw-boned pilot, outfitted me with a helmet equipped with a speaker and earphones so that we could talk.

Originally from the state of Washington, Dan had met his wife, Lynn, at Bible school, and I found that similar meetings among their number had been commonplace. The wife in such a union invariably was skilled in nursing or teaching, often both. On the face of it, these were simple, hardworking, pious people from America's provinces come to spread God's word, and they not only preached the Gospel, but brought fundamental messages of Western hygiene as well.

Borneo was outside the "ring of fire," the honeycomb of volcanoes that makes up much of Indonesia, but isolated volcanic cones from another age, weathered by succeeding ages, rose from the jungle like great stone deities. We flew under a gray canopy of cloud that afforded gentler light than the harsh sea of sun that habitually enveloped us, and it often rained but quickly cleared, the heat drawing from the primeval earth a ground fog resembling a thousand bivouac fires.

In the distance on our southeast horizon rose the southern arm of mountains, but in the expanse between them and our position, the smaller, isolated peaks magnetized the frequent squalls that hurtled across the landscape. One such mountain was a square rock a thousand feet high, another weathered volcanic cone. According to Dan, it had no name. When we passed it, I could see that it was not a single rock but two towering chimneys rising from the same base.

Our first destination was called Riambatu, a Dayak village of three hundred people secured in a crown of hills west of the main ridge of southern mountains. I couldn't see the dirt strip until we passed low over a saddle, then banked before a peak to sideslip into our approach. A tribe of long-nosed monkeys swung through the trees at the edge of the jungle, and a large red orangutan sought cover in the brush. The wind sock at the runway's edge hung limp, and the squall that had preceded us by minutes had scarcely settled the dust when we touched down.

We were met by a dozen natives and missionaries and kids of both races. Except for an emergency radio in the village, the occasional MAF flight that called here was this community's only link with civilization. With the airplane came mail and gossip from the very distant outside world. An energetic man from Texas introduced himself as George, while his son, a blond, strapping boy of eighteen, began unloading the cargo: sacks of mail, medical supplies, food staples, and, most important for Dan, the drum of reserve fuel he liked to have on hand at each strip.

George and Dan discussed what to do with the fuel. If it was left unattended, the tribesmen would steal the liquid for fires as they had done in the past, evidenced by the empty drums beside the strip. George had an idea: he would organize a group of "trusties" to bear the precious stuff to his own bungalow.

As the plane was being loaded, I struck up a conversation with Ted, George's son, ostensibly discussing the flora and fauna of this part of the island, though I was pleasantly distracted by something else as the boy talked about where the fishing was best and where it was not safe to swim because of crocs. I looked at his younger sister with her Dayak playmate and then looked back at him, enjoying the family resemblance: the shock of blond hair, the wide smiling mouth. These are good, contented kids, I told myself, and they sprang from good, well-meaning people. They are the measure of the cohesiveness these missionaries tacitly enjoy, and I envy them their purposefulness and happiness. The God they worship is not the son of human pride.

The group waved at us as we taxied and took off and continued to wave until we were out of sight.

A country of uninterrupted wilderness lay below us as Dan sought new landmarks on this next leg, and ahead under a billow of cumulus cloud higher peaks, six thousand feet, appeared on the horizon, and beyond them the upper basin of the Kapuas. When the river appeared, it flowed unhurried and unpausing, savagely and austerely beautiful, flashing like light on a serpent's scales.

I distracted myself from the roar of the engine by imagining what disparate forces lured white people here and the essence of the baggage that accompanied them. If I still felt a lurking temptation to dismiss these soldiers of Christ as hypocritical do-gooders after the manner of American television evangelists, it was as ludicrously inexact as it was unjust. They lived hard lives and met daily challenges with a peasant astuteness and cunning, and they regarded the snakes and snares of this world as a fighting man regards a minefield. The wife of one missionary had taken on the Herculean task of rendering the dialect spoken in her village into phonetics and was compiling a dictionary.

The night Doyle had dropped by the hotel, I had asked him why he had chosen his vocation. Expecting a sermon, I was met with an embarrassed smile that barely shielded his altruistic conviction. "I don't really know," he said. "I suppose it's a man's lot in life to do his best to make the world a better place to live in, while remembering that the results are bound to be mighty small. That, and to tend to his own soul." Camus or Sartre might have said the same thing, substituting "responsibility" or "validity" for "soul," thereby diluting the wisdom and power of this simple truth.

The missionaries brought Psalm 91: "I will say of the Lord, He is my refuge and my fortress. . . . Thou shalt not be afraid for the terror by night; nor for the arrow that flieth by day. . . ." But Joseph Conrad, with his seaman's papers and sea chest of personal demons and dark powers, had no such faith in Christian divination. The silent voice he heard in these parts was "the immense indifference of things."

Sulawesi (Celebes): The Funeral and the Hajj

SULAWESI, or Celebes as it was known when it was a part of the Dutch East Indies, is the world's eleventh largest island and the fourth largest in the archipelago after New Guinea, Borneo, and Sumatra. Lying east of Borneo across Macassar Strait and west of the Moluccas or Spice Islands, it is perhaps the most curiously shaped island on the globe, with four distinct peninsulas that form three major gulfs. There are inland freshwater lakes, one of which has been sounded to nearly two thousand feet, and the entire island is covered with forested mountains, natural barriers that have fostered diversity among its fauna as well as its tribes.

South Sulawesi is the southwestern peninsula of this sprawling, tentacled island, and it plunges down into the Flores Sea. Near its western tip is Ujung Pandang, called Macassar in Joseph Conrad's day. I was curious to meet the native Bugis of this part of the island, who along with the Dayak tribes of Borneo figure so prominently in Conrad's novels. The Bugis by reputation were a devoutly Muslim, churlish, seagoing people marked by their contempt for Westerners, a hatred springing from their many armed confrontations with the Dutch.

After my return to Java from Borneo, I found a Bugis schooner bound for Ujung Pandang at Surabaya's waterfront. As I was

curious to meet the Bugis on their own terms, I negotiated a fare
of fifteen dollars and a carton of kreteks with the skipper.

(Notes from a Diary) Dawn of the third day out of Surabaya.
It has been a mercifully dry crossing of the Java Sea, with steady
winds and gentle swells to Ujung Pandang, but my bones ache
from wakeful nights on deck. Amidships, I join several of the crew
taking our breakfast of fish rice and hot chili *sambal*. The skipper
is a rail-thin man, sleek as a sea bird and blackened by the sun,
squatting on his haunches and sipping his tea. Naked save for a
sarong, he issues no orders. While a boy swings topside to adjust
the sails for hauling in, the crew of a dozen does everything by
rote, making spontaneous adjustments to wind and sandbar.

This Bugis *pinisi*, dating from the last century, is a three-masted
prahu, thirty feet wide amidships, with port and starboard oars
reaching deep beneath the keel. The peculiar configuration of the
craft originated in the day of the Phoenicians and Romans, and it
passed centuries ago to the Bugis from the Portuguese. The Bugis
made their own modifications, and the pinisi remains unique
among seagoing vessels. Apart from a cabin over the stern for
charcoal cooking fires and a few bunks, there are precious few
comforts. Space is for cargo, below and above decks, and these are
hearty, tough sailors, who know and expect privation and scorn
luxury.

We enter the harbor, a hub for international shipping trade:
for centuries it thrived as a gateway to the Spice Islands. Macassar
was seized by the Dutch in 1669, and Fort Rotterdam remains its
vestigial guardian. Built on a site occupied by a succession of native
forts, it is the most obvious link to a past when this was one of
the most important Dutch colonial ports of the archipelago. Now
in ruins, it is an edifice the size of two city blocks, with thick
reinforced walls to withstand cannon shot and siege. The walls of
white stucco over brick catch the early-morning sun, and the roofs
of terra-cotta tile are steeply pitched, their russet hues lending a
somber presence.

We make port north of the city where a Bugis village spills along the banks of a refuse-ridden side channel, docking at a maimed godown of rotted timbers. My shipmates have regarded me with bemused curiosity, a bleached but game alien and infidel in their midst, but the hospitality abruptly ends after we tie up fore and aft for the frantic unloading of cargo—rice flour and sugar. A peremptory farewell and I am standing in the heart of a Bugis settlement.

"They were a numerous and an unclean crowd, living in ruined bamboo houses, surrounded by neglected compounds, on the out-skirts of Macassar," wrote Conrad in *An Outcast of the Islands*, published in 1896, and his description is apt today. For the first time in Indonesia I feel myself to be an intruder. The stares from the men and women are palpably hostile, though I have been in the islands long enough to recognize the curiosity as well.

The women, many of whom wear caftans, have bright scarlet lips stained by betel nut. Their faces are white with rice powder, both a beautifier and protection from the sun. I have not seen such makeup before in the archipelago, and when I become accustomed to this artifice, the ghostly, painted masks seem not the stuff of theater but somehow seem to deepen their Bugis identity.

For centuries the enterprising Bugis sailed the Eastern Archi-pelago in their pinisi as freebooters, adventuring as far as Aus-tralia. Fierce and coarse by reputation, these *orang laut,* or "people of the sea," still sailed the islands now, but as determined traders. They were still coarse and aggressive swaggerers. Small wonder "bogeyman" is believed to be derived from "Bugis."

Today is Saturday, and the villagers are idling on the piers, their beached boats surrounded by litter and flotsam. The black-hatted men are darker by half than their women. One old man is on his knees picking through a heap of garbage, vying with three goats. The air stinks of burning trash. I walk past the wharves to the sea wall, where I am accosted by a group of young boys, one of whom pulls up one leg of his shorts to taunt me with his uncir-cumcised penis in a parody of masturbation, while the others hoot with glee. Behind him looms an old mosque with the gingerbread of the last century adorning its cupola, conferring a decayed dignity on the squalor.

I walk in search of a becak driver. A man sitting against a shack holding two fighting cocks glowers at me, showing his teeth like a rabid dog. His mouth is so filled with dentist's metal that his face resembles a rough-cut jewel ripped from the earth. As I pass, he sets the cocks against each other as if to dramatize the menace of the place. The old man sifting through garbage is still on his knees when I mount the becak and the driver sends the bicycle rickshaw forward. A breeze stirs up the dust, and I am relieved when we cross a stagnant network of canals and enter the city.

Alfred Russel Wallace, when he visited Macassar in 1856, noted that it was the first Dutch town he had visited and found it "prettier and cleaner" than any he had yet seen in the East. But in the more than 130 years since the naturalist's visit, Macassar had suffered more than a change of name. Such a major port as Ujung Pandang, with a population of a million, ought to be imbued with the spirit of Conrad's Marlow and Lingard: its having seen better days ought to suggest a seedy charm, but I find it a motley place, with low faceless concrete buildings and corrugated tin-roofed bungalows scattered southward from the fort. Far more tangible than charm is a sense of desperation. Cripples and beggars are no less insistent in demanding money than the becak peddlers at heel, sounding their bells for a fare. The teeming, poverty-ridden, charmless city seems a picture of living death.

I take a room in a hotel on the waterfront and at dusk watch the Bugis night fishermen perched like crows upon their outrigger skiffs against the fading light, preparing their nets and charcoal fires. Afterward, I have a dinner of barbecued octopus on the hotel roof overlooking the harbor, and the luxury is welcome after the spartan sea voyage.

Off the dining room is the hotel's disco, the city's center for nightlife, so I stop in before going to bed. The place is packed, but strangely so. In the whirling, surreal light of the dance floor be-

neath the turntables roosted above, young men dance together to
Western rock in the absence of female Bugis company. The bizarre
pairings and the contagious music produce an exercise that is
blandly mechanical: the hip gyrations quivering with sexual in-
nuendo are anesthetized by the exclusion of women, except for
the occasional butterfly intent on a pickup. This is a reminder that
South Sulawesi is fiercely Muslim and this place is off-limits to
unmarried Bugis girls.

After watching for a few minutes, I turn in. Tomorrow I shall
hire a Land Rover and driver to explore South Sulawesi.

My Bugis guide was Dumah, a young married man with finely
chiseled features and a quiet, unassuming manner rare for a Bugis.
He spoke no English, so we communicated in Bahasa Indonesia.
Dumah's appetite for the sizable chunk of cash the trip would
bring him was at war with a prejudice descended to him from his
people, a revulsion against visiting the hated Christianized Toraja
tribe to the north. When we shook hands to cement our arrangement, the corners of his mouth twitched.

At the settlement north of town, Dumah pulled up to his bungalow, where he left money for his wife and collected his own
things for the trip while I waited in the Land Rover. Soon a crowd
of curious Bugis surrounded the vehicle. One timid young woman
veiled her face while peering at us, while an obstreperous mother
with a naked infant boy shrieked *"Gula-gula!"* and *"Rupiah!"*
through obscenely painted lips on a rice-powdered face. When I
demurred, she pointed to her baby's uncircumcised penis, making inscrutable exclamations punctuated by horrific shrieks of
laughter.

I recalled the boy taunting me with his penis and the laughter
of the others. Beyond what seemed an obscene gesture, I could
find no explanation for the preoccupation with a child's foreskin.
Circumcision was practiced among Malay Muslims as an initiation
for boys nearing puberty, though I had heard that some males
endured the procedure as young as nine or ten. Whenever they

underwent the procedure, at the hands of a medicine man, it was a proud if painful experience. Among Malays, as far as I could learn, the circumcision of girls required by Islamic law was largely a symbolic exercise without mutilation.

We departed Ujung Pandang under a steaming ten-o'clock sun. Roads in Sulawesi, as in all Indonesia, are few and deplorable, even when paved. Narrow, potholed, and treacherously banked, they are a less cheering legacy from the Dutch than the breweries.

We hugged the coast for the first leg of our drive to Rantepao in the center of Toraja country, and when we cleared the outskirts of Ujung Pandang, the countryside opened out into fine grazing land and rice fields irrigated by a network of streams and rivers. To the east the mountains rose abruptly to a height of ten thousand feet, a sawtooth range of limestone rock drawn against the sky with deep, sheer cliffs and ravines. When we turned inland from the coast, we began a steep ascent through the highlands, following the Sadang River, which we crossed and recrossed, its brown waters far below us in a gorge. "Such gorges, chasms, and precipices as here abound, I have nowhere seen in the Archipelago," Wallace noted in 1857.

In these Bugis highlands, verdant rice fields glistened in the light muted by rain-cloud cover. For centuries this part of Sulawesi knew only slash-and-burn techniques of rice growing, but when wet-rice cultivation was introduced after the Dutch conquest, mountainsides were terraced and local streams harnessed for irrigation. Men and women alike wore special sarongs, wrapped about the shoulders and hanging down in back, to ward off the chill in these higher altitudes.

Respecting Dumah's silence, I thought better of grilling him about the unworthy Toraja, who like the Bugis had migrated to the island from the Southeast Asia mainland before recorded history.

The Toraja, isolated by the rugged mountains of Central Sulawesi, had warred with the Bugis for centuries but remained remote from the West until the turn of the century, when the Dutch sought to control them, quelling pockets of resistance in two years. Christian missionaries soon followed to claim the Toraja as theirs, and this served to sharpen the Muslim Bugis' hostility. Even so, the Bugis traded with the Toraja to gain coffee and slaves and introduced such blood sports as cockfighting, which became an integral part of the Toraja's lavish funerals. Such funerals suggested a highly stratified society ruled by an aristocracy, and ancestor worship, as in Bali, had a rigid place among the Toraja's polytheistic beliefs.

Before the Dutch invaded their country, headhunting was practiced, and the sacrifice of slaves or prisoners at a royal funeral would provide servants for the afterlife. Since taking on the outer garment of Christianity, the Toraja now sacrificed pigs and buffalo. But the animist Toraja had difficulty accepting the notion of one supreme being, excepting the chief god of a clan or village, and so the notion of God had continued to be a tenuous one, notwithstanding the efforts of Christian missionaries and Suharto's Pancasila. More to the point, a funeral with its elaborate trappings remained a grand and expensive preparation for the deceased person's journey to the next life. Ceremonies of savage bloodletting continued, while the church at once turned its head and extended its hand, accepting cash payment generated by such grand occasions.

The road leveled out at a misty plateau, and the astonishing Toraja houses told that we had entered their country. The houses, called *tongkonan*, were constructed of thatch and woven bamboo, with high gabled roofs shaped at either end like the prow of a ship or the horns of a buffalo. They faced north, toward the home of the gods, with a talisman of buffalo head and wide expanse of horns at the front. These were the houses of the nobility, with similarly constructed rice barns within their compound to protect the harvest from rats and the rain.

At dusk we entered the edge of the green, cultivated valley that was Tana Toraja. Boys rode on the backs of buffalo, guiding them home across rice-field dikes in this high country, whose main cash crop was coffee. Rantepau was little more than a large settlement, with few places to stay, but I found a clean losmen, while Dumah elected to guard his vehicle by sleeping in it.

"I know, tuan, that I am your driver, but I cannot enter the funeral compound of the Toraja." Dumah was speaking over morning tea, and he had reacted as though slapped when I asked him to accompany and guide me in protocol. "The Toraja are infidels. Do you not know that they slaughter pigs by the hundreds for their feasts? That the Toraja drink alcohol?"

"I don't know that I am welcome," I said. "I hire you to help me, and now you refuse. How do I manage?"

"It is sinful for me to accompany you, and I answer for it on the day of reckoning. Buy packs of cigarettes and dispense them to the relatives, but do not remain among the Toraja for long. They are an unclean people. Sometimes curiosity is not such a good thing," he said, glancing heavenward. "The Toraja are fit to be slaves. Today I drink their coffee, but I scorn them who grow it. They are ignorant hill people who know little of the great world."

I had hoped a funeral would be in progress, and one was. It would last seven days and nights, a measure of the deceased dowager's wealth and high social standing among the Toraja. Though a sign at the edge of the funeral compound read "Turist Stop!", I was not challenged when I entered the outdoor compound, to discover myself the only Westerner present. The church was perhaps a thousand yards away on a rise, but in the foreground stood various pavilions to serve the complex rituals already in progress. Hundreds of trussed pigs suspended from wooden poles were borne into the compound in an endless parade and left squealing and defecating in a muddy heap while they awaited transport to the butcher's block. Scores of tethered buffalo likewise awaited the ax and knife.

Despite the stench, upwards of a thousand people sat around inside and out, on sarongs spread on the ground or on the floors of the open-sided pavilions, eating large slices of hide-singed, burnt, and bloody hunks of pork, served in large, hollowed pieces of bamboo with rice and vegetables and washed down with an alcoholic drink called *tuak*. High over the central pavilion, the death house where her body lay in state, an enlarged color photograph of the deceased noblewoman kept vigil over the proceedings as preparations continued by way of elaborate ritual to send her soul to *Puya*, the afterworld.

I did not seem to be an unwelcome guest, and no one seemed interested in my cigarettes. A preadolescent schoolboy from a nearby village approached to practice his English and exchange addresses, and when I gave him my pen, he became my host.

"You must sit there," he said, pointing to a small covered pavilion with open sides. I hesitated, for these were rows of folding chairs for family and friends, but the boy was insistent.

"This is the funeral of my grandmother," he said. "And you are one of us, a Christian. And you have a companion?"

I told him that I had a driver from Ujung Pandang, but that he had elected not to come to the ceremony.

"The Bugis are bad and dirty heathens," he said. "He is not welcome here."

I selected a seat among family members who had come from near and far to view the next stage of the weeklong ritual.

A procession of exquisitely veiled young women wearing bejeweled, full-length dresses of saffron and magenta began a processional from the death house to a pavilion adjacent to ours, where the immediate family of the dead matriarch gathered. They marched in a slow, stately fashion that made a sharp contrast to the squealing of pigs at the slaughter block, first bearing tobacco, then drinks of tuak and tea, and finally food.

In the middle of this solemn processional, I shifted my weight and the legs of my chair slipped through cracks in the makeshift floor with a crash, sending me tumbling over in a back somersault, nearly spilling me into the pig-fouled mud. The entire compound broke out in riotous laughter exempting no one, not even the handmaids whose movements were as elaborately studied as dancers'. My interruption of this solemn occasion seemed almost welcome, as if fabled ritual needed the unanticipated to season it. Pretense was acceptable if it could be brought low by pratfall from the unexpected. As an outsider, I was the unwitting source.

When I left the compound, the crowd erupted in applause and good-natured cheers.

I found Dumah at the vehicle smoking a cigarette with taciturn deliberation and told him what had happened. For him the incident was no cause for mirth.

"Did I not tell you they are an unclean people?" he said. "The fall was humiliation enough. Suppose you land in the mud? These people eat pigs, tuan, *pigs!*"

For the remainder of the day we explored Tana Toraja's many villages to see the grave sites and their unique *tau tau*. These were life-sized, carved wooden likenesses of the dead that gazed from high ledges, guarding the graves of aristocrats and receiving offerings from those who came to pay homage. The Toraja buried their dead in caves hewn a hundred feet up in the faces of sheer cliffs, a deterrent to grave robbers, and they were interred with valuable earthly possessions for the long journey to the hereafter.

"This is no way for men to be buried," Dumah said, exhaling smoke in hisses. "Imagine dying with the fear that robbers climb rocks like monkeys to pick over your remains. The Toraja have no shame."

He was adamant in remaining with his vehicle, while I took the inevitable half-mile walk along the dikes of the rice fields to reach the cliffs. Here the strange wooden effigies, weathered to pastels by the years, gazed out from precipitous heights like wan, ethereal mannequin-gods.

That evening I returned to the funeral compound to discover that on a makeshift screen beneath the portrait of the deceased lady, a Chinese-language kung fu film was being shown to an enraptured outdoor audience, while a man translated in an anemic monotone the English subtitles.

We left Rantepao in the morning as nineteen buffalo were slaughtered, while the festivities continued. Our route took us out of Tana Toraja's pristine cultivated valley to cross the eastern range of the central mountains, bathed in cloud. There was little traffic in the mountains, so little that harvests of coffee and cloves spread on sheets in patches of sunlight impinged on the right-of-way; when we slowed to a crawl to pass, the blue mountain air was sweet with the spice. Breezes soughing over the peaks were speckled vermilion and gold, black and emerald-green as swarms of butterflies crossed the road at every switchback—shades of fiction's notable collector, Stein of Conrad's *Lord Jim*, who sought his "specimens" among the human community as well as lepidoptera.

The drive along the Bay of Bone passed through delta country, a network of rivers and crocodile-infested mangrove and palmetto swamps that stretched inland to the foothills. At a hamlet the road veered away from the coast, seeking the rich farm land of the interior and passing through Bugis market towns. By dusk we arrived at the inland city of Sengkang, a small provincial capital on a large freshwater lake in the heart of Bugis land. The shoreline of Lake Tempe was marked by a nexus of hamlets constructed over the water on stilts, the houses connected by rickety bamboo bridgeways.

"Here you are accorded Bugis hospitality," Dumah said, stopping before an expansive bungalow on a hill overlooking the lake.

I was greeted at the door by a handsome middle-aged woman with bunned hair, dressed in a blouse and sarong. Inside were several younger women and girls performing various chores, but no men. This was no losmen but a private home. I was shown to my room and told dinner would be served at seven.

· · • · ·

By nightfall the common room had been transformed into what resembled a royal refectory, and the young women of the afternoon were now crimson-lipped and rouge-cheeked, with long, loose hair reaching past their shoulders. They attended me dressed in tribal finery: varicolored diaphanous bodices woven of gold and silver thread, silk sashes and sarongs, gold tiaras of leaf and flower and studded with pearl, similar necklaces and earrings, and soft, black, pointed shoes. The angles of the room had been softened by folds of bright silks, and large cushions were placed on the floor around a low table.

Four of the girls were of marriageable age, sixteen or so, and even the youngest, who was perhaps thirteen, was considered a woman. They wrapped me in a silk sarong and placed a faux-gold crown on my head before bidding me to sit cross-legged on the floor, while they fetched dishes of soup, meat, rice, vegetables, and fried crab in banana leaves as well as fresh grilled fish from the lake, before taking their seats around me.

Several times during dinner the mood was interrupted by great shouts from the streets. When I finished I stepped outside on the veranda, where I was joined by Dumah.

"It is the hajj," he said.

It had begun to rain. Hundreds of pilgrims were en route to Mecca, arriving in bemos clogging the thoroughfares or already arrived in Sengkang, waiting in the drizzle for the midnight buses that would bear them to Ujung Pandang for their flights to Saudi Arabia.

We listened to the din rushing up the hill from the city below. The hajj, a pilgrimage to Mecca, was the crowning achievement in a Muslim's life. The Great Mosque and the *Ka'ba*, which housed the heavenly stone given by Gabriel to Abraham, drew pious Muslims from the world over, and this spiritual magnetic field charged voyagers to Islam's holiest city with an uncommon zeal.

"It is best not to go down, but if you do have a look, take care," said Dumah. "Leave your money belt locked in your room."

I walked down the slippery, mud-covered stone steps leading from the veranda to the steep cobbled street, where I found myself in a river of several thousand frenzied Bugis, the pilgrims themselves huddled together in the rain and the curious who were to be left behind parading backward and forward in the square before the mosque.

Evening prayers had ended. Most of the women were veiled, and they clustered near the sanctuary, while men and boys walked the streets arm in arm in groups of four and five. The smoking warungs in front of the mosque did a lively business. The air was electric, with everyone feasting on the mysterious promise of the hajj.

It was frightening to slip from the silken refuge of the bungalow a few hundred yards down into a cavernous Bugis stronghold, seeking a kinship that tasted of the forbidden. But the Arab laws of hospitality had accompanied the Koran to a remote town in South Sulawesi. Though not of the hajj, I was a pilgrim among pilgrims. Standing before the mosque, I pretended to appreciate the severity of its beauty, fully aware that the air I breathed was saturated with an orthodoxy from which I was excluded.

By now, the rain had intensified, and the buses for the pilgrims had not yet arrived. The leavetakers, many with black umbrellas, sought whatever shelter they could find, and I headed back to the bungalow. An old man in a black skullcap left his place among the pilgrims to cross the road and grasp my hand, a show of peace and goodwill. I wished him and his companions well on their holy journey, and in a chorus they blessed me in return.

Dumah rarely smiled, but he was smiling when he met me at the veranda. "When a Bugis makes money, he buys gold," he said. "When he makes more, he goes to Mecca."

I heard the buses arrive and depart in my sleep as the rain continued.

The next evening Dumah dropped me at the torchlighted night-mare that was Ujung Pandang's port.

"Mind your purse," he warned, and extended his hand as I closed the door of the Land Rover.

A thousand becaks were caught in the port's potholed maze under a hot, heavy wind. Finally the hysterical cries of the Bugis were silenced by the boat whistle's scream.

North Sulawesi curves eastward, then north toward Mindanao in the Philippines across the Celebes Sea. On a detailed map the two large islands resemble two magnetic poles, the space between dotted with islands like dancing particles. At nearly two degrees north of the equator on North Sulawesi's tip, Manado is the northernmost Indonesian city in the eastern half of the archipelago. To reach it by motorized vehicle from Ujung Pandang requires a grueling thousand-mile expedition of ten days. A faster, if more circuitous, route is by ship.

The *Rinjani* sailed between Jakarta and Sorong, one of the remotest ports of the archipelago, on the so-called bird's head peninsula of Irian Jaya. After departing Ujung Pandang on this outward run, it called first at Baubau off Sulawesi's southeastern arm. Once a pirate stronghold and slave trade center, Baubau was a protected, stench-ridden Bugis port on Butung Island that, when we anchored the next afternoon, offered little to see save the feverish energy at the waterfront.

When the *Rinjani* cruised out of the roadstead and cleared the southern tip of Butung Island, she faced a day-and-a-half run across open ocean to Ambon, the capital of the Moluccas, or Spice Islands. By late evening it was clear that we had entered another weather pattern, for the sea boiled and buckled under the cutwater. Dawn brought a steady rain and an overwhelming grayness that rendered the horizon indistinct.

By contrast to the larger islands of Indonesia, Ambon appeared insignificant on a map, but this nucleus of nowhere was situated at the center of a large vortex, the hub of a wheel of curvilinear islands and centrifugal seas that created its own climate. Now, in early July, the rain was incessant.

Cursed by inclement weather, Ambon was also a remote cross-roads for places in the "spiceries" that were even remoter: the Banda Islands in the Southern Moluccas, as well as the former sultanates of Ternate and Tidore in the north, not to mention Irian Jaya. Ships proceeding northwest to Manado also called here.

Ambon, known as Amboina or Amboyna during the centuries of the spice trade before the Dutch monopoly was broken, had galvanized the attentions of the Western colonial and trading powers. Five hundred years ago one of the most important ports on the globe, it was today one of the archipelago's many backwaters. Its deep, long horseshoe harbor, protected by green hills and mountains, resembled a Norwegian fjord, and it had been a strategic Allied harbor in World War II, when the relentless pounding of Japanese bombing attacks had destroyed Ambon City and the remaining vestiges of Dutch colonialism. A new, ugly metropolis of concrete blocks and corrugated-tin roofs had been built atop the ruins of the old. Hotels were few, ramshackle, and expensive.

It was three days before I could leave. The freighter I had planned to take to Manado canceled its run, and flights were grounded because of the rain and poor visibility.

"I've never seen so much rain," I said to a Dutch engineer staying at my hotel. "It's dispiriting."

"It's the southeast monsoon," he said. "The Australian winter causes it. Only on Ambon does it rain this much. Two hundred forty inches of rain at this time of year alone. But there's no avoiding Ambon. To go to hell from this part of the world, you have to go through Ambon."

On the Fourth of July I escaped the drenching depressions of Ambon. The flight lifted off during a brief lull in the weather, and when we had completed our circle and were headed north to cross the equator, the land was obscured by monsoon clouds that resembled those you would see before a blizzard. It was not until we had departed west from Ternate in the Northern Moluccas and were halfway across the Molucca Sea that the configuration of weather changed—drastically so. The vivid, mingled sea of sun, blue water, green reefs, and the reflecting rice fields of North Sulawesi appeared like a fading dream.

Manado was a lively city full of Chinese shops and kung fu cinemas. The inhabitants here were Minahasan. These tribes had been animist headhunters in this northern extremity of Sulawesi before European colonization, but with the arrival of the Dutch, they had accepted Protestant Christianity willingly, and many tribes had embraced the Roman Catholic faith offered by Jesuits. For centuries these people had known the outside world through trade, but trade to the north, through the Sangir and Talaud Islands to the Philippines, as well as east to the Spice Islands. Indeed, Manado, considering its Catholic population and its proximity to Mindanao, seemed as much a Philippine as a Malay city.

On this northern edge of the Malay Archipelago, vast expanses of sandy scrubland and stretches of palmetto gave way to marsh and tidal inlets and rivers. To the north, volcanic cones rose abruptly from the water like great netherworld monsters, and puffs of cloud hovered over the surface like steam from boiling seas.

I found a fishing camp where outriggers plied the offshore reefs and enjoyed a brief respite while my clothes, still sodden from Ambon, dried. It was a quiet, modest place with polyglot visitors who came for some of the finest diving in the world: the odd, bearded German backpacker and his buxom wife, who sunbathed topless; the aloof French boy and girl; a gay couple in the antiques business in Sydney who shared the Christian name John and talked of opera.

Many of the natives feared the water, which they believed to be inhabited by spirits who regarded divers as intruders. On cloudy days the dearth of sun muted the subcurrents, rendering the depths in less vivid hues. With a guide called Boy, I explored the flues and caves of a giant coral chimney with barracuda for company as well as fluttering rays, sand sharks, schools of blue fish swimming vertically, moving nests of golds and blues, then blue heads with silver bodies in sharp outline against the ink-dark depths.

The convivial evening meals included grilled bluetail tuna served on a palm leaf by Boy. The owner of the camp was a thin, fastidious Javanese named Loky who spoke excellent English and bore an eerie resemblance to Jacques Cousteau. He kept his guests entertained with stories of native superstitions that had come into play when he had built his camp: he had been required by the locals to appease the spirits of the deep through elaborate ritual.

"Where do you go next?" he asked me on my final evening.

"Back to the Moluccas," I said. "I passed through Ambon to get here."

"I must warn you that the Moluccas are among the loneliest places in the world," he said.

"I've had a taste of that," I said. "I was trapped in Ambon for three days and took away a bag of wet clothes."

"That's nothing," he said. "Ambon is the capital of the Moluccas, a cosmopolitan city. But if you were trapped in Ambon, imagine being marooned in the outer islands. There are a thousand of these so-called Spice Islands. Once they were the center of the world's attention, but today they are totally forgotten. The coral reefs and deep seas that isolate them will only enhance your sense of dislocation."

"I've been to Borneo," I said. "How could the Spice Islands be more remote than a rainforest?"

"It's a different kind of remoteness," he said. "Borneo's wilderness is a presence to be reckoned with. The Moluccas are one of history's odd accidents. Those islands exist in the past tense. There is no presence to be reckoned with because the presence came from the outside world, and now that presence has long since fled. You will see what I mean soon enough. And there's another thing," he added. "Something you already know if you've been to Ambon."

"What's that?"

"It rains a lot this time of year."

The Moluccas:
Spices and Fire

$\mathcal{H}$ISTORY HAS NO PRECEDENT for the Spice Islands. There are roughly a thousand of them, and on a map they lie as minuscule as flyspecks in the middle of the Malay Archipelago, today comprising one of Indonesia's twenty-seven provinces. Though it takes brushing up on your geography to find them, for centuries they occasioned the rise and fall of empires whose seats of power stood on the other side of the world. They fired the imagination of the Roman scholar Pliny and beckoned Sinbad the Sailor.

From the time of the Renaissance, their remoteness and exoticism provided a theater, a sort of fashion show of power in world history. The participants were Eastern cartels and Western nations, with each season bringing a new rage while successors with new leases of affection waited in the wings. Their history rings out with such names as Vasco da Gama, Ferdinand Magellan, Sir Francis Drake, and Francis Xavier, the missionary and cofounder of the Jesuit order, who traveled these islands to save souls and called them "islands of divine hope."

But it was earthly hope that altered the vision of an already progressive age of exploration. Four centuries ago spices were not only the most significant force in the world's economy, but as well the harbinger of Western colonization in Asia. Before the arrival of the European ships, spices with their Edenic scents and tastes and their preservative properties were made available in Europe only by Arab traders, who brought them overland to sell at extortionate prices. Literally worth their weight in gold, the cloves, nutmeg, mace, cinnamon, and pepper from these islands induced the invasion of the East by the European powers, spawning a new age of revolutionary economics based on credit, the rise of a rudimentary international banking system, and ultimately free enterprise.

The spice trade underwrote the Italian Renaissance and prompted the discovery of America. The Spice Islands, or Moluccas, were the East Indies Columbus meant to find when he chanced upon the New World in 1492, but the Portuguese, who rounded the Cape of Good Hope to cross the Indian Ocean two decades later, were the first Europeans bent on exploiting them.

The port and fortress of Malacca had been Southeast Asia's most important trading center for centuries. Situated northwest of the future city of Singapore on the Malay Peninsula, it presided over the narrow straits separating the mainland from Sumatra. A strategic, fabled gateway, it saw every European visitor to these parts, traveler and adventurer alike, from Marco Polo to Magellan. The Portuguese seized Malacca in 1511, poising themselves for the invasion of the mysterious "spiceries," whose exact whereabouts remained elusive.

Guided by Malay pilots, they traversed the Malay Archipelago via Java and Nusa Tenggara to Ambon at the center of the Moluccas, another gateway long since discovered by Arab and Chinese traders. Three hundred miles to the north were the island sultanates of Ternate and Tidore, producers of cloves, and a hundred miles southward lay the tiny Banda group, a scattering of islands with a total area of forty square miles at high tide, which were the world's only source of nutmeg and mace. "When God gave trees to the world," went a local saying, "He gave the nutmeg tree to Banda, and to Banda alone."

For hundreds of years Malay, Chinese, and Arab traders had controlled the spice trade, buying for a pittance cloves, mace, and nutmeg on the spot, and shipping the precious cargo through the Straits of Malacca to the Persian Gulf, where it was unloaded and carried by caravan to the Mediterranean and such major ports as Constantinople, Genoa, and Venice for distribution throughout Europe. Just how precious these spices were as a commodity manipulated by middlemen almost defies comprehension, even by today's most jaded economist. In his study *Indonesian Banda*, Willard A. Hanna reveals a startling fact of this early commerce that inevitably drew competing colonial powers into the fray, staining the Molucca seas with European blood. The value of the spices increased one hundred percent each time they changed hands, from the native on a Malay prahu or Arab dhow, to the Chinese middleman, to the traders in the dusty bazaars passed by desert caravans crossing the vast Asian wastes.

When they arrived in the Spice Islands in 1512, the Portuguese were intent on controlling the trade and could count on realizing a thousand-percent profit on their cargo in Lisbon. For their part, the islanders, who had long known of the popularity of their produce in Europe, were curious to meet these new, fair-skinned comrades-in-trade, and initial negotiations were peaceful. But trade unmarred by violence was not to last.

Contentious parties in the sultanates of Ternate and Tidore already struggled with each other for control of the clove trade in the north. Now, with the European threat, the Javanese dynasties, which had brought Islam to these islands, and the northern sultanates began a protracted struggle with the European powers for preeminence, often forming strange alliances. Ternate and nearby Tidore, for example, bitter enemies in trade, each sought an alliance with the Portuguese.

For most of the sixteenth century Ternate and Tidore were the focus of the Western invaders. Indeed, their exploitation by the Portuguese weighed heavily in Magellan's efforts to persuade the king of Spain to finance his circumnavigation of the globe. Having been among the Portuguese who visited the Spice Islands from Malacca in 1512, Magellan became convinced that the Moluccas could be more easily reached by following Columbus's example, sailing west, than by the long, difficult voyage around the Cape of Good Hope and through the Malacca Strait. The great navigator's expedition arrived in Ternate in 1521, though Magellan had met his death in battle in the Philippines earlier that year. The Banda group in the south would suffer little outside interference during the sixteenth century. But the later arrival of the Dutch would change all that.

The Portuguese hold on the Northern Moluccas was tenuous, and the Europeans eventually engendered widespread hatred among the natives. The Portuguese fled Ternate in 1575, and at the beginning of the seventeenth century the Dutch entered the archipelago with better ships and weaponry to gain their own monopoly in the clove trade of Ternate and Tidore in the north, as well as the nutmeg and mace trade of Banda in the south.

The Dutch were ruthlessly cunning in their mercantilism. They murdered native leaders, enslaved the islanders, and leveled clove and nutmeg trees throughout the Moluccas, except in the few places where they exercised rigid control through *perkeniers,* or estate managers, over this new, phenomenal wealth which literally grew on trees. They marked up prices over a thousand times. Their monopoly changed the balance of power in the world.

Until the mid-eighteenth century, it was generally held that trees and plants could be grown only in places where they were found. The German botanist Georg Eberhard Rumpf (1627–1702), writing a hundred years earlier, for example, suggested that cloves were a gift of God to the Moluccas, "beyond which, by no human industry, can they be propagated or perfectly cultivated." But a Frenchman named Pierre Poive disproved this theory by smuggling small amounts of clove and nutmeg seedlings to Mauritius, while the British secretly exported plants to India, Africa, and Grenada in the Caribbean, thus ending the monopoly and relegating the Moluccas to the state of economic stagnation in which they remain today.

The location, configuration, and size of the Spice Islands and the distribution of power among them not only reflect the curious drama of Malay and colonial forces but highlight some attendant historical ironies as well. Ternate, Tidore, and the Bandas are so tiny as to be invisible on a globe, yet their yield of spices held an expectant world hostage for centuries. While the British "gentlemen adventurers" sent by Elizabeth I to settle tiny Run Island in the Bandas in 1601 were not the major players in the Moluccas that the Portuguese and Dutch were, their expulsion illuminates one curious vicissitude of history. The treaty known as the Peace of Breda in 1667 required that the British relinquish their claim to Run, hardly more than an atoll with no fresh water except rainwater, in exchange for a larger, though still small, island owned by the Dutch—Manhattan.

Despite its proximity, Ternate is a world away from the sunny brilliance of North Sulawesi, and my small freighter plowed reluctantly the heavy seas of the Northern Moluccas, until the three islands materialized like smoke in the rain. Tidore lies a half hour by longboat to the southeast of Ternate, and both islands are equally close to the larger island of Halmahera, sprawling with its tentacles to the east. Ternate, six and a half miles in diameter, and Tidore, scarcely ten miles long, are so tiny and such strange-sounding names to contemporary Western ears that it is difficult to believe the hold they had on the imagination of an earlier age. In *Paradise Lost* John Milton describes a fleet

> by equinoctial winds
> Close sailing from Bengala, or the isles
> Of Ternate and Tidore, whence merchants bring
> Their spicy drugs . . .

We steamed into the sanctuary of Ternate's small port. The dark, saturnine townspeople who had gathered at the waterfront watched the unloading of cargo with morose curiosity. Though the original settlers here were Malays who established a monarchy that evolved into a sultanate with the arrival of Javanese traders, there is a lot of mixed blood in the Moluccas. Before the arrival of the Europeans, Papuans were brought here from New Guinea as slaves to serve the clove trade, and the races have intermingled over the centuries.

I disembarked and walked in the drizzle into town along the single road that encircles the base of Gunung Api Gamalama, the active volcano that makes up the entire island, rising in a nearly perfect cone from the sea, its summit washed in rain cloud and smoke. The town was marked by shades of native and faded colonial grandeur. The sultan's palace, now a museum with little to see, stood off the road in a grassy field, perfectly framed and proportioned by the backdrop of volcano rising behind it. When Wallace passed through Ternate in 1858, he found the royal residence "now a large, untidy, half-ruinous building of stone," and little had changed between the naturalist's visit and mine. In the middle of town was the seventeenth-century Dutch fort, crumbling and gone to seed, its visitors chickens and goats, the entrance guarded by a long-nosed monkey tethered to a post.

The town, visited by Magellan and Sir Francis Drake in livelier times, was ghostly quiet. Two hotels near the waterfront, decrepit structures embedded side by side in a mudbank, were full with a teachers' convention from nearby Halmahera. I was lucky to find a vacancy in a brothel on the edge of town and arrived in a downpour.

Two young women greeted me in the lobby under quietly rotating ceiling fans, a light-skinned girl and one whose darker Melanesian prettiness was undermined by a seizure of giggles. I caught a whiff of disinfectant, and from the back rooms near the garden came female voices as well as scullery noises. There were no clients.

In an odd way, the place seemed representative of Ternate. The town itself was like a desanctified church, empty of parishioners and slightly sinister. I wondered how it had differed in Wallace's day, if it had differed at all. The spice monopoly had been broken by then, and no other perceivable forces had been at work. There were neither industry nor tourists here.

An older woman, part Chinese, rouged, and sultry, entered through an arched doorway. "'Allo Meester Ingerris Jones," she said.

"I just need a room for a couple of days. Can you rent me one?"

"A room, sure, Meester Jones. This hotel. Anything you want."

By evening it was still raining quite heavily, but the proprietress, whose name was Soroya, assured me that the restaurant adjacent to the hotel had the best kitchen on Ternate, with island specialties of stewed bat and a land crab that fed on coconut. In the rainy darkness I walked the short distance to the restaurant, a dim, crowded place with red candles flickering on the tables, and took a seat near a table of Javanese merchants from Jakarta.

Apart from the customary flirtatious byplay, the fact that I was a guest in a paid room appeared to exempt me from the hustling games of the butterflies. "Meester Jones" somehow stuck, and the girls sang it out when I passed, the familiar but formal greeting issued by domestic servants to a gentleman at home. As "Meester Jones," quite simply, I belonged. Now my exemptive status was extended to the restaurant, where from my neutral position I could observe the interplay and the missed cues between the homegrown and the odd assortment of visitors.

The convention of teachers out from town accounted for the brisk business at the other end of the room. They sat in rows of chairs facing a lectern where a man was giving a speech. Beyond was a table laden with food that grew fly-ridden and cold, and when the speech ended, an amplified band played dance music, including Christian hymns, but no one danced. Soroya's girls were gathered at a large table and chirped like songbirds as they watched the proceedings, which ended after an hour to polite applause. The teachers formed an orderly queue for their dinner.

While the girls were Soroya's to manage, the restaurant was

the province of her husband, Oscar, a nervous, raffish man who wore his hair in dreadlocks. Throughout dinner he remained with the conventioneers, while Soroya, attired for evening in a low-cut dress, sat at my table, well out of his earshot.

"Why anyone come to Ternate?" she said. "There nothing here except clove trees on the mountain." She looked up, shaking her head at the tattoo of steady rain beating on the roof. "Where you go when you leave Ternate?"

"The Banda Islands."

"Bandaneira? Not good to go. Travel stop to Banda. Mountain blow up."

Before I left Jakarta, the news had been full of reports about an eruption of Banda's active volcano, resulting in widespread damage and loss of life. There were conflicting stories on Banda's accessibility, but Indo Avia had recently resumed its twice-a-week flight there out of Ambon.

"Four hundred miles away. Nowhere. Lonelier than here," she said. "And this a lonely place. Only my girls, and me."

"Who sees the girls?"

"Who? Anybody. Them. Tourists." She nodded toward the contingent of schoolteachers.

"After hymn-singing?"

"You okay?" she said. "You happy? You hotel guest."

"I'm okay," I said.

"Oscar businessman," she said looking in Oscar's direction. "I businesswoman. You shy, Meester Ingerris Jones? Okay, I make joke." She laughed.

I was gaining a new appreciation of Ternate, gloomy as it was. As it had for centuries, it held sway as the most important city in the Northern Moluccas, or, better put, the only city. And as the only city, it was the wicked city for those seeking diversions among its fleshpots. People from nearby islands clustered here like moths around a flame. Though it saw few outsiders, it attracted such "tourists" as the teachers from Halmahera. There were tourists on Ternate, but they didn't arrive in Boeing jets: they were borne across the straits from Halmahera, Tidore, and Hiri by motorized longboat.

"That disease, AIDS," Soroya said suddenly. "What you know? I know nothing. They speak no AIDS in Indonesia. Is true it started because a man *pam-pam* a monkey?"

"That's what I've heard, but I don't know."

"Was it a male or female monkey?"

"I don't know. I don't know that it matters now. It's a dreadful thing that so many innocent people . . ."

She leaned toward me, touching my arm, and spoke in a perfumed whisper. "No one is innocent. Have you not read your Genesis?"

I was up and about before first light. The rain had abated, but the hotel was flooded from the night's downpour. After breakfast I packed some fruit and departed, determined to see the island despite the weather. In town I took a bemo to the volcano's slopes. Gunung Api Gamalama was beautiful in its almost perfect roundness, even in the wet, the steady drizzle softening the dawn light into perpetual shadow. This lofty, mercurial mountain was now at rest, but having erupted twice in the last ten years, it was capable of breathing flames.

The sun was up when I started climbing for the fifty-six-hundred-foot summit, first through the cobbles of a small village, past the cultivated holdings along a pathway, through a broad field where cattle grazed and goats were tethered, to a fringe of wood, where the path began its meandering way toward the peak.

The lower slopes had fine stands of bamboo and palm, but soon these gave way to acacia and wattle trees, which in their turn stopped abruptly. The mountain had not been climbed in this wet season, and I lost the path in a nearly impenetrable jungle on a narrow saddle. When I reached a clearing, the tantalizing summit emerged from a heap of gaseous cloud. Below, the vivid green quilt of the landscape stretched to the sea.

The only sound was the cold wind passing the saddle, rustling the undergrowth. From the mountaintop a sudden rain cloud began tumbling down the slope, so I quickly made camp and rode out the squall, lunching on fruit. At noon I set out for the summit, and after climbing hand over hand up the warm pocked stone, I stood gazing into the smoldering crater. I felt a momentary panic and shivered, feeling like a lost man caught between two centuries but belonging to neither. Then I felt a rush of exhilaration as the heat burned my cheeks and my ears adjusted to the silence, broken only by the whisper of wind.

When I descended, the rain picked up and I had difficulty maintaining my footing in the mudslides. By late afternoon I stumbled onto a clove-tree grove beside a farm hut.

Cloves were picked before they flowered, and dried in three days to a deep brown, but in this weather the process was painstaking and uncertain, and each brief appearance of the sun elicited frantic activity by the farmers at this altitude. The natives who lived on these slopes used an ingenious suspended network of bamboo aqueducts crisscrossing the trails to bring water from the mountain streams to their huts.

I was about to continue my descent when a farmer emerged from the hut and approached me.

"The oldest clove tree in the world is near here," he said in Bahasa Indonesia. "Do you want to see it?"

He explained that Indonesians used a Chinese name for the spice, *cengkeh*. "In the olden days the Chinese emperors like cloves to sweeten the breath of their women," he told me. A few minutes later we stood next to a massive tree with a trunk several feet in diameter.

"More than two hundred pounds a year from this tree alone," he said. "Records tell us it is nearly three hundred seventy-five years old."

I made a spontaneous connection. The tree had been planted just after the reign of Elizabeth I, in Shakespeare's day, before his retirement to Stratford, during the period that saw *The Tempest*.

Shipwreck, a lonely island, magic, witches, and monsters seemed appropriate references on Ternate. I asked the farmer if the Dutch had planted it.

"After the Dutch," he said. "After the Dutch destroy all the clove trees on Ternate. For them, they want all the clove trees on Ambon and Banda. So my people plant trees in secret." He offered me a kretek and lighted it for me. "Cloves originate here," he said. "But now we cannot afford to grow them, and we grow other crops to make ends meet. The prices for cloves we get are too low, so it's not worth it. The big people control the market, and they don't like competition. It's as simple as that."

"Who are the big people?" I said.

"In the old days it is the Dutch," he said. "Now it is the Indonesian government."

He invited me inside his bungalow for tea and cakes. His wife was a fat, pleasant woman with a large mole on her chin sprouting black hairs. After serving me, she planted herself in a chair, where she remained immobile, smiling and belching audibly. There were two daughters: a beauty of nineteen, and a schoolgirl of eight who returned from her studies in a white burnoose and caftan and took my right hand and touched her nose to the back of my palm.

When I left, my host gave me a sack of cloves. "Please do not forget us," he said. "Pray for us."

In the evening I returned to the restaurant. I had just ordered dinner when Oscar appeared at tableside and took a seat.

"You know, Meester Jones, bats are a certain cure for asthma," he said. "You like?"

I was having stewed bat and coconut crab for the second night running. I had never tried bat, and it was delicious. The land crab was as succulent as a Maine lobster. "It's very good," I said.

It became clear that Oscar, like his wife, felt incarcerated on Ternate. While Soroya managed the butterflies, he ran the island's best restaurant, admitted to keeping a mistress, and had seen

enough of the world to want a certain kinky underside of it se-
questered with him on lonely Ternate.

"Ellie is my girlfriend," he said as I was finishing dinner. "And
now because I am now your friend, Meester Jones, I want to share
her with you." He nodded toward a fragile young woman at a
nearby table, who looked first at Oscar, then at me, smiling with
uncertainty.

"No, thanks." If Ellie's beauty was undeniable, it was all the
more so because she seemed an apparition in the soaked hell of
Ternate. But I had no intention of paying court to her. I sensed
that Oscar's voyeurism masked a tawdrier profligacy.

"You like Soroya?"

I excused myself and bolted for the hotel in the drizzle.

Before falling asleep, I thought about Ternate and the dislocation
the island's remoteness induced in a stranger. Ternate appeared
aimless and disconnected, the aimlessness underlain by a pathos
personified by the clove farmer on the slopes of the volcano. My
thoughts shifted to Banda and another volcano that had in its fury
dominated the news. I anticipated tomorrow with fascination and
dread.

The Moluccas:
The Sultan of Banda

I WAS TRAVELING to the Bandas with the hope of meeting a man called Des Alwi, a native of Banda but a figure of some wider reputation in the archipelago. He had been born into the aristocratic Baadilla family, whose patriarch had made a fortune in pearls, and as a boy he had come to know such men as Muhammad Hatta and Sutan Sjahrir, anticolonialists exiled by the Dutch to Banda in the 1930s. Later leaders in the independence movement, Hatta and Sjahrir adopted Des Alwi as a protégé and saw to his education in Java. School in England followed, and after independence Des Alwi entered the new nation's diplomatic corps.

When discontent with Sukarno's policies fostered the Permesta Rebellion in 1956, Des Alwi was the rebels' spokesman in exile. After Sukarno's overthrow in 1967, he became a successful businessman in Jakarta, amassing a fortune that led to extensive holdings in the Bandas, including cinnamon, clove, and nutmeg plantations, and two waterfront hotels on the island of Neira. Now a widower in his sixties with grown children educated in the West, he was known, not facetiously, as "the sultan of Banda." I carried a letter of introduction.

In an hour's time the plane out of Ambon began a steep bank on its descending circle toward the small strip built by Des Alwi, affording me only a kaleidoscopic glimpse of the nine clustered green islands that were the Bandas, marred only by the burnt slopes of Gunung Api. Though the Banda group belongs to the Spice Islands by virtue of its flora, geologically it lies at the tip of a great chain of active volcanoes running through Sumatra, Java, and Nusa Tenggara, continuing eastward in a hooklike curve that terminates in Banda.

The narrow strait separating two of the islands—Neira and Gunung Api—created a natural harbor that was guarded by two old Dutch forts. The realization that these tiny, forgotten islands had once charged the competitive instincts of the Western world, resulting in fortunes being risked and wars waged, was oddly unsettling.

Wallace visited Banda for the first time in 1857, and his description of Gunung Api is noteworthy. ". . . Close opposite the town is the volcano, forming a nearly perfect cone, the lower part only covered with a light green bushy vegetation. On its north side the outline is more uneven, and there is a slight hollow or chasm about one-fifth of the way down, from which constantly issue two columns of smoke, which also rises less abundantly from the rugged surface around and from some spots near the summit. A white efflorescence, probably sulphur, is thickly spread over the upper part of the mountain, marked by the narrow black vertical lines of water gullies. The smoke unites as it rises, and forms a dense cloud, which in calm damp weather spreads out into a wide canopy hiding the top of the mountain. At night and early morning it often rises up straight and leaves the whole outline clear."

Wallace's description of Gunung Api at slumber is striking in that it remained valid for the next 130 years, despite periodic rumblings, until the eruption that preceded my arrival. However, in regarding Gunung Api, Wallace heard a silent voice serving notice of a potential natural disaster.

"It is only when actually gazing on an active volcano that one can fully realize its awfulness and grandeur. Whence comes that inexhaustible fire whose dense and sulphureous smoke for ever issues from this bare and desolate peak? Whence the mighty forces that produced that peak, and still from time to time exhibit themselves in the earthquakes that always occur in the vicinity of volcanic vents?"

The annals of vulcanian time are recorded without regard for the affairs of humankind and count minutes and hours in centuries and millennia. Volcanoes inhabit a capricious world of absolutes, with no intermediate shades between the extremes. On Ternate's slumbering Gunung Api Gamalama I had warmed my hands over brimstone in the earth's belly as though the crater were a brazier. But Banda's Gunung Api had awakened after an eighty-seven-year sleep like a dragon snorting fire.

On the runway I approached a man who seemed to be greeting the handful of passengers on my flight.

"Can you tell me how to find Des Alwi?" I asked.

He brightened. "I am Des Alwi."

He was large for an Indonesian, with a rotund chest and broad, sloping shoulders that gave him more the look of a bear than a man. He was gregarious and a natural host.

We reclined and sipped coffee on the veranda of his hotel facing the still smoldering Gunung Api, rising twenty-one hundred feet out of the sea a half mile off Neira. Its green eastern side had not been ravaged by the eruption two months earlier. At the town dock a hundred yards down the beach, a small freighter was loading tuna for transport to Sorong on Irian Jaya. Immediately below us a young fish eagle screamed from its perch in a jackfruit tree.

"It's a nestling from Gunung Api," Des Alwi said. "I discovered it and a female chick after the eruption. But as they grew, they fought. I had to separate them.

"The animal life in the Bandas is unique," he continued. "No monkeys, but plenty of wild boar and pigeons. We grow coffee here as well, and the variety we have thrives at sea level."

"And nutmeg?"

"Indonesia still produces nearly eighty percent of the world's nutmeg," said Des Alwi. "That's a surprise to most people."

"After reading about the broken Dutch monopoly of colonial times, it is a surprise," I said.

"But only one percent of Indonesia's exports comes from the export of spices, so it's not like the old days."

"What about Grenada's nutmeg production?"

"Grenada grows most of the rest. In fact, when the U.S. invaded Grenada in 1983, production ceased, causing world prices to climb. Indonesia invited Grenada into its cartel. Little did we know that the Dutch would resurrect themselves to haunt us. A Rotterdam consortium gave us fits. Undercut us by encouraging a black market. Prices crashed, and our poor farmers have suffered. No, we may produce the lion's share of nutmeg, but Banda has never recovered from the old days." He smiled. "You see how the lines are drawn," he said. "It's odd how history repeats itself with new variations. Things change, but not really.

"But collapsed nutmeg prices are nothing compared to the collapse of that," he said, nodding seaward at Gunung Api. "Come," he said. "I want to show you something."

A boatman and launch awaited us at the dock beneath the hotel. As we pulled into the channel, Des Alwi explained that it was his habit to circle the volcano and inspect it daily.

From the hotel veranda the view of Gunung Api was of its green eastern slope, with the only clue to the recent eruption offered by a series of interconnecting lava flows that scarred this side two thirds of the way down from the summit. These resembled outcroppings of black rock except for the telltale sticks that used to be trees. Sulphuric smoke drifted into the air from the still-soft, black lava mudbanks, but I was unprepared for what awaited as the launch began our clockwise circumnavigation of the mountain.

From summit to base the mountain was burnt black, as if from weeks-long napalm bombardment; so devastating had been this attack that, seemingly, nothing would grow here for a hundred years. The slow cruise of the boat and the proximity of the smoking nightmare prompted hellish images: grim pictures of World

War I France, the no-man's-land beyond the wire barricades and trenches. But those desecrations were merely man-induced. This was a hideous parody nature had played on herself.

The trails of lava flows crossed and recrossed themselves, plunging downward at various degrees, and here and there were portioned off by the ash-colored skeletons of trees mummified by lava.

"Put your hand in the water, but be careful," said my host.

We were a hundred yards offshore. I reached into the water but withdrew my hand quickly, for the water was nearly scalding, like a boiling sea on the dark side of the moon. I tried to imagine the awesome forces beneath us, the recent eruption only a murmur of what might happen.

"The water is hotter than yesterday," he said.

On the western side, where the open surf of the Banda Sea pounded the island relentlessly, the water had cooled and the only sign of life was a lone blue egret sailing past, its brilliant plumage catching the sunlight in sharp relief to the overwhelming grayness.

The patches of settlements had long since been deserted and destroyed. On the fateful early morning of May 9, 1988, more than two thousand villagers had fled this island when Gunung Api had erupted, sending fireballs, as reported by airline pilots, ten thousand feet into the air.

"It's no small wonder that only four people died," said Des Alwi. "One was an old man, my boat builder, who refused to leave. He sought refuge in a mosque and was overcome by lethal fumes. Two high school boys who returned for their transistor radios were consumed by falling waves of lava. Then a young woman fled with her infant daughter, though when she reached the canoe, she realized she was holding a pillow."

As we rounded the southern face, I could see that where there had recently been two craters, as in Wallace's day, there were now six, each belching forth smoke and debris in a disconcertingly unsteady rhythm, the wind carrying the soot across the narrow, shallow strait that kept large ships from entering the harbor from this side.

"Before the eruption people would come here just to climb the volcano," said Des Alwi. "It doesn't take long, but I insist that climbers set out before sunup because of the heat. There was a Dutchman staying at the hotel who suffered a fatal heart attack after the climb. He was forty-eight, and his wife blamed me, saying that I didn't supply him with enough water for the climb. She was a half-breed, a very strange woman. After he died, she converted to Islam. Then the story gets odder still. She was trampled to death in Mecca."

Once clear of the strait, we emerged again into the deep blue lagoon of the harbor, where canoes laden with fruit and other stores crossed waters as still as a Canadian lake. The boatman cut the engine as we coasted to the hotel dock. I looked back to see the marred but green soft face of the eastern slope, which masked the nightmarish horror of what lay behind it.

Later in the day we walked through the town. It seemed a forgotten sanctuary echoing rites of distant customs and old wars. Neira was dressed in a North European cut of clothes: it was portioned into square blocks commanded by the ancient forts over which had flown successive Portuguese and Dutch banners.

"Somerset Maugham was quite taken with Banda," said Des Alwi as we walked. "You know, he set one of his novels here, *The Narrow Corner*, but he called the island something else."

Des Alwi greeted each person we passed by name, often stopping for a brief chat, until we reached the museum. It was an airy Victorian mansion with shady porticos. Inside, paintings, engravings, weapons, porcelains, and man-sized Portuguese earthenware urns told of Banda's brutal colonial history.

"I grew up in this house. It belonged to my grandfather and many of these things were his," said Des Alwi. "Artifacts keep turning up. Old cannon, muskets, coins from all the Banda islands."

The terrible deeds the invaders had inflicted upon the natives resounded here. In the 1620s, as governor-general of the Dutch East Indies Company, Jan Pieterszoon Coen, then in his early thirties, envisioned an unassailable commercial empire for his nation that would stretch from Japan to India. Coen was a visionary whose zeal was matched with equal portions of efficiency and ruthlessness. It was Coen who established the Dutch capital in Batavia, now Jakarta, and seized the Bandas, established slave-labor plantations, forced out the competing, undermanned British from their garrison on tiny Run Island, and established a monopoly so potent that it lasted until the Napoleonic Wars two centuries later. With the Dutch monopoly broken, the Bandas, like the rest of the Moluccas, were forgotten.

For every tyrannical Coen, there was a martyred native leader such as Pattimena, and the portraits that hung on the walls of the museum, grim on the one hand and noble on the other, told who they were even today.

There were signs of a softer, more domestic Dutch presence that had passed into Des Alwi's family, legacies of the perkeniers who thrived in this lonely outpost, homesick for a Holland left generations before: a brass bed from France; a smoked-glass chandelier hanging precariously from the tall ceiling over a set table; glass-encased cupboards of wood imported from Bali, displaying Chinese porcelain bowls as well as monogrammed delft plates; a Victorian settee of native hardwood. These were manifestations of a Neira that had worn a broad-brimmed hat against the sun but dressed for dinner.

There were as well reminders of a more recent past. An old framed photograph on the wall showed Des Alwi as a student dressed in cricket whites; another pictured him as a young man with Muhammad Hatta, later vice-president of Indonesia. Des Alwi wound up an old gramophone with a blue porcelain speaker, "His Master's Voice" emblazoned in gold letters, and an old 78-rpm bawled out, "You sent her an orchid, you sent me a rose," a Jean Shepard rendition, American country and western to complete the anomaly.

Neira was not destined to outgrow its tin-roofed days. There were a total of four vehicles in the Banda islands, and they were all in Neira. Outside along the main street, shops were scattered among the colonial buildings gone to seed. A Dutch church, representing colonialism in a more settled era than Coen's, dated from 1873. It had stark white Corinthian columns set off by the gray-blue trim found on delft china.

Various trees and bushes lined the streets on the way to Forts Nassau and Belgica: acacia, jackfruit, papaya, and cassava plants with their succulent roots. Fort Nassau lay in ruins at the base of a hill at the southwest entrance to the harbor and marked the old shoreline, long since reclaimed by Low Country engineering; the seemingly unassailable Fort Belgica at the hill's crest had provided defense by cannon and musket from either direction. Entrance was gained through a vaulted archway stale with the scent of fecal matter into tunnels beneath walls twenty-five yards thick. We climbed the winding steps of a corner tower to reach the battlements, overgrown with weeds the height of a man.

Except for the impotent cannons gone to rust, the fort resembled not so much a defense post as a monastery. Below the battlements the interior walls opened out onto the courtyard, with arched doorways alternating with similar but raised windows that partitioned off individual cells. But the fort nonetheless reflected the strategy of 350 years before. Its cannon were pointed toward the deeper northwestern reach of the strait, for at its western end the water was as shallow as three meters, a depth that would rip the keel from a warship. Thus in the days of square-riggers, the capital of the Banda Islands had been made impregnable to attack. Today the fort that had once protected Neira was a refuge for goats and graffiti-happy lovers.

"The Minister of Population and the Environment is coming in a few days," explained Des Alwi as we took the hotel launch across to Lonthor Island. "We want to put on a good face."

While Des Alwi oversaw work on one of his cinnamon groves, I followed a teenaged boy to see Fort Hollandia. We climbed steep stone steps and followed a winding path up to the fort, high on the central ridge of the island, which was covered with a scattering of fifty-foot nutmeg trees. The fort, constructed by Coen in 1621, had been damaged by an earthquake in the mid-eighteenth century, and only three walls remained, enclosing weeds and stone.

The view was astonishing. Tiny Run Island lay six miles to the west, where the British settlement had been blockaded by Coen's Dutch forces and the island's nutmeg trees destroyed by an invasion. Though the British had remained for another decade, they had eventually left, fearing a massacre at the hands of the Dutch, and the island, Britain's only legitimate claim in the Spice Islands, had eventually been ceded to Holland in exchange for Manhattan.

When I descended the ridge to rejoin Des Alwi, I found him surrounded by a group of villagers.

"A boy just gave me a handful of Dutch coins for the museum," he said. "One may be valuable. I have a book in my office that should tell us."

He handed the coin to me for my inspection; it bore the date 1856.

"Let's have tea," he said.

The launch tore past Neira to a tiny bungalow at the opposite end of the harbor, where we stepped onto a small dock. The boatman left us and in minutes returned from the hotel with a pot of hot tea, cups, cakes, and a book for Des Alwi's perusal, while the sun settled behind Gunung Api, setting the sky ablaze.

"This coin is worth five thousand U.S. dollars," he said after consulting his book. "Come see. There are a lot more where these came from."

By chance, a small fishing boat entered the harbor, and Des Alwi gave a quick order to his boatman, Djumat, who sped out to intercept the fisherman.

"I'm buying a fresh tuna for our dinner tonight," he said.

In minutes the boatman returned with a large tuna. "It's a gift for Des Alwi," Djumat said in Bahasa Indonesia. "The fisherman won't take Des Alwi's money."

Des Alwi smiled and shrugged. "I was away from Banda for twenty-five years," he said. "When I returned, you cannot imagine what a sorry state I found these islands in. Most of the nutmeg trees had been destroyed during the Japanese occupation and the old perkenier estates were a mess. The government cared nothing for us. I lobbied furiously for an airstrip, a doctor, better local government. Do you know why they call me 'the sultan of Banda'? My family is the local aristocracy, *orang lima*, we say. The governor of the Moluccas lives in Ambon. He has no idea of the customs here, so I must interpret local *adat*. He doesn't resent me. Quite the contrary. I must settle disputes and solve problems. Restitutions if an offense is committed, distribution of inheritance, local civil matters, things like that. Tonight after dinner at the hotel, we're having a meeting of townspeople to discuss harbor pollution. There's a movie afterward. Lots of kids will come.

"You'll enjoy the movie," he said. "A documentary on the Bandas. I produced, directed, and wrote it myself."

A combination of things played off Des Alwi's ursine appearance: energy, intelligence, goodwill, cunning. I sensed, too, if not a measure of the huckster in his noblesse oblige, at least an acute sense of his own destiny in the Bandas. He seemed a throwback to an earlier age, the legendary king returned after years of exile to claim a throne rightfully his.

Suddenly the sunset was shattered by a procession of two small ships entering the harbor with rock music blaring forth from their speakers. Each was filled to capacity, and makeshift clotheslines decorated the stern, whose hull was more rust than white paint, with a trim of jaundice yellow. The crafts had a similar list to port as they rocked and rolled with the grim authority of an old bosun's mate past us toward the town dock.

"They've come from Seram for the soccer tournament," said

Des Alwi. "Seram versus Banda, a fierce rivalry. The first boat has the players and the second the fans. A fifteen-hour voyage. They'll be here a week."

We followed in their wake back to the hotel and arrived as it grew dark. Before dinner in my room I took from my pocket the nutmegs I had randomly picked on Lonthor Island. I split open one of the plum-sized fruits and saw the white meat used for making preserves. At the fruit's center lay a smooth, coral-colored seed the size of a large grape. The skin of the seed, when peeled away, felt and looked like tough yellowish-red flower petals. This skin, which would be dried, was mace, costly because one "nut" could produce only so much. Stripped of the mace, the nut was ready for grating, as nutmeg. Once more valuable than gold, the freshly picked nutmeg was now a mere souvenir from a place and time that had fired the European imagination during the Renaissance, luring royalty and adventurer, soldier and priest—shrinking the globe.

At dinner we were served the fisherman's gift of tuna, not only grilled, but in other preparations as well: smoked, sashimi, even tuna jerky.

"Tuna is our meat staple here," said Des Alwi. "They are very plentiful here in the Banda Sea. You will see when you cross to the other islands."

"I thought I'd visit Run tomorrow," I said. "I have to see the island the Dutch traded for Manhattan."

"Take Djumat and the boat. Man Ali will be your guide. Run and Ai will make a fine day trip. There are tanks if you want to dive. You will learn much about Banda underwater. You will see."

As we finished dinner I heard crowd noises from the narrow street behind the hotel, and when the meal ended a servant opened the doors to admit scores of men, women, and children for Des Alwi's seminar on harbor pollution.

I studied an ancient Dutch map of this tiny archipelago; it was amazingly accurate. The group ran only fifteen miles east to west.

Neira, Gunung Api, and Lonthor offered each other mutual protection from natural and human invasion by virtue of their half-moon configuration and proximity. Run and Ai, by contrast, were isolated far to the west, as distances went in the Bandas, and anchored in extraordinarily deep seas. These tiny islands tantalized on the near horizon.

There was something else about the Bandas: they were unique, one of history's green puzzles, unchanged in shape and texture on the Banda Sea for millennia but now bereft of their historical implications, save for ruins and buried shards. Therein lay their fascination.

Djumat had a distant, taciturn manner, while Man Ali was a friendly young man who had a good command of English from listening to cassette tapes. He fetched a regulator, weight belt, and tanks from Des Alwi's diving locker, and I found a pair of old U.S. Navy UDT duck feet among the hotel's odd collection of flippers and masks, and we got under way.

The surface was glass-smooth as Djumat rounded Gunung Api and urged the outboard across the open sea for Run. The sky was alternately bright and overcast, and the occasional squall raced across the horizon. Schools of dolphin often broke the placid water, but the feeding tuna were spectacular: flocks of screaming seabirds revealed where they were by feeding on the smaller fish these yellowfins preyed upon. Whenever such a frenzy occurred on our course, Djumat released a line to troll and unfailingly pulled in one of the edible predators.

An hour later we were in the lee of Run. There was a narrow spit of land on the northeastern side, where the British fort had once stood, facing the Bandas' main deep-sea corridors and the old Dutch threat. The rest of the island appeared unassailable from the sea because of its series of interlocking reefs. Coen, however, had managed to seize the island and destroy the nutmeg plantations after a prolonged blockade. A settlement of perhaps a few hundred people appeared on the north shore. Even these settlers, fishermen, depended upon rainwater, for the island has no natural springs. A small ridge of forested hills ran on an east-west axis, but beyond the fishing village the island appeared uninhabited. Run Island was a quiet, ghostly, green place and mocked any attempt to make it what it was not. Run in exchange for Manhattan, one island for another, an even swap in a global choose-up game.

"There's not much to see at Run," said Man Ali, adjusting my tanks, "except down there."

Djumat cast anchor two hundred yards offshore on a reef in six feet of water, on the edge of a great drop-off whose depths were obscured by an inky darkness. Wallace had noted in the Bandas that "living corals and even the minutest objects are plainly seen on the volcanic sand at a depth of seven or eight fathoms," but Wallace had made his observations from the surface.

Exploring underwater held more discoveries. When I rolled into the water a large ray glided beneath me. Most of the shallow-water fish were delicate and feathery. There was the occasional bamboo fish trap. Besides the multicolored coral, the reef was studded with giant clams, and at fifty feet nearly man-sized groupers. At a hundred feet, where the face of the reef was nearly vertical, I could see how extraordinary, strictly from a geological standpoint, Run and the rest of the Bandas were. Volcanic in origin, Run rose out of a Banda Sea of awesome depths, while from the surface it seemed to float with its neighbors in astonishing isolation.

Run is the westernmost of the Bandas, so when Djumat turned toward Ai, we were guided in the distance by the nearly geometric configuration of Neira, Lonthor, and Gunung Api, the volcano rising serenely to belie its angrier nature.

"There's more to see on Ai," said Man Ali, as Djumat cut the engine in a slight chop of surf and beached the boat.

"We are here until the tide carries us out," said Djumat in Bahasa Indonesia, and I turned to see the offshore reef sending up spray.

We lunched on smoked tuna and fruit in the shade of a coral

wall and soon were joined by a group of children, the youngest about four, who had been fishing the surf in dugout canoes. All but the youngest carried small machetes, *parang,* used to cut into hard green mangoes. After initial timidity they were friendly and accepted gifts of bananas with self-conscious courtesy. They invited me to see their village, so Man Ali and I followed them, while Djumat remained with the boat.

The village was at the edge of forest down the beach. Upon entering, I realized that it had been a Dutch settlement and dated from the early seventeenth century, if not before. The streets were laid out neatly and were being swept by women with large straw brooms. Dugout canoes fashioned from almond trunks lay overturned beside each stucco house; this was a community of fishermen. Each house had a cistern fed by an elaborate network of bamboo gutters, for, as on Run and the other outer islands of the Bandas, rainwater was the only fresh water to be had.

A church, perfectly preserved and still used for worship, bore the date 1611, and behind it was a cemetery with elaborately engraved markers from the same period. This was the era when Dutch munificence had fueled the Dutch master painters. Frans Hals had been in his prime at thirty, Van Dyck twelve, and Rembrandt five years old when the church was built.

"So this is a Christian community, Man Ali?" I said.

"Christian and Muslim. There's the mosque," he said, pointing to a much newer structure down the way, with its own graveyard.

"Christians and Muslims together in such a small village and no problems?"

"No problems here."

It seemed an ideal community, and I believed him.

Later, on the return run to Neira, Man Ali returned to this theme. "I am a Muslim and I am obliged to be a good Muslim, but many of my friends are Christian. It does not matter here."

"And Des Alwi?"

"Des Alwi is Muslim, but his wife was a Christian from Sulawesi."

I remembered that Des Alwi had taken a drink of scotch before dinner. "Is Des Alwi a good Muslim?" I said.

Man Ali laughed but did not answer.

Several days passed, and as the arrival of Emil Salim, Indonesia's Minister of Population and the Environment, was imminent, Des Alwi had suggested that I extend my visit another couple of days. The minister was to fly into Ambon by jet from Jakarta, then transfer to a small Indoavia charter plane. As the charter would be returning to Ambon empty of passengers, there would be room for me. Eager to visit the other islands of the group as well as to see Des Alwi in his official capacity as head of the welcoming committee, I readily accepted.

On the morning of Emil Salim's arrival, Man Ali, an only son with seven older sisters, took me to his home to meet his mother. As we walked through Neira's streets, I saw that flower and crepe-paper garlands and Indonesian flags hung from every conceivable lofty spot to which they could be appended, while every citizen moved about in tribal finery. In the harbor two large *kora kora*, war canoes, were readied for a race. Bands played, and the atmosphere was festive.

By lunchtime Des Alwi was elegantly turned out in a batik shirt and dark dress slacks and was in radio contact with officials in Ambon, who advised him in the early afternoon that the minister and his party were airborne en route to Banda. We got into the hotel van, and Neira's four vehicles proceeded in a parade to the airport, where dancers, young women with bouquets, and a chorus of uniformed schoolchildren awaited the flight.

When the airplane appeared, a great cheer went up, and with the efficiency of a stage director Des Alwi saw his reception committee positioned, while I stood well to the side. The plane touched down, taxied to the reception area, and the minister, his wife, and his aides and their wives stepped onto the tarmac to be warmly greeted by the sultan of Banda, music, and flowers. When the brief ceremony ended to polite applause, Des Alwi guided the minister and his wife toward me.

Emil Salim was gray and dapper in matching shirt and trousers, his wife smiling and well groomed in a blue cotton suit and pink blouse.

"You come here from San Francisco?" said the minister as we shook hands. "I went to Berkeley," he said with a knowing chuckle.

When Des Alwi guided them toward the vehicles, the pilot signaled to me, and I climbed into the aircraft.

I found Ambon in a rare dry mood for this time of year. The blast of sunlight dried the puddles of water, and breezes swayed the tall palm trees. Push-bike becak drivers cruised the streets in the heat, and the city turned out for the weather. Banda's weather normally reflected Ambon's, though now it was the quirky reverse, with Banda's warm southern front overriding the Moluccan capital, pushing Ambon's rain north.

The airline and shipping offices were closed for the day, so I took a room in a hotel and struck up a conversation with a young Japanese woman sunbathing in the garden.

Michiko, a pretty, edgy native of Osaka and the incarnation of Japanese consumer chic, had been in Ambon for several months as the sole representative of a Japanese tourist agency. In a sense, she was the point woman for Japan's second invasion of Indonesia. This new onslaught, however, was not to be carried out through the marshaling of troops and weapons but with tourists armed with a vigorously strong yen against the rupiah and dollar.

Michiko wore shorts and a halter and garish pink-rimmed spectacles and worked in the garden with colored pencils, composing brochures and maps while listening to Simon and Garfunkel cassette tapes.

Her agency's courtship of the hotel had assured her both privilege and attention, which she received with the mild tyranny of a spoiled princess. Michiko's pink figure was less than fetching, but she claimed she was constantly ogled by the male staff, much to her resentment. Her manner with the hotel staff was moody and bracingly peremptory. After snapping at a waiter who brought the wrong drink, she complained about her predicament as she perceived it.

"I am a free woman, but they"—she swept her arm as if to include all the men of Ambon—"watch my every move. I feel as though I am in jail. What must I do? They won't leave me alone."

"But you're here on business. Why not make that clear and not take things so seriously? It seems to me that you are free to set your own boundaries, within reason. Maybe sunbathing where there's no pool is going a bit far. What's tough for them to handle is that you're a foreign woman alone in a Muslim society."

"Yes," she said, examining a sunburned arm. "I am Japanese."

Japan was offering Indonesia a bigger box of candy than the United States: $6 billion a year in foreign aid to our $90 million. The personification of this trade-off was Michiko, lonely and haplessly rigid, on reconnaissance for the impending invasion.

Since I had to wait until the next day to secure passage to Irian Jaya, I was curious to see a place outside the city in the mountains. The village of Soya Atas lay thirteen hundred feet up the slopes of Gunung Sirimau and was clothed in mystery and legend regarding a number of unexplained disappearances. Stories were legion. Supposedly, in colonial times the daughter of the village raja became enamored of a Dutch official. Her father refused to condone the match, and the girl drowned herself in despair. Her restless spirit, however, continued to haunt the place. I asked one of the waiters about Soya Atas.

"Oh, it is true," he cried. "It is not good for you to go there. Her spirit takes Western men, even children."

"Why children?"

"She is denied children by her own father. But man or child it is always the same. Her victim disappears for a few days and turns up, often dead, as often in a trance. Only a drink offered by the raja from his own well can cure this trance, but there is no memory afterward."

"There are documented cases?"

"Many documented cases," he said, and explained that the most famous kidnapping occurred just before World War II, when the Dutch governor-general disappeared from a house above the city, was lost for three days, and afterward was found in a trance. A drink from the raja's well brought him around, and he could not remember what had transpired.

I had heard of this case. Apparently it was well documented and had been much written about, but I hadn't associated it with Soya Atas.

The shadows were long in the late afternoon when the taxi pulled into the courtyard of the tiny village. It was as silent as a tomb. There was little to see in Soya Atas, so I instructed the driver to wait and hiked up the trail beyond the village, passing a stream where women in sarongs were washing clothes. After a half-mile climb, the path leveled out at an ancient meeting place of stone megaliths and seats. I mounted a throne and gazed south across the Banda Sea toward Gunung Api, a magnificent view. Afterward, I washed my hands in the "Devil's Urn," said to cure illness, induce prosperity, and spawn requited love. Dusk was settling in, so I hurried back down the steep trail to the village.

At breakfast the next morning in the small dining room, I was seated next to a table at which a group of Indonesians and Westerners were launched into an intense discussion over coffee turned cold. Without eavesdropping, it soon became apparent that there was trouble.

"I don't think I'm being unreasonable at all," said a young woman speaking in French-accented English. "You've had six weeks to conduct your investigation and so far you've turned up nothing."

"We're doing all we can," rejoined a middle-aged Indonesian man in an olive-drab uniform. Another Indonesian member of the party, also in uniform, remained silent.

"But you've just arrived from Jakarta."

"My department has been working on this case night and day. Of course, this is important to us. But you must realize that people, how do you say, drop out, disappear in these islands all the time."

"My husband wouldn't just disappear."

As the discussion continued, the divisiveness sharpened, as an Indonesian woman in a floral-printed dress translated into French for a bearded Westerner in a dark suit. Finally, the young wife, now greatly agitated, abruptly got up and left, terminating the meeting.

"Please assure her we're doing all we can," said the middle-aged officer to an angular, sallow-faced Westerner, who, I guessed by his accent, was a New Zealander. "Now I must have my breakfast."

In the lobby beside the desk a small Xeroxed poster told the sketchy details of a missing Paul Henri, a dark-haired, square-jawed man of thirty-one, last seen at the Cendrawasih Hotel across town.

I took a seat in the lobby, and the New Zealander came over.

"I only arrived yesterday," I said. "What happened?"

"My business partner," he said. "His toothbrush, the equivalent of six thousand in U.S. dollars, all his clothes were found in his room. Everything was there except his knapsack."

"That much money?"

"He had a lot more on him at the time he disappeared. At least thirty thousand."

"What sort of business are you in?" I asked.

"We're furniture importers. The best acquisitions are in the field, and of course we pay cash."

"Who are the other people?"

"The older uniformed chap is the head of the missing persons' bureau from Jakarta, and the other is his man here. The bearded fellow is from the French Embassy and the woman in the flowered dress is his translator. They're from Jakarta as well. The wife is out from France. Just arrived. The posters just went up this morning. It's a hell of a mess."

"It sounds it. How much do you know?"

"Not a lot. He had talked about going to Seram, the island north of here, but it's not like him just to disappear. The odd thing is the hotel didn't report him missing. They just kept charging another day's rent for a whole month, running up his bill. Can you believe it? The government is taking it seriously now that the embassy's involved. They closed the hotel pending the investigation."

"I would think that somebody at the hotel would be interested in that cash in his room," I said.

"I couldn't find it. Government agents did. He had it stashed away, so maybe the room boy wasn't wise to it."

"Any leads at all?"

"We met with a guy, the last person to see him, an Ambonese, but his story doesn't jibe with what we already know. The police backed off. He's some sort of Mafia figure here in Ambon, and the police are afraid to hassle him."

"I wish there was some way I could help," I said.

"Thanks anyway," he said. "The police mentioned that village Soya Atas, said the spirit might have taken him, but I don't believe that shit."

"I went up to have a look late yesterday," I said. "It's a spectacular view."

"That's the only reason to go up there," he said. "Well, if you'll excuse me, I'll go prepare my statement for these Jakarta chaps. I can't believe Paul would just slip away to Seram without telling anybody."

"I wish I could do something. I hope he turns up okay."

"There's nothing to do, really. The leads are pretty bum, and now it's in their hands. Now that the embassy's lighted a fire under them, they ought to get cracking. How long are you here for?"

"Just passing through," I said. "En route to Irian Jaya."

"Thanks for your time," he said, "and good luck."

Later, when I was about to leave the hotel on my errands, I passed Michiko in the lobby. She was dressed in a pantsuit.

"You're not out in the garden in such nice weather?" I said.

"I'm leaving," she said flatly. "I called Osaka this morning."

"Why so suddenly?"

"Did you not see this?" she said, pointing to the missing-person poster.

"I saw the people from Jakarta at breakfast," I said. "The poor fellow's wife's taking it pretty hard."

"I hate this place. It's horrible and evil, and the people are dark and dirty. I'm afraid something may happen to me. I'm going home."

Irian Jaya:
Among Farmers
and Warriors

(Notes from a Diary) $\mathcal{T}$ HE NATURAL DRIFT in the archipelago seems eastward and back in time to be swallowed by the past. In the Spice Islands the past manifests itself as shades: faded portraits; walled forts decorated with graffiti; Run Island, abandoned by the British in 1628. You take away a sense of nostalgia. In Irian Jaya, whose Western extremity is only two hundred miles east of Ambon, I anticipate a different sort of past where nostalgia has no place, where the past collides with the present, where Stone Age people live in the twentieth century.

Irian Jaya is the western half of the island of New Guinea, the world's largest after Greenland. My destination is Jayapura, situated on the north coast near the Papua New Guinea border. It is the easternmost city in Indonesia, but whether you travel by plane or ship, it is a circuitous journey from anywhere to get there.

My flight proceeds due east from Ambon for the southwest coast of Irian Jaya, which appears in late afternoon as a massive country, less an island than a small continent of wilderness, with coastal river country giving way to towering mountains carpeted with rainforests green and thick as playing fields. We put down at Timuka, a landing field dug out of palmetto swamp that services the Freeport copper and tin mines a hundred kilometers inland through inhospitable country. All passengers must deplane and enter a Quonset hut crowded with startlingly black people, mine workers and their families waiting to board. They wear Western casual clothes, jeans and T-shirts, and have closely cropped hair. The steaming close quarters reek of dirt and sweat, and a fastidious Javanese engineer in the next seat holds his nose as a silent rebuke to the Irianese.

Once again airborne, we fly in darkness north to the island of Biak, off the northwest peninsula of Irian Jaya known as the "bird's head." Biak was a strategic base for the Japanese and then the Allies in World War II, and today military helicopters crouch on the edge of the runway, a reminder that the Indonesian government regards Irian Jaya as a highly sensitive province. After a Spartan night under mosquito netting, we begin the final leg at dawn, southeast along the north coast into Jayapura, the capital of Irian Jaya.

The western half of New Guinea, an area the size of Spain, has been the Indonesian province of Irian Jaya, or West Irian, or simply Irian, since 1963. If Africa was the "Dark Continent" of Sir Richard Burton's day, this country is measurably darker, even in the late twentieth century. Alfred Russel Wallace described his first impression of the island, gained from a ship's rail. "I looked with intense interest on those rugged mountains, retreating ridge behind ridge into the interior, where the foot of civilized man had never trod." That impression dates from 1858 and is scarcely less valid today.

If Irian's interior has remained largely unassailable by outside influences, it nonetheless has tantalized Eastern and Western imaginations alike by virtue of its primordial vastness and mystery. In the ancient days of the Hindu kingdoms, traders from Sumatra and Java sailed Irian's waters, though the country was known to them as Djanggi. Holy books of that age tell of "the island at the tip of Samudranta," with a mountain range eternally covered with snow. In the eighth century Chinese traders reached the island and called it Tung Ki, though they considered it a part of the Moluccas and traded for its spices. Irian was later ruled in name only by the Tidore sultanate, then as well by the successive Western powers who laid claim to and ultimately abandoned this uncivilized, ungovernable land so rich in resources and promise.

Anthropologists have estimated that the original inhabitants of New Guinea migrated here thirty thousand years ago, though it is uncertain where they came from. One theory, based on Papuan similarities to Australian aborigines, is that the Irianese came from the south, first to the great plains of the island before moving into the mountains. Then, supposedly, during neolithic times, came an influx of Melanesians from the islands east of New Guinea, bringing tools for farming, hunting, and warfare as well as cowrie shells for money, which you can still find in the interior.

Today, apart from scattered mining operations, lonely missionary outposts, pockets of separatist guerrillas, and the heterogeneous population of the coastal settlements, little has changed. The natives of the interior, scores of tribes differing in language and culture by virtue of their isolation in a hostile landscape, have remained essentially as they always have been, peoples largely ignorant of the outside world.

The Portuguese, who along with the Spanish were the first Europeans to claim discovery of this large island, named it "Ilhas dos Papuas" after the Malay word *Papuwah*, or "Fuzzy-Hairs." As if to underscore this point, the Spanish captain Ynigo Ortiz de Retez landed on the north coast in 1546 and, thinking that the natives resembled the Negroid peoples of the Guinea coast of West Africa, called the land "Nova Guinea." Though the chart of the noted Antwerp geographer Abraham Ortelius (1580) shows Nova Guinea as an island, its enormous size and configuration, as well as the presence of outlying islands, left the question open for another seventeen years, until Luis Vas de Torres circumnavigated it.

In the seventeenth century Dutch navigators appeared after Holland's conquest of the Moluccas, followed in the eighteenth by French and English explorers, with James Cook in 1770 rediscovering the Torres Straits, which separate the island from Australia. During this period, and extending well into the nineteenth century, scientific observers visited here, most notably Wallace. There were also several surveying expeditions, but these were confined to the coastal areas, and very little knowledge was gained of the interior or its people. The island was not crossed by a Western expedition until 1897.

Like the other islands of the archipelago, New Guinea was not spared the claims of rival nations during the long colonial period. If these contentions were less bloody than the intrigues and battles that tell the history of, say, the Spice Islands, it was because the rivals had neither the madness nor the method to exploit the fiendishly inaccessible interior. That interior, the home of hundreds of ethnic groups, each with its own language and culture, remains so today.

New Guinea consists of a long central mountain chain of complex formation, a northern coastal range, and a country of small hills on the south coast, together with the alluvial surfaces formed mainly by the rivers under equatorial rains. Outside the ring of fire, some of its mountains rise above the snow line to sixteen thousand feet and have glaciers, giving credence to the reports of early Hindu travelers. But most of the mountainous interior is covered with dense rainforests and divided by countless writhing gray rivers, which foster isolation and often mutual hostility among the many tribes who war and trade with each other.

The Dutch, Germans, and British divided the island among them until World War I, but this division was inconsequential to the island itself because the interior remained unknown to white men. Germany relinquished its share after the Great War, while Britain ceded its territory to Australia, which after World War II and the tyrannical Japanese occupation united the colony and trust as a single territory. This in turn became Papua New Guinea, which achieved its independence in 1975.

But Dutch New Guinea was to become Irian Jaya. It strains

credulity that this western half of the island of New Guinea is a part of the nation of Indonesia, but then this diversified country has been governed so shrewdly that political miracles are commonplace. Therein lies a tale.

In the beginning the Dutch had little use for so vast and wild a country, beyond an official claim and settlements on the coast, but when nationalistic fervor seized the Malay Archipelago after the Second World War and the Dutch surrendered the East Indies to President Sukarno, West Irian was not similarly deeded. While Holland prepared the island for self-rule, Sukarno insisted that all the former Dutch colonies be forged into his new nation, despite Irianese protests fomented by the Dutch. In 1962 the Dutch capitulated to international pressures, springing from a fear of Soviet aid to Sukarno, and Indonesia took over West Irian in a year's time, but with a provision that allowed Irianese self-determination by the end of the decade.

On the face of it, it was a simple choice: whether to declare independence or remain a part of the nation of Indonesia. But the dynamics of Irian Jaya's political history have been most rigorously played out since. An elaborate charade took center stage when the Indonesian government, in an agreement with Irianese leaders known as the "Act of Free Choice" under United Nations supervision, hand-picked a collection of elders who in the process of *musyawarah*, or consensus, unanimously voted in favor of Jakarta. Such bald ballot-stuffing fueled violent objections from many pockets of resistance and subsequent Indonesian retaliations that have continued to the present.

Other factions have plagued West Irian's future as well. The border dividing West Irian and Papua New Guinea is a troubled one, less because of mutual hostility between the two nations than because of the presence of the Free Papua Organization, or OPM, which with its grievances against the Indonesian government, mostly involving traditional land rights, battles for self-rule and seeks refuge across the boundary in Papua New Guinea. Unsur-

prisingly, the OPM has attracted outside agitators, mostly mal-
content Malays from other islands, who continue to mount
terrorist operations.

There is another force at work in Irian Jaya, the government's
transmigration program, which strives to relocate a million new
settlers in the 1990s, though many Malays, most notably the Bugis
of South Sulawesi, have moved to Irian Jaya on their own. A less
charitable explanation has the Bugis preying upon the unworldly
Irianese, their exploitation the latest measure of the inexorable
history of the archipelago.

(Notes from a Diary) It is an hour's drive into Jayapura, or
"Victorious City," from the airport along an asphalt road that is
nearly the only stretch of highway in Irian Jaya. It was constructed
by Allied forces under General Douglas MacArthur when Jayapura
was known as the Dutch colonial city of Hollandia. The road winds
through limestone hills, circumnavigating a deep freshwater lake,
danau sentani, fished by Malays in dugout canoes. If the Baliem
Valley is a highland plateau where tribes have lived much the
same way for thirty thousand years, Jayapura's history is absurdly
recent by comparison, though hardly negligible.

We pass Hamadi Beach, the site where the Allies stormed ashore
under Japanese fire in the spring of 1944. Now the relics are nearly
a half century old: a rusting Sherman tank, along with the occasional half-submerged landing barge and sunken vessel lan-
guishing in the surf. After taking Hollandia, MacArthur launched
his invasion of the Philippines from another coral-studded beach
near here.

The road descends from the hills to the city, surprisingly com-
pact with a handsome harbor, a miniature Hong Kong, nearly
enclosed by jungle-covered mountains that slope steeply to the
sea. Seen from the heights of the road winding in from the airport,
Jayapura and its harbor look inviting, but once in the city this is
all revealed as illusory. The influx of Bugis from South Sulawesi
gives Jayapura, Irian Jaya's capital, its Malay stamp.

Jayapura is not an Irianese but an Indonesian city inhabited by Malays, Irianese, and people of mixed blood. Shantytown shacks at the edge of the city cluster around fetid canals. Streets lined with undistinguished structures, storefronts, massive white banks and government buildings, some new and others not so new, run parallel before converging at the harbor. Children play on the sidewalks, pulling toy automobiles fashioned out of empty kretek packs with thread spools for wheels. On one corner a lone man squats at a cardboard box working a numbers game. Across the street a man hawks snake oils, essence of sea horse, and other curatives.

It is easy to walk anywhere in fifteen minutes, but this convenience is undermined by a feeling of entrapment. Except for the harbor with its boats lining wooden piers, mountains surround this breezeless city pounded into submission by a relentless sun. Behind, to the south, the mighty Van Rees Range guards the interior, while at the waterfront on the north the busy deep-blue harbor beckons like a mirror of freedom.

Jayapura is no place to linger. At night the waterfront is frequented by prostitutes and pickpockets; at midday the streets are nearly deserted. Shops close for the afternoon in deference to the searing heat and reopen at five.

At the bank I meet another Westerner, an alert, gregarious missionary from Canada who introduces himself as Lawrence and explains that he has returned to Irian Jaya after a year's home leave.

"Any Westerners you run into here are bound to be missionaries, right? Otherwise, why would anyone want to come to Jayapura?" He laughs. "I'm famished. How about lunch?"

We have fried rice and noodles in an open-air place shaded by a canvas awning secured to trees. Lawrence blesses the food and as we eat ponders the best way for me to make application to enter the interior. He explains that the police and army work in tandem. In effect, the police are an administrative arm of the military. It is they who process applications for travel permits.

"The authorities are paranoid regarding the rebel situation," he tells me. "And with good reason. A month ago forty Irian tribesmen near my village were ambushed and killed by non-Irians. Let's go to the Mission Office and talk to Ted. He'll know the best way to proceed to get your *surat jalan.*"

At the office I learn of the restricted areas in Irian Jaya, or, more accurately, the shorter list of unrestricted ones. Missionaries are given special dispensations to live in troubled areas, and it is extremely difficult, according to Ted, a cordial man of middle years, for a non-missionary such as myself to gain permission to enter restricted zones. Such areas are blacklisted for visitors as trouble develops. A visit to a village open last month might be impossible this month, and so forth.

"I don't think you'll have much trouble getting permission to visit the Baliem Valley," says Ted. "Just make sure you're dressed properly when you apply. Backpackers come here all the way from Germany and make the mistake of calling on the police wearing beards and lederhosen. The police don't appreciate such attire. They get a two-day permission, if that. If you look respectable, you might get a month."

The police compound is not far from my hotel. I am directed to offices resembling the administrative rooms of a military barracks. The atmosphere that greets me is convivial and male, and the officers chatter among themselves in Javanese over tables heaped with paperwork. I apply for my travel permit, presenting my passport and the required photographs, and am told to return the next day.

The beleaguered agents at the Merpati office across the street tell me over the cracklings and sputterings of a two-way radio that there is little hope of flying into the Baliem Valley in the next few days because of an insistent low cloud cover. The valley is a mile above sea level, often socked in, and hazardous for aircraft more often than not.

"We're reluctant to compile a manifest," says a hatchet-faced woman. "Why make up a list if the flight is not cleared to enter the valley?"

"Why not make it up anyway, just in case?" I say.

"*Belum*. Because passengers are angry with us if the flight is canceled. One flight goes into Wamena today, but it is not allowed to leave because of the low cloud cover."

"That is a good sign in one way, but not so good in another way," I say. "Let us pray that the weather clears."

"Pray all you want to," she says. "Who can predict the will of Allah that is already written, but not yet written for us to read?"

I find diversion at the hotel. The manager is Mr. Sunan, a tall, slender Javanese with an understated elegance about him. He has been lured away from Jakarta to run the hotel here, and it's a losing proposition. Displaced in Jayapura, he wants nothing so much as to return to the capital and its circuit of international hotels.

"It's this brochure," he says in the evening. "Can you help me with it?" He has made stabs at an English-language brochure advertising the hotel, and it's full of howlers.

"I can rewrite it," I say. "Can you get me a typewriter?"

I make the fixes and in the morning take the copy to Mr. Sunan in his office, where we are joined by a pale, willowy young Javanese woman called Susi, who also works at the hotel.

"I must go home and pick up my daughter for school," Mr. Sunan says to me. "Will you come with me?"

We make small talk en route to his house, a modest bungalow on the edge of town, where he introduces me to his wife, a pleasant, matronly woman in her mid-thirties, while his daughter, a shy child of eight, climbs into the back of the hotel van. After we drop her at school, he steers our conversation.

"You met Susi at the hotel. What do you think?"

"She's lovely. Having such attractive young women around must make your job easier."

"We're lovers. I'm taking her to Jakarta next summer to marry her. I've already spoken to her parents."

This revelation bowls me over. Mr. Sunan is a married man with three children, but under Muslim and Indonesian law he is entitled to two wives, provided he secures the permission of his first wife. Though it flouts government policy, men of the most militant Muslim sects in Indonesia are known to take as many as four wives, as allowed by traditional Islamic law. That such permission from the first wife is not easily forthcoming hardly matters, because women in most of these islands have little recourse and few resources.

There is nothing provincial about Mr. Sunan: he is neither Borneo chieftain nor Sulawesi sea captain. He is suave and worldly, smugly so, with the distinct mark of the West on him. I suspect he would be at home attending a cocktail party in San Francisco.

Later, when Susi is off-duty, I accompany him to her house, where he is to drop a package off. She lives off a road that climbs a mountain adjacent to the city. Mr. Sunan parks the van and leads me down several flights of stone steps past foraging chickens and goats to one of several ramshackle bungalows. Babies are crying and dogs barking. I wait outside while Mr. Sunan enters, pausing first to pat the head of a three-year-old girl, Susi's daughter born out of wedlock, but not by Mr. Sunan. Shortly, Mr. Sunan, wearing the look of a man in love, appears with Susi.

She is radiant, a ripening plum of a woman who I suspect gets by on her looks and a scent she throws off that intoxicates Mr. Sunan. Beyond that, she strikes me as passive and dull, having settled at age nineteen into her role as Muslim woman and wife.

"So you're looking forward to returning to Jakarta?" I ask Mr. Sunan later over tea.

"More than you can imagine," he says. "The owner of the hotel is Chinese. I'm having a difficult time running the hotel because he's stingy with the payroll, and he pays me only when he feels like it. Now he wants proof that I can attract Western tourists. That's the reason for the brochure. Do you blame me for wanting to return to Jakarta?"

.   .   .   .   .

Dawn on Friday. The weather has cleared, and the Merpati seventeen-seater lifts off the runway. Our southwest course climbs over foothills that give way to steeper ridges bisected by silver rivers cutting through limestone hills. This country remains impenetrable, broken only by the occasional riverside clearing and isolated settlement, whose inhabitants speak their own dialect and that of their neighbors upriver or beyond the next ridge, where their world ends.

Such clearings are few and far between, though occasionally the waterways broaden out on plateaus, revealing sandbars and rich fields for such indigenous foodstuffs as yams—but only along the riverbanks, for all else is jungle. On such a plateau the river winds its way like an endless python from its source to the south and west, then doubles back on itself, repulsed by a southern wall of towering mountains rising out of the sea of green. The river is far too shallow to accommodate any but the lightest craft, bamboo rafts and dugout canoes, and far too remote from the unseen coast toward which it twists itself to serve as a means for trade with the outside world.

But as we continue on our southwestern course, the plateau rises yet again into foothills and another ridge, one after the other, evidenced by new cloud formations as the mountains create their own weather, beyond which lie new spines of ridge. Now we approach a range of mountains more awesome, with precipitous cliffs wearing glaring faces of chalk, nature's parody of the rice powder favored by Bugis women. These mountains are the northern border of the Baliem Valley, and the white cliffs appear to support the black rain clouds that guard the valley like ghostly gods. Small wonder that the mile-high Baliem Valley was not discovered by white men until 1938. But a more telling miracle is that bits of steel and cowrie shells, and little if anything else, somehow made their way into this interior from the coast over centuries of trade.

With the guardian ridge behind us, the aircraft descends quickly, dropping out of gray cloud into a valley halved by the torpid brown

Baliem River rising to meet us. This is the country of the Dani, farmers, swineherds, and warriors, who live in villages of thatched huts, which we see just under the treetops as we approach the Wamena strip and touch down. The plane taxies to the small terminal, a tin hut, where curious black people, the men naked except for penis gourds and the women bare-breasted in grass skirts, line the runway and regard the iron bird that carries people from a world they neither know nor desire to know.

Wamena is a frontier town in the Old West sense, an Indonesian outpost imprisoned in a valley five thousand feet above sea level, forty miles long and ten miles wide, fringed by mountains. Barely thirty years old and settled first by missionaries and then by the Dutch government, it is laid out in square blocks of corrugated-tin-roofed bungalows that sprawl over a large area with no town center. The police station is across the street from the airport, next to the jail, a single cell inhabited by a dozen black men peering out. Naked children play on the asphalt runway, until a siren warning of approaching aircraft scatters them.

The market and a collection of warungs are at the north end of town, and beyond the market is a cinema. The few motorized vehicles are bemos, which travel the mud roads connecting a few native villages. As everything has to be airlifted in, prices for imported goods, from gasoline to bottled water, are high. The local economy, such as it is, remains securely in Bugis hands. Women run the shops, while their men operate the bemo lines.

A black boy, dressed in shorts and a T-shirt, collects my bags and leads me a thousand yards through the streets, past scores of silently curious Dani people, to an encampment, a collection of thatched bungalows situated around a central refectory. I take one of the huts.

The grounds of this encampment are a strange sight. Natives from nearby villages congregate here, men sauntering among the bungalows, women with babies squatting here and there with artifacts to sell and, barring success in that enterprise, silently waiting for handouts.

I leave the grounds to find a place for lunch, and quickly have company. A black youth, with a hole in the cartilage of his nose the size of a dime for the traditional boar's tusk worn by warriors, follows me. He speaks some Bahasa Indonesia and is eager to serve as my guide for the day. I find a small café and enter, while the boy remains outside.

I order fried noodles and a beer, but the proprietor laughs.

"You cannot get beer or any alcoholic drink in Wamena," he says in good English. "It is forbidden by the Indonesian government for the Irianese tribesmen to drink it, because when they do, they get drunk, cause trouble, and get thrown in jail."

"How can they get alcohol?" I ask.

"The Bugis smuggle it into the valley and sell it to them. Of course as Muslims, the Bugis do not take alcohol themselves, but they have no scruples about selling it to the Dani, who get drunk, steal, and kill. The Bugis care only about business. Then the Bugis police arrest the drunk Dani. If they cause trouble in jail, the Bugis beat them. At night they get noisy. If you pass there at night, you can hear their cries."

Mr. Dan is a lean, hardened, articulate Malay who has led many lives. A former crocodile hunter now turned guide and restaurateur, he explains that his people are Ambonese, but that he was born in Irian Jaya and has lived here all his life. Since giving up crocodile hunting, he has been engaged in various entrepreneurial schemes in Wamena, and is awaiting the day when tourists will flock here.

"Drop by again," he says as I leave. "Come in whenever you want, and we'll talk."

I follow the boy to the market at the other end of town, passing scores of Dani men and women walking in the streets. The town seems a picture of chaos. Everyone walks everywhere with an inimitable pigeon-toed gait, men, women, and children alike with no covering for their heavily callused feet. The thin gourd, or *horim*, worn by the men covers the penis from its base at the testicles, and is worn erect, secured around the waist by a cord.

The Bugis have another name for it, a derisive one: *koteka,* from the Indonesian word meaning "tail." But by the Dani this age-old dress code is scrupulously observed. I remember that my Jakarta friend Stan had visited the Baliem Valley and told of a guide whose sheath was lost in a swift stream he was crossing. Rather than expose himself to certain humiliation, he elected to remain in the water until a replacement could be provided.

It is soon evident what village a man hails from by his facial features, as well as the ornaments that adorn his bare body. Though skin color is universally blue-black, one group of men has flat noses and thick lips, while another has the fine aquiline profile engraved on old coins. The women are large-boned, round-bellied, and buxom, with closely cropped hair, and wear *noken,* or head or shoulder utility bags of dyed, knitted tree-bark fibers, necklaces of seashells, and grass skirts that rest below the abdomen.

The market stinks of sweat, produce marinating in the sultry heat, and the feces of trussed pigs lying on their sides in the mud. The few Dani men of the market idle about, smoking homemade cigars while their women, with nursing infants and toddlers, run the stalls. A soft rain begins to fall, and later in the day when the wind picks up, it will turn cold. Regardless of the weather, the dress, or lack of it, of the Dani remains the same, any chill warded off by a layer of pig fat covering the skin.

I had thought the custom of amputating a woman's finger down to the second joint as a sign of mourning was outlawed by the government, but the practice has not ceased. Invariably, the older women are missing portions of fingers, but what catches my eye is a young widow covered in yellow ashes, silently holding her baby, with one finger a bloody stump.

A sullen atmosphere weighs heavily in this place, the merchants eyeing us impassively, while in the market's interior, Bugis women conduct their own business from behind stalls despite the wretched smell of swine, which they deem unclean. They sell goods from the outside world: cigarettes, sweets, bottled water. It is a surreal picture of two worlds in uneasy coexistence, worlds that can never touch beyond the marketplace or the jail.

I buy water for an exorbitant price and fight off a spasm of nausea from the foul odors before I reach the outer confines of the market and fill my lungs with the humid air. Then I see something extraordinary. An ancient man, white-haired and toothless, with reptilian skin, sits against a shed among the squealing pigs, next to an old woman with shriveled breasts. I have never seen a human being who looks so old, a look emphasized by his milk-white eyes, which reveal that he is blind. I ask the boy to speak with him. In a voice barely audible, the old man discourses for a few moments, and the boy translates.

"He is over a hundred years old," he says, "but he doesn't know exactly how much older. The passing of years confuses him now, but there are records in his village that can tell his exact age. He has many wives and many pigs, and so he is a wealthy man. He fights in many wars and slays and eats his enemies, though no longer because he cannot see to kill and he has no teeth."

"Ask him if he remembers the first white man in the valley," I say.

The soft voice now speaks more animatedly, and a crowd gathers. "Oh, yes," the boy translates. "Fifty years ago. A bad time because the Dutch and after them the present government change our way of life. They even give us a name that is not properly ours. Worst of all are the missionaries. The Muslims think us unworthy of conversion, but not the Christians. Though the outsiders of the market, the people who call themselves Bugis, are not worthy of the pigs they scorn, the Christians nearly wreck our economy. Years ago they bring many cowrie shells from the coast, so that a cowrie shell for a long time loses its value. They also bring in steel axes, but we still prefer stone, because our stone is harder. Our ancestors use stone and so do we. That is our way.

"And pigs. Those yellow women of the market do not understand pigs. Pigs are everything to us, just as the urge to wage war is a part of our nature. What is a man without women who bear children, and pigs and land and his own village, and enemies to defend himself and his people against? Life is simple if you follow your own laws. If you do not, life is not so simple, and you lose your way in the world. If you are a white man and do not feel welcome here, it is for a good reason. You lose your way and are not welcome."

The gravelly-voiced elder speaks with impunity won by his advanced years. The boy and I leave in the drizzle to find the river that bisects the valley. We reach its banks after a half hour's walk through fields lined with cone-shaped thatched huts, passing grass-skirted women of varying ages carrying baskets of foodstuffs, who hurry past us fearfully.

It is nearly dark when I return to the hut. Small groups of Dani crowd around fires for warmth or position themselves near the bungalows. Mothers are seated with infants, while their older children peer through cracks in the thatch. The men remain aloof, hugging their arms against their bodies to ward off the rising chill.

The refectory is operated by a bearded Irianese with a crazed look and a feverish, impulsive manner that barely masks a violent nature: I see him as the prototypical half-breed not to be trusted. He directs me to a table where the staff of mostly young girls is seated. A fleshy, talkative woman called Sari serves me a meal of rice and stringy meat.

"Where are you from?" I ask her.

"Everywhere," she says. "Sumatra, Surabaya, Sulawesi, Ambon, you name it. You want a massage?" she says with a leer and a loud laugh.

Sari has cast herself in the role of camp follower, with her own portable canteen to minister to the needs of the troops: Brecht's *Mother Courage* transported across time and space, from the Thirty Years' War to a different battlefield in Irian Jaya. Her present circumstances are a momentary convenience, and as a Malay woman, and a woman of pleasure at that, her actions expose her darker-skinned partner, the crazed Irianese, to public ridicule. By dinner's end, the atmosphere is tense.

"I go with anyone I like," she says. "Too bad for him."

"I must leave," I say.

The rain has abated, though the cloud cover obscures the heavens, and there is no light when I walk the streets. Wamena after dark is a ghost town in the middle of nowhere, and yet it is charged with a flammable atmosphere, as though it were a city anticipating an undefined calamity.

I walk past the jail. Mr. Dan was right. I hear cries, but they have a special stylized cadence and a strange timbre, as though it were a staged affair—as many of the Dani clan battles are. That the battles are staged doesn't alter the fact that real deaths result, and that these cries sound stylized doesn't mean the lamentations are not genuine.

On my way back to the camp I pass a house where a party with loud rock music is in progress, the revelers oblivious to the night and the cries from the jail. Although its placid surface suggests otherwise, Wamena is a town divided by turmoil and fear.

I have difficulty sleeping this night after an intruder somehow gains entrance to the bungalow. I awake with a start, and he flees as noiselessly as he entered.

Over the course of my stay in Wamena, which stretched into a fortnight, I had many interesting conversations with Mr. Dan, who explained much of the valley's lore to me and suggested which of the villages would treat me hospitably when I passed through and which would attempt to extort payment.

One day, after hiking for hours, I stumbled on a village market along a path that in the intermittent rains had become slick with mud and pig excrement. The market was a noisy, open-air affair. At one end a group of mourning women had gathered, bound by their shared public show of grief: the stumps for fingers, the yellow ash covering their bodies, and one girl barely past puberty suckling a pig. "It is customary here," said a Bugis woman wandering among the stalls. She spoke with contempt. "If her infant dies, she must nurse a pig. Her milk is too valuable to waste. Imagine, nursing a *pig*."

Yet there were signs of consumer invasion of the most basic sort: here and there the red-lettered T-shirt worn by a youth whose nose had been surgically prepared for the boar's tusk; the naked old man shielding himself from the rain with a rare black umbrella, while the women squatted at their stalls in the befouled mud, seemingly oblivious to the elements as they counted their rupiah notes from sales of pineapple, yams, and dried fish. White parrots and cockatoos flitted and squawked in the nearby trees.

Nearby was the bungalow of the district superintendent, where I, as an outsider, was required to report. He was a self-important man of mixed Malay and Irianese descent accorded status by the government but by no one else. Pompous and officious, he intoned about modernization under a crucifix on the wall that remained in the fixed, green-eyed stare of a stuffed monkey perched nearby.

"There is a mummy in a village not far from here," he said as I was taking my leave, and he pointed the way.

I hiked for thirty minutes along a path so slippery that it was impossible not to take an occasional spill, covering me with mud and slime from head to toe. Even so, I had to enjoy the valley's beauty despite the rain. Like the Romans of Caesar Augustus's day, the Dani were warriors, but they were farmers as well, and the countryside was not only cultivated but portioned off by stone fences. The Baliem Valley is an oasis cradled in a primeval wilderness, and this was so when it was discovered by Richard Archbold, who in 1938 landed by seaplane in a nearby lake. "From the air the gardens and ditches and native-built walls appeared like the farming country of Central Europe," he wrote. And so it has remained.

I had to climb a fence to enter the village. It was typical of its kind: an enclosed compound filled with smoke from a cookhouse, thatched dormitories for men and women, and pigsties. Men and women slept separately. Children under ten stayed with the women and the older ones with the men. If a man wanted to sleep with one of his wives, she was commanded beforehand to sleep near the door, while the other women remained on the level above. Then he mounted her downstairs.

Most curious were the mummies of the valley. The Dani traditionally cremated their dead, but these mummies predated living memory. No one knew how old they were, reputedly hundreds of years, but they were few in number and kept under wraps in special quarters and were regarded, as were many things in the valley, with great superstition.

I flashed a thousand-rupiah note, and the men offered stiff handshakes all round to seal the bargain. One old man went to fetch the mummy from a central hut, while the others puffed tobacco and waited. A ragged ledger appeared, which I surmised was a guest book. With it was a ballpoint pen, and both were handled with the same reverence accorded the mummy when it was brought out. The mummy was a blackened, rock-hard thing with a great gaping mouth; it was frozen in a seated position, with the headdress and shell necklace of a wealthy man. I inspected the corpse with curiosity and a show of reverence, but the smoke coming from the cookhouse watered my eyes, and I soon took my leave.

It was nearly dark when I arrived at the edge of Wamena, where a five-year-old plant generated the town's electricity from a sluice of the Baliem River. Near it was an ancient suspension bridge constructed by the Dani of vines and stone-hewn planks.

"Only here in Wamena of all Irian Jaya is water used to generate electricity," said an Irianese schoolmaster, greeting me before his one-room school adjacent to the plant. He led me across the bridge, which was in a state of disrepair. When we reached the other side, he said we should go no farther.

"Do you see that field?" he asked, pointing to an open area a thousand yards distant. "That is the war area where the Welesi tribe fights the Kurima. When they fight, they fight to the death with spears and bows and arrows, even though it is forbidden by the Indonesian government. Whenever they fight, there are many deaths. Their ancestors keep the conflict alive. These tribesmen are nominal Catholics, and after the battle the priest lectures them from his pulpit. But his sermon falls on deaf ears, even though his parishioners have no homes to return to because they've all been burned. But of this you must speak to Mr. Dan. He knows far more than I. I've been away from the valley."

"But you are Irianese," I said.

He shrugged. "Not by education," he said. "But for these people it is a small world. The valley is only so long and so wide."

"When was the last war?" I asked.

"Last month," he replied.

As we walked back toward my camp of bungalows, he explained that in Irian Jaya the Indonesian government had been required to buy land from the Dani to build the city of Wamena as it now stood.

"This practice is scrupulously observed all over Irian Jaya because of the requirements of the United Nations charter. This in itself differentiates Irian Jaya from Kalimantan on Borneo, where the powerful government and private industry consortia engineer exploitation of native lands and resources."

I had doubts that Irian Jaya had been or was to be treated any differently from Indonesia's other provinces. The U.N. had been impotent twenty years before over the question of self-determination for West Irian, and the Indonesian government had brooked no recalcitrance on the part of Irianese tribes or political separatists. The past, after all, was prologue.

As we walked, we passed a naked man whose penis gourd was greatly oversized and secured by a red cloth. "He is of the Lani clan," said the schoolmaster. "They wear bigger koteka not because they are more manly, as they would have you think. They wear them because they can carry money and cigarettes in them."

As I left him at the edge of the camp and headed for my bungalow, the loudspeakers from a nearby mosque summoned the

Malay faithful to sundown prayers. Here, that seemed the oddest anomaly of all.

Most days I spent hiking through the valley alone, following scrupulously Mr. Dan's directions to avoid being extorted by unfriendly clans who would collect a fee of one kind or another, money or cigarettes, to let me cross their tribal lands. The villages I did visit were friendly, and I was able to exchange cigarettes for handicrafts. On the mornings when the rain clouds collected over the surrounding peaks, allowing sunlight to flood the valley, the Baliem Valley bore an eerie resemblance to Jackson Hole, Wyoming, nestled in sharp relief against the Grand Tetons—an illusive impression that vanished at the sight of tribesmen.

But I saw other apparitions, more tangible but equally strange. Late one morning I stumbled on two Viennese university students eating their midday rations beside a stream. They were clean-cut, friendly young men who were spending their summer holiday trekking through the valley. They had huge packs and a lot of camera gear, heavy loads. We lunched together and shared experiences, while they produced a bottle of wine brought from home and unfolded a superb German map of the island. I regarded it with envy, for it was impossible to find a map of such exactitude anywhere in Indonesia. The students recounted with good humor the problems they had encountered with the Dani during their expedition.

"It's crazy," said Owe. "We've had nothing but trouble with porters. We agreed on three thousand a day, and then at day's end, the porters insisted on ten thousand. We hope to get more reliable help when we return to Wamena."

I suggested that a good source in Wamena might be Mr. Dan.

"It's really weird," said Martin. "We agree on a price at a village, the guide agrees to accompany us for our entire holiday, and yet when we need to cross a river to proceed, he won't do it because the land belongs to another, unfriendly tribe."

"So he leaves, and here we are," said Martin.

"As long as you can make it to Wamena, you'll be okay," I said. It was a four- or five-hour walk for me, traveling light, but longer for them.

They brought news of the outside world and a level of conversation addressed to concerns and events that seemed so distant as to be nearly nonexistent. Talk shifted among opera, sports, politics: a pleasurable interlude catalyzed by wine and conversation.

Life at the camp had its own tempo, with odd variations from time to time. For several days I was the camp's only paying occupant and, as well, the object of speculation and curiosity among the Dani squatters and the camp staff. I was bewildered by the incorrigible Sari, wondering whether she was dim-witted or simply playing her Mother Courage role, so open and nonchalant and riotously funny were her propositions at whatever time of day. Rebuffed, she would belch loudly and leave in a huff, only to return alone or to tempt me with a pubescent scullery maid.

Only once was I relieved of my solitary status. I was reading late in the afternoon when I heard a shrill woman's voice speaking English. "These accommodations will not do. We need five bungalows, not four, and bring us hot water, not cold!"

I looked outside to see a Japanese tour director admonishing the manager, his head bowed, while the group of Japanese tourists, looking lost in their designer clothes among the naked Dani habitués, watched.

The woman got what she demanded for her group, and I was a beneficiary of her assertiveness. That evening, when the mandis were filled for bathing, I received hot water for the first and only time. Inevitably, when water, hot or cold, was brought me, the black man who brought it poured the several buckets into the mandi and then took a seat on the floor and simply stared at me. I went about my business, while he remained a full half hour and then wordlessly left.

There was also the inscrutable boldness of the Dani squatters. Late that evening I heard hysterical screams and rushed outside prepared for a bloodbath. The Dani had stolen a camera from one of the Japanese huts and made their escape. The Japanese, infuriated and terrified, remained in their quarters for the rest of the evening and were gone by charter airline shortly after dawn the next day, cutting their week's visit by six days.

On my last day I dropped by Mr. Dan's restaurant. I thanked him for his suggestions and guidance during my stay in the valley and happened to mention the camera theft.

"It is a great mistake to allow the Dani on the premises of that camp," he said. "No one understands them except the anthropologists, and they understand them only for themselves. Least of all does the Indonesian government understand them."

"And the Christian missionaries?" I said.

He laughed. "The missionaries may claim that the Dani are Christian, but deep down even the converts are animists. The missionaries cannot understand why they make war against each other, but how do you erase the traditions of thirty thousand years? All the original inhabitants of the Baliem Valley are called Dani, but the different clans wage war among themselves. The Mokoko in the river valley fight with nearby clans who threaten their ancient land rights. Then there are the Kurima and the Woma, and their enemy are the Sugogmo, the Hetigima, the Hepuba, the Minimo, and the Welesi."

"Why do they fight?" I asked.

"Why do they fight? Their ancestors tell them to fight. They fight over land, women, and pigs. These things are interrelated and cannot be separated one from another. Let's say I have two wives. If one runs away to another clan, they must pay in pigs. If they don't make the payment, that makes war. When the Dani fight, they fight with spears, bows and arrows, axes, bush knives. Whole villages turn out, hundreds and hundreds of warriors. They attack early in the morning. At night they cannot tell who is the enemy, and they are terrified of ghosts. To die in the dark would be very bad for them."

"What does the government make of all this, and how do they attempt to control the Dani?"

Mr. Dan laughed. "Like most governments they are naive about their own people. After a war the appointed government officials come in and try to make peace at government expense. They call the warring factions together to make peace. They order the slaughter of pigs, which the government pays for, and have a big feast. Everybody leaves happy, and supposedly that's the end of it. But it is not. The government doesn't know the customs, what these people really carry inside them. After three months, there's another war. The last war was last month between the Kurima and the Welesi. Even the priests cannot stop it. The Dani are what they are. The Bible may be God's word to the priests, but not to the Dani.

"At the end of the last war, the military came from Jayapura and asked me what could be done about the Dani. So I said to them that they must learn to see the people carefully. The military do not understand the insults of the Dani, how a challenge is issued and responded to. If one clan cooks pigs, it can insult another clan by giving it raw meat. Cooked meat is a gift. Uncooked meat means blood. If a clan is given raw meat by another, they respond with a similar insult: by offering cooked yams, then dropping them, and with a heel grinding them into the ground."

"What does all this have to do with the political situation regarding Irian Jaya?"

"Why, absolutely nothing," Mr. Dan cried. "The people in the Baliem know nothing about self-determination and care less. Their world is here. Self-determination to them is a vague concept brought from the coast. On the coast there are many educated black people, and they are very clever. Like the schoolmaster you met. Jayapura is an Indonesian city, but there is a strong separatist movement. But in Biak or Sorong, the intellectuals all claim that they are leaders of the separatist movement. They believe the Indonesian government is corrupt, and they want no part of it.

"But the government for its part is almost helpless in its

naïveté," Mr. Dan continued. "They argue that it is wrong for villagers to dance without clothes because 'all our people are within one nation.' There is simply no logic to that way of thinking. If we cannot give the Dani jobs, how can we require that they wear clothes? If you have clothes, you need soap. And to buy soap, you need money."

"What do the Dani do with money when they get it?"

"Oh, a few buy clothes, shorts, T-shirts, but most save the money to eventually buy a pig. But clothes for these people are something they don't understand any more than they understand what a bank is, and they haven't understood anything but koteka, grass skirts, and cowrie shells for thousands of years. It gets cold at night, so you wonder why they don't spend money on clothes. From where would they get clothes? It is simply not in their tradition. Clothes make them sick. They believe it, and it is true."

Mr. Dan led me to a map of Irian Jaya on the wall. "But the Dani are civilized by our standards compared to these people." He pointed to an area south of Wamena and the great central east-west mountain range that bisects the island. "This is country of the Cain people. They are naked and live in trees. They have absolutely nothing. Absolutely nothing!"

I was ready to continue my journey to Sumatra at the opposite end of the archipelago. Even though I had a seat on the Merpati flight out of the valley in the morning, I had an overwhelming urge to call San Francisco. The month had already turned. It was August first. Guided by its huge monolithic dish, I took the short walk through Wamena's streets to the new telecommunications center, where you could call anywhere in the world via satellite.

While waiting for the call to be put through, I realized that I was standing at the edge of a battlefield where men still slew each other with Stone Age weapons.

Medan:
Indonesia's Wild West

S UMATRA IS INDONESIA's large, westernmost island, reaching from the tip of Java northward through the Indian Ocean, past the Malay Peninsula and toward the mainland of Burma. Though it is as richly variegated in its mountains and rainforests, lowland swamps and jungles as Borneo and New Guinea, its proximity to Southeast Asia's mainland has given it an accessibility denied those larger islands and a place on European maps since ancient times.

Some scholars have speculated that the Taprobane of Pliny was not Ceylon, but Sumatra. It was the first island in the archipelago to receive the Hindu migrations, and by the seventh century Sumatra was the seat of a powerful Hindu kingdom. In the thirteenth century Arab traders brought Islam to Aceh in the north of the island, and the new religion spread southward. In the Padang highlands are ancient inscriptions calling Sumatra "the first Java." As Java's neighbor, it has remained through the centuries a sort of vassal country to the superior Javanese kingdoms, a status that has fostered a mutual dependence. Marco Polo's reference to Sumatra as Java Minor was an apt one.

An Italian, Ludovico de Varthema, provided Europeans with the name Sumatra in 1505. But the Portuguese were the first Western power to establish a trading post on the island, in 1509, though they were driven out at the end of the century by the Dutch, who in turn withstood claims by the rival British over the next three centuries.

Lying between six degrees north and south, so that the equator divides it into two nearly equal parts, Sumatra is the largest, after Borneo, of the Great Sunda islands of the Malay Archipelago. Over 1,000 miles long and 250 miles wide at its broadest point, it is nearly four times the size of Java, as large as California, and almost the size of Spain.

Smaller islands off the west coast rise from the edge of the submarine platform of the Indian Ocean and serve as an outer barrier. A high mountain chain runs along Sumatra's western coast, descending eastward to a great expanse of alluvial flatlands, seamed with a network of rivers. The mountain chain, known as Bukit Barisan, contains numerous volcanic peaks ranging in height from five thousand to twelve thousand feet. In fact, this mountain range consists essentially of two folding, parallel chains with a vast valley between that is broken into separate sections by the intrusion of volcanic massifs. Along this valley lies a string of volcanic lakes, the largest being Lake Toba in North Sumatra, the largest lake in Southeast Asia.

Because of the wall of mountains that runs along the western coast, the rivers on this side of the island are largely unnavigable, while the eastern rivers pass through wide delta plains and coastal swamps, providing access to the interior for oceangoing steamships.

Sumatra and Java, once joined, are now separated by the narrow Sunda Strait. The striking difference in animal species between these two large, nearly touching islands led Wallace to hypothesize that their initial severance was very ancient, and was followed by joinings and separations over a long period, while successive waves of animal migration produced the anomalies of species so characteristic of the archipelago. Curiously, Wallace devotes only fourteen pages to Sumatra in his masterwork, *The Malay Archipelago*.

The naturalist confined his travels and research to the southeast, eschewing the north and west as "a part of the island entirely in the hands of native rulers."

Then there is Sumatra's diversity of inhabitants. Borneo's Dayaks and New Guinea's Papuans, while diverse among themselves, are essentially homogeneous peoples, and anthropological interest in them springs from their isolation from the outside world. Sumatra's tribes, by contrast, have maintained their cultural identities along one of the world's oldest trade routes. Here is an entire world within an island, a world more laden with exotic paradox today than it was in Marco Polo's thirteenth century, when the Venetian journeyer was detained for a lengthy stay in Aceh after traversing the Strait of Malacca on his return to Europe from China.

I sailed north from Jakarta's port, Tanjung Priok, past the Riau Archipelago, still a haven for pirates, toward Singapore at the entrance of the Strait of Malacca: a stormy, three-day passage through a southwest monsoon, squalls known as "the Sumatras." The *Lawit* churned northeast through the strait, coasting among the crocodile-infested mangrove swamps of the island's southeastern lowlands, to arrive in a calm at Belawan in North Sumatra. This is the rank, fly-ridden port that serves Medan, the largest city on the sixth largest island in the world, situated some three thousand miles west of Jayapura.

After dinner on my last night aboard ship, I stood at the bow rail in a soughing wind with Dr. Halim, a fastidious Javanese dentist from Jakarta.

"I think Somerset Maugham was right about Asian cities," he said. "For him they were all alike, and he couldn't visit them without a certain malaise."

"I haven't seen two that are alike," I said.

"He would respect that. A city is a different place to everyone."

"What do you think of Medan? I'll be stopping over for a few days."

Dr. Halim shook his head. "Medan was formerly a rich area for the Dutch," he said. "You can see the estates near the city and the old mansions still standing. But I must warn you about Medan. It is Indonesia's Wild West, with its own Mafias and rackets, crime, and prostitution. Its Batak inhabitants are the most offensively aggressive people in Indonesia. There are both Christian and Muslim Batak tribes in North Sumatra, and they are scattered from Medan south to Lake Toba. They are as tough and strong as they are dishonest. When they turn up in Jakarta, they take to the streets as purse-snatchers and pickpockets, and they're no better in Medan."

He paused to scribble some names in my notebook by moonlight. "Hank and Jake have lived in the city for years, and if they're in town, they can be helpful. Give them a call. But Medan is the most disorganized and undisciplined city in the entire Malay Archipelago," he said finally. "Take my word for it, and take care."

I found a teeming metropolis situated on North Sumatra's coastal plain, whose white buildings and Moorish archways were the dual vestiges of Dutch colonialism and Arab expansionism in trade and Islam. Motorized and push-bike becaks prowled the streets day and night past the shops, restaurants, and bars. Medan is Indonesia's third largest metropolis, after Jakarta and Surabaya, and is as polyglot a city as any in Indonesia: among its citizens are Chinese, a handful of Europeans from the oil-boom days of the 1970s, Indians, Arab descendants, Javanese, and a mingling of tribal Sumatrans, with Bataks making up the majority.

My hotel was an old Dutch colonial building with airy rooms and shaded verandas protected by large Moorish arches. It stood across a busy avenue from a green, manicured field with a small grandstand and racetrack, though the field was now used by schoolchildren for soccer and volleyball.

Flame and palm trees before tile-roofed buildings dating from the turn of the century lined the avenues. Houses facing the side streets had rounded corners, and windows carved out of pastel walls were shuttered against the sun. Troops of boys and girls in school uniforms walked the streets, many of them with pieces of cloth tied over their noses as a shield against the noxious fumes of the becaks. The city's great mosque had been conceived in Middle Eastern light, with the lofty archways of the octagonal dome supported by pink marble columns, and beyond its park-enclosed minaret and reflecting pool stood the sultan's palace, now a museum whose faded green and blue formal rooms were rented out for weddings and other private functions.

Inside the mosque, upwards of a hundred men were curled up on the cool marble floor, fast asleep. It was a day when women were forbidden to enter, and the men sought escape from their wives and domestic humdrum here.

As I walked, I saw vestiges of Medan's Dutch past, when its principal exports had come from plantations worked by indentured servants, producing rubber, tobacco, and palm oil.

I stopped before the mansion of a Chinese Mafia lord who had prospered decades before in the ganja trade. The house sat behind open gates off the street, and as it seemed a museum of sorts with its open doors, I entered to find a lush, unfurnished hall of Islamic tiles, with three grand chandeliers. The house was empty, so I walked around, hearing my own footsteps, while the sunlight caught the dust on two ancient mirrors with flamingos etched into the glass.

In the rear room hung a portrait of the patriarch and his wife, as well as an oil portrait of the lady in long dress and bustle, and a grand piano. There were snapshots of better times than today on the wall: a yellowed picture of a teenaged boy playing a piano, smiling family portraits, teenaged girls in tennis whites. Behind the mansion was a large birdhouse near a Buddhist shrine.

Suddenly, I heard piano music upstairs. Someone was practicing a Schubert impromptu. I quickly left the way I'd entered.

Medan had always been a boomtown, and the haphazardness with which buildings were placed reflected that. A small mosque stood next to a Chinese bakery, and two doors down the street was a dive called "Flora Massage." I entered to find four or five men steaming in the perfumed smoke, waiting their turns for more lascivious exercises. Across the street was a dancing school where tiny Chinese girls in pale blue tutus and pink slippers giggled at me through windows, but when I tried to enter, they squealed and scattered with timidity and delight. On the corner was a Protestant church, and at five in the afternoon men in shirtsleeves, smelling of cologne, arrived with their women in flowered dresses, their faces and necks powdered white. Loudspeakers outside the church filled the streets with hymn singing and the Pentecostal spirit.

By dusk I had wandered far afield, and hailed a motorized becak to return to the hotel. The driver was talkative and complained alternately of an oil leak and the Medan police. On a potholed side street, before a cinema featuring *Fatal Termination*, he stopped for oil, which a woman dipped from a large drum under a canopy of clotheslines, while a traffic policeman watched us. "Police no good in Medan," the driver said, holding a hand aloft and rubbing his thumb against his fingers. "Police bad."

At nightfall the city began its transformation. Outside the hotel I caused trouble leading to a vicious fistfight by inadvertently violating becak protocol. When a Batak driver asked an extortionate fare, I shunned him and hired another at my price, a move that goaded the first driver to pounce on the second. Dr. Halim had not underestimated Medan's proclivity for violence. I walked quickly away as blows were savagely exchanged, waving off the other drivers who swarmed like hornets around the hotel. I moved down a dark covered sidewalk flanking the wide, busy avenue in search of a particular restaurant, passing beggars, street people, and prostitutes working the dark blocks. Scarcely a doorway I passed hadn't been claimed by itinerants.

"Apart from the obvious advantages, living here's a bit difficult. It's a question of learning who to pay off, and that takes a little time," said Jake.

"But essentially it comes down to this," Hank added. "There's the Chinese Mafia and the Batak Mafia. If you pay the top man in each, the smaller people leave you alone. The protection racket has a rather poetical name. Called 'the night guard.' But if we don't pay, there's trouble."

I had telephoned Hank and Jake from the hotel, and we had met at a bar with paneled walls, Japanese lanterns, cozy booths, and other trappings of a private club, a hangout for expatriates. A tape deck played "Too Young," the Nat "King" Cole ballad of the fifties, rendered in Chinese, and comely Batak girls served drinks.

Hank was a tall American in his late thirties who operated rafting safaris on the Alas River through the inhospitable rainforest of Aceh province across the island. He shared a house in the old Dutch quarter with Jake, a balding New Zealand wildlife photographer of medium build, who was working under a grant from Mobil Corporation in a large reserve in Aceh. Hank was married to a Batak girl, who had borne him a son, while Jake had a live-in girlfriend.

"My Land Rover's outside," said Jake. "We thought we'd have dinner in Chinatown. It's a grungy place with natural air-conditioning, but good food."

We wound our way through the dimly lit byways of Medan, past smoking warungs and shops selling cigarettes, medicines, stolen automobile parts, stereos, and TVs, to find the restaurant on a narrow dirt street. Cooking was done in large woks over a flaming grill on the edge of the street, and we sat at one of a few tables crowded together inside. It was so sweltering that the cook was stripped to the waist, and as we ordered plates of seafood and vegetables the rush of cooking chilis wafting in the air made our eyes water.

While we sipped beer, waiting for our food, a young boy with mournful eyes and a rag for polishing shoes crawled around on the floor, which was littered with food and cigarette butts. When the food arrived, we ate quickly, using for napkins rolls of toilet paper placed on the table in egg-shaped dispensers. Afterward, we ran into a couple of Australians outside.

"We're going to the red-light district," they said. "Come along for the ride."

"They've just moved here," said Jake, as we fetched the Land Rover. "Medan's red-light district is something to see."

"But not like the old days," said Hank. "The seventies during the oil boom. Medan is dead now compared to then."

The red-light district was a street of bars, each with live music and a dance floor, though inexplicably no dancing was allowed. In these places the atmosphere was sleazy. When Batak teeth were bared in such places, they were shown to bite the feeding hand. I sensed that if etiquette was violated in Mafia-controlled Medan, an outsider could end up not in jail but dead. Hank and Jake were clearly in their element, teasing the girls with mock displays of affection, while our new companions, Felix and Greg, were intent on something more.

As we barhopped, I saw that all the establishments operated in the same manner. Even though the girls were prostitutes, gems of a rough cut, a certain protocol had to be observed even in the ordering of drinks. The "waitresses" each represented a different kind of beer. There was an Anker girl, a Bintang, a San Miguel, a Beck's, and so on, so the girl whose beer was not selected had herself been rejected. She was paid a cut of whatever she sold, whether her beer or her body. Though ordering a beer was not tantamount to choosing a girl to take to bed, it opened the door of possibility. There were rooms upstairs for sex on the premises, but if you wanted to take a girl to a hotel, such matters as working shifts had to be taken into account and negotiated. Felix and Greg seemed intent on the latter course.

The rigid protocol seemed at odds with the appalling raunchiness of the clubs. Hank and Jake appeared to be acting out the libertine's charade for the benefit of the fresh recruits. As the evening wore on, Felix became more eager, while Greg began to falter in the presence of a girl called Marina, who sat next to him.

"If you wanted, you could be in bed right now, couldn't you, mate," said Jake to Greg. "I mean if that's why you're here, it's so easily arranged."

"Mood counts for something," said Greg.

"Moonlight and roses is it, mate?"

"Something like that."

Marina's beauty was typical of the islands, unblemished save for a slightly pocked face and a few welts of scar tissue on her slender arms. Her seeming lack of self-consciousness masked her vulnerability, and on closer inspection one could recognize the ravages of her class and trade. Her fingernails were broken and dirty. She opened her mouth to reveal a space where a molar was freshly missing, and I had no doubt that the tyrannical pimp who managed the girls had served up the blow. She was eighteen, a Batak Muslim, and had borne a child out of wedlock.

"I'd like to go back to the first bar," said Felix. "A girl there I liked."

When we returned to reclaim Felix's girl, he made the overtures, but she slipped out just as the place was closing, confounding Felix.

"You lost that one, mate," said Jake.

Hank spoke up. "Best to get them alone outside, if you want to take them off the premises. You never quite know why. Boyfriend, boss, other girls. But get them alone, and all is cool. It's funny, but that's the way they are."

I wanted to take the late-night air, so hired a push-bike becak back to the hotel, chatting with the Batak driver in Bahasa Indonesia. He was a Christian from a small village near Lake Toba, a married man trying to support a family in Medan, and very poor, with only the clothes on his back. But he had a soft-spoken, amiable dignity.

"What is your name?" I asked after giving him mine.

"Karl Marx, tuan."

German missionaries had ventured into North Sumatra's Batak interior in the last century, and such names were commonplace in this part of the island. At the hotel I retrieved some old clothes and took them back to the street for Karl Marx. My gift forged a sort of allegiance, and thereafter he became my driver in Medan.

Before retiring, I looked into the bar. A group of Acehnese were sipping cups of coffee in the lobby. Medan was a transit stop for these pious travelers, for they were returning to their homes in the north the next day from the hajj.

Medan required that it be met on its terms, and I began to feel comfortable blending myself into the passing silhouettes against the flickering background of this nomadic city with its drifting pulse. I could appreciate Medan's external absurdities and contradictions, its surface movements, without expecting any revelations beyond them. Medan seemed material for a painter's canvas: strangers on the edge of society, urban disintegration, the tragic crossed with the absurd.

By Dr. Halim's reckoning, the Bataks of North Sumatra were infamous for their churlishness. He had explained that *Batak* evolved from an old Malay word meaning "robber" or the more damning "pig eater." No doubt Medan's "Wild West" reputation sprang in part from this widely held prejudice against the Bataks. But the next morning I struck up a conversation in English with two young women who were playing cards beside the hotel pool. They were university students enjoying a day off, and immediately seemed manifestations of the obverse side of Medan.

"Would you like to spend the day with us?" they said after introducing themselves as Erma and Tetti.

These were nice, well-bred girls from affluent families, who, although Batak Muslims, were not unmindful of consumer chic and repartee. They sparkled in Western jeans and designer blouses and drove an old, beat-up roadster. Tetti was the third of six daughters, a tiny young woman who wrestled with the large steering wheel. During the drive to Erma's house for refreshments, I learned that they were studying business administration at Medan University. Later, I discovered why: their fathers owned tobacco plantations and had no male heirs.

Erma's house was in a wealthy section of town. We passed through a gate that had to be unlocked by a male servant and entered a Mediterranean-style drive with a garden and patio beside it. The spacious, high-ceilinged living room was decorated with Balinese paintings and Javanese furniture. Pieces of kitsch, dime-store figurines and the like, along with plastic flowers in vases, decorated every flat surface. A steep staircase led upstairs.

Erma's parents were away, but she showed me a family portrait taken on the occasion of her older sister's wedding. The bride looked beautiful in the traditional red gown and gold crown of Batak Muslims, and Erma, who in the picture had not yet budded, smiled shyly. The mother looked proud, and the father, surrounded by so many daughters, wore a demeanor of weary contentment.

"Would you like to see the crocodile farm?" said Erma. "It is nearby."

The natural habitat of these man-eating reptiles was the coastal mangrove swamps, but at this place, only a few miles from town, they were raised and slaughtered for their hides. We arrived to find buses as well as a contingent of police. Clearly, something extraordinary was going on inside. We entered and I recognized from my hotel a group of Japanese visitors from Ichihara, headed by that city's mayor, and their Medanese hosts, including the mayor of Medan.

The place was a ramshackle collection of pits and ponds, cinder-block and corrugated-tin enclosures, containing hundreds of crocodiles of various sizes, the largest ones thirty feet long. The largest reptiles swam in a central black pool, feeding on chickens, which they caught in their jaws when tossed to them by an attendant. The fastidious Japanese women held handkerchiefs over their noses in a futile effort to fend off the atrocious odor rising from the pits, while a small orchestra of reeds and gongs beat out a tune as prelude to a ceremony that was a sort of laying on of hands.

The Japanese mayor was presented by his Medanese counterpart with a ceremonial robe, as well as a five-foot stuffed crocodile.

Handlers brought out smaller, live specimens, which the visiting mayor was invited to inspect.

The mayor incautiously touched one three-foot beast forward of its hind leg, and with lightning speed the crocodile swept the visitor's hand into its open jaws with its tail and snapped its mouth shut. The mayor cried out in pain and terror, while the compound was frozen in horror. Handlers stilled the reptile and pried its snout open to free the badly lacerated hand. The mayor, pale and faint, was made to sit while his wife and a host of others crowded about to fan him and the host mayor wrapped a handkerchief around the wounds.

The daughter of the wounded mayor burst into uncontrollable sobbing; another woman vomited, and yet another fainted, while most of the group bolted for the exit. But the poor man's misfortune was also the subject of amusement and ridicule by some Batak onlookers out of earshot of their own mayor. Clearly and by any measure, this celebration of a tourist and trade agreement between these new "sister cities" had ended badly.

Outside we heard sirens in the distance as the dignitaries were borne to hospital, and I wondered which eminent gentleman, the mayor of Ichihara or the mayor of Medan, had suffered the greater loss of face.

We drove away from the city into the flats of the coastal plain. The countryside, the most developed part of Sumatra, was alternately burned over and cultivated: we passed bulldozed acres of palm; then green rice fields and shepherd boys tending buffalo, often napping on the animals' backs; then forests of rubber trees, plantations leased if not owned by Goodyear, and the foul-smelling rubber factories, serviced by a railway.

Our destination was Tetti's family home and tobacco plantation, a vast expanse of sprawling fields connected by a network of red-clay roads around a spacious country house reminiscent of the large peach and cotton farms of the American South. This plantation was in fact a tobacco company.

We stopped first at a long open-sided tobacco shed, a *bangsal,* where heaps of tobacco were dried under thatched roofs of coconut palm. The heavy clumps of rich-smelling leaves were spread and turned by peasant women from Java, transmigration workers, and descendants of the indentured servants brought here by the Dutch in the 1930s. The girls explained that this drying process took sixty days, and then the harvest was shipped from the port of Belawan to Germany, where it was made into cigars.

The plantation house was a lovely, spacious, century-old Dutch farmhouse, or rather two houses, for the kitchen was separated from the living quarters by a patio. There was a large, scrupulously clean mandi, where I washed for lunch. I then joined the girls in the roomy parlor cooled by ceiling fans.

When I emerged from my wash-up, Tetti had gathered her mother and five sisters to meet me. *Ibu*, or the mother, was matronly, her natural beauty faded, but she was proud of her brood of daughters. Tetna and Ida were Tetti's older married sisters and lived, counter to Batak patrilineal custom, with their husbands on their father's company premises. Tuti, Yuni, and Nova were younger. All were mischievously pretty; their ages spread from sixteen to twenty-two.

As was customary, I had removed my shoes before entering the house. The marble floor was cool to the feet, the walls whitewashed, and the heavy, hardwood-framed, overstuffed furniture, which had been made on the premises, was slipcovered in cotton to match the walls. As in Erma's town house, figurines decorated the tables, and the vases overflowed with plastic flowers. Tetti put a Stevie Wonder tape on the cassette player.

Ibu joined us for lunch at the foot of the table on the patio, which was shaded at either end by a mango and a rain tree, and as the only male I was seated in *bapak's*, or the father's, chair at the head. Here at home all ate in the Muslim style, with the right hand, washing the fingers in individual water-filled glass bowls. My place alone was set with silverware, but I followed their custom. Servants passed plates of chicken sweetened with sugar and tomatoes, eggplant stuffed with fish, potatoes flavored with red-hot chilis, and spinach laced as well with the fiery pods, all accompanied by warm tea. A dessert of fresh fruit followed.

At ibu's prompting Tetti spoke to me. "Please, Char-les, you must not reveal the secret of our tobacco processing. Our company is world famous, and my father would be very angry if a competitor learned our methods. He believes we have the finest tobacco in the world."

By chance, a searing ray of sunlight pierced the tree canopy, falling on me, and in time it settled on Erma, seated to my right. Without ceremony, she shifted her chair to the shade, catching my eye as she moved.

"It's the sun. I don't wish for my skin to become darker. You are fair, but we are not." Her tone was apologetic.

"What difference does it make?" I said.

It was a rhetorical question, because to them it did matter. Under Dutch rule, the Anglo-Saxon attitude had held that these islands were a land of coolies. I guessed that not even Sukarno's incendiary rhetoric to the contrary on the occasion of his nation's independence had removed this deeply ingrained feeling of inferiority. Essential to an Indonesian lady's toiletries was a battery of cosmetics and creams, bleaching agents labeled with false promises.

We left at midafternoon, dropping Tetna and Ida at their houses, and returned to the city. The girls insisted that I visit their favorite shopping center, where there were boutiques featuring Western designer clothes. I treated them to sundaes and banana splits, which they relished, at an ice cream parlor, and afterward we window-shopped.

Tuti, who was nineteen, had joined us, and saw this opportunity as her own cue.

"Will you buy this for me, Char-les?" she said in English, holding up a blouse, "and I'll be your friend girl."

"You mean 'girlfriend,' " I said. "You do not have to be my girlfriend. Let me buy something for everybody."

The others politely declined, while I bought the blouse for Tuti. Tetti was appalled and berated her sister icily, and when we returned to the car, Tuti was penitent.

"They are angry with me," she said of Tetti and Erma.

"They want you to be a lady. They think you are naughty to ask a man for a gift."

"They are envious and jealous."

"Hardly."

"No," said Tuti, crestfallen. "It's only a joke." Suddenly she burst into tears.

That evening, my last in Medan, I had dinner at a sidewalk café near the hotel. It had a film-noir charm, with whirling overhead fans, and white-jacketed waiters and batik-clad waitresses serving patrons seated at small tables in oversized rattan chairs. A middle-aged woman pianist with a two-man percussion backup played Western music from old sheets and spineless books: "Danny Boy" and Dave Brubeck's "Take Five." Well-heeled young locals hung out here, the girls in blouses and skirts and the boys in baggy pleated trousers.

When the pianist finished a set, she folded her music and made her way to my table.

"Forgive me," she said, taking a seat. "I want to speak English and don't often get the chance." She was a dark, homely woman with a nervous tic.

"Where do you come from?" I said.

"Goa, in India," she said. "I came to Medan many years ago with my father, a musician who taught me how to play the piano. Since his death, I've been stuck here."

"You don't like Medan?"

"It's a dreadful place, don't you think?"

"It's a complete city," I said.

"Completely mad, I think. I've never been happy here. My father was Portuguese. He was never at home in Medan. The people resented us, and they still resent me."

"Why is that?"

She shrugged. "We came from India. We were outsiders. They treated us terribly. If we stood in line at a store, at a bank, at a theater, when it came our time to be served, they would do all they could to discourage us. They would refuse to serve us or if they did, because our money was as good as anybody else's, they would overcharge us. Since my father's death, they are even worse to me. Why? I don't know. Perhaps because of my Indian and Portuguese blood, they see me as superior. But I really don't know why."

"That's no fun."

"The Chinese are the worst," she continued. "They are a minority, but a bigger minority than us." She paused to rummage through her bag and produced a thick sheaf of papers.

"I want to emigrate to Australia," she said, laying the documents on the table. "Will you help me by writing a letter proposing me for citizenship? A letter like these?"

She presented them for me to see. There were perhaps a dozen testimonials in all, presumably from anyone with an English name who happened to pass through.

"I'm an American, not an Australian," I said. "I'm afraid I wouldn't be much help."

"Please," she said, writing her name and address in a palsied script on a slip of paper, then giving it to me. "You can be more help than you think."

"Okay," I said and pocketed the paper. "Good luck to you."

"God will love you for this," she said. "I'm here three nights a week. Please come in again."

"I'm leaving tomorrow," I said.

"Where will you go?"

"I'm taking a ship to Banda Aceh."

"The Acehnese are difficult people," she said after a moment, "the most militant Muslims in Indonesia. Though I have not been to Banda Aceh, I know that it is very different from Medan. The Acehnese are not friendly to Westerners. They fought a terrible war against the Dutch at the turn of the century. They do not like white people. I don't think that you'll be welcome in Banda Aceh, but I shall pray for you."

She rose quickly and returned to the small bandstand, and I could see that she exercised some tyranny of her own over her percussionists, who were mild-mannered and deferential. While she tore into a dusty book of Americana in deference to me—"Old Black Joe," "Camptown Races," "Dixie," "My Old Kentucky Home," "Moonlight on the Wabash," "Shenandoah"—I wondered if her troubles were not born of her own superiority. When I left, I sensed her nervous stare following me into the street.

Outside, groups of becak drivers squatted in semicircles, talking and puffing cigarettes, Karl Marx among them. When he saw me, he pushed his becak over.

Sumatra:
The Edge of the Jungle

*M*Y ACEHNESE DRIVER pushed his taxi as aggressively as he had bargained, along the narrow road from the port, approaching the city through a broad, flat valley of palm-covered farmland that spread, then gave way eastward to the large range of mountains that bisected the island. Westward the sun glanced off the Indian Ocean where the small island of Sabang floated in the glare.

We entered the city, winding past the Moorish covered sidewalks and the shop signs in Arabic script, which betrayed Aceh's proximity to the Islamic world west of the Bay of Bengal. There were only two other guests in the spartan hotel buried in the dust of the city, both businessmen from Jakarta, who sipped hot tea in tall glasses at opposite ends of the small lobby, while the call to prayers rose in the late afternoon.

Here in Aceh subtle, contradictory forces were at work that had me suspended and dislocated. I was more prepared for the taciturn stares of the Acehnese when I disembarked than for the strangely melancholic sunlight that plunged through the clouds in great shafts, creating a cubistic canvas in chiaroscuro. The atmosphere was charged with an otherness that made Medan seem a world away, rather than a mere three hundred miles.

Though the distance was less one of geography than of mood, geography counted. Banda Aceh was on the northwestern tip of

Sumatra, and its seaside plain was isolated from the rest of the world by mountains and sea as well as by Acehnese severity. Just offshore from the city, Sabang Island, connected to the mainland by ferry, marked the westernmost point in Indonesia. You could stand on its outer beach and look across the Indian Ocean toward an invisible Africa. India was to the northwest, and beyond it Arabia, the Fertile Crescent, and then Europe. From here the world seemed finite and this place a lonely outpost on its edge.

These days no one came to Banda Aceh, the "Doorway to Mecca," but that had not always been so. Marco Polo passed through Aceh in 1292, was a guest of Aceh's Islamic sultanate, and reported that he had sighted a unicorn, most likely a spotted rhinoceros native to Sumatra. In 1585 Aceh's autonomy was suggested in a grand letter from its sultan to Queen Elizabeth I of England, signaling the beginning of a trade agreement between the two nations that would last for four centuries. "I am the mighty ruler of the Regions below the wind," the sultan wrote, "who holds sway over the land of Aceh and over the land of Sumatra and over all the lands tributary to Aceh, which stretch from the sunrise to the sunset."

Banda Aceh's days of glory were the seventeenth century, when it was a center for international trade as well as for spiritual and intellectual life. Poets and scholars resided here, and such exports as gold and camphor, pepper and tortoiseshell departed for the West.

This multifaceted supremacy resulted in Aceh's challenging Portuguese autonomy in the northwestern part of the archipelago: that challenge led to war and Portugal's abandonment of Malacca, Aceh's biggest commercial rival, across the strait on the Malay Peninsula. The long-standing treaty with the British enabled Aceh to trade actively with Singapore, an arrangement that continued until the Dutch and the British signed their own treaty in 1871, undercutting the earlier agreement.

With the British disavowing Aceh, there was no force to prevent a Dutch occupation. After the Acehnese sought support for their autonomy from the American consul in Singapore and an ensuing document of friendship was forwarded to Washington, the Dutch declared war against Aceh in 1873, ensuring nearly four decades of bloodshed.

Banda Aceh is immutably Acehnese. During my short stay in the capital, while I arranged for an expedition down the island, it became clear that the city's fabric remained largely unstained by the West. As well, its citizens had crossed their Muslim practices with animist ones of a more distant time, and this became apparent when shadows lengthened. Dusk was the time when people felt most vulnerable to evil spirits. As I walked through a square where warungs were being prepared for evening, I heard the terse and ominous chanting of the *dukun*, the native doctors hexing these unseen, mischievous powers.

"Happy's" was a Chinese place across the street from a market reeking of fish. The restaurant was brightly lit, with overhead fans and a screened door to keep out the swarms of flies. Nightly, an ancient blind couple felt their way through the entrance to beg, and a sober-faced boy guided them to my table. Giving alms to the poor was a tenet of the Islamic faith, so I habitually dug in my pockets for change, while a cat curled up at my feet.

After dinner and the passing of the malicious hour, the streets were transformed, the edginess in the air receding. I half expected the women of Banda Aceh to be veiled and reclusive, but the ones at the warungs were suddenly gregarious and eager to engage a stranger. Dr. Halim had told me that despite the rigid Islamic culture, which usually weighed heavily against female rights, Acehnese women enjoyed a great deal of independence and were willing to shed blood for it. In quiet times a woman was known as "the one who owns the house," but during the protracted war with the Dutch, some of the fiercest guerrillas had been women. Cut Mutia, the most heroic of these women warriors, was venerated here, and her house was open to the public.

But there was segregation nonetheless. The men sat at curbside tables drinking strong-smelling, sweet coffee and making loud, boisterous conversation. There were no women in these makeshift sidewalk cafés. Nightlife here, as in all Indonesia, was street life, and conversations lasted well into the morning hours, with caffeine rather than alcohol the drug that loosened tongues. Aceh produced the finest ganja in Indonesia, and if Acehnese scorned alcohol on religious principle and cultural habit, they had no compunctions about spiking their coffee and curries with marijuana buds.

By day the central mosque was a sight to lift up hearts. Situated in a paved circle surrounded by a confusion of avenues, it glowed in the morning light as if it arrogated to itself all the virtues of Islam, superseding previous visions. It was not an ancient structure. The Dutch had begun the present building in 1879 during a lull in the forty years' war by way of mollifying the Acehnese after the torching of its predecessor, and it had been completed in 1957, when the last of its five jet-black, wooden-shingled domes had been erected over the sun-bleached white walls.

I removed my shoes and entered beneath a clock with Arabic script for numbers, found a seat against a wall on the cool marble floor, and enjoyed a cross-breeze while pretending to busy myself making notes. I remained until noon prayers, when the faithful came with their rugs, all of Middle Eastern design and some made of plastic. The women offered their prayers in a rear area roped off from the front, where the men were secluded, and prepared for worship by wrapping themselves in oversized robes, removing their street clothes, then shimmying into their white caftans while allowing the larger robe to fall at their feet. Two young women arrived on a single motorcycle, and one waited while the other took off her denim skirt under a robe, slipped into a caftan, prostrated herself uttering prayers to Allah, reversed the procedure, and, once again in her street clothes, passed the caftan to her companion.

If there was a sameness about many Indonesian cities, Banda Aceh was singular, marked by local history. The nearby Dutch cemetery was a vast field of headstones, for more than two thousand Hollanders were buried here, mostly young men barely twenty years old slain by the Acehnese. Dutch money maintained this burial place. Baked by the sun on the edge of a scruffy field stood an old C-47, mounted as a statue upon a pedestal; it had figured strategically in Indonesia's independence movement and was celebrated as the genesis of the country's air force.

A short walk away was the Gunongan, a palace of clandestine walkways and hidden baths, built for the wife of a seventeenth-century sultan. In front of the museum sat a large cast-iron bell dating from the time of Christ that had been given by the Chinese emperor as tribute to the Acehnese.

The museum nearby featured weapons from the Acehnese wars as well as traditional ceremonial clothing. The girls of the museum were friendly, while the male students who sought me out to practice their English were more sedate.

"How many Muslims are there in the United States?" asked one.

"What do Christians in America think of our Muhammad?" asked another.

These were questions to which I'd given scant thought, but my circumlocutious answers were listened to courteously. Still, an unalterable fact remained: I was an infidel among believers.

My two drivers for the expedition south were called Tonku and Tomy. They were tall, erect, earnest young men. Together with our short supply of provisions, we filled the jeep. Neither Acehnese could read the map even to find his village, so I refolded the map and put it away. These young men had never left their province, so maps were irrelevant to the conduct of their daily life.

We set off in the morning, driving toward the Indian Ocean, passing rice fields ringed by palm trees against a backdrop of mountains and the occasional buffalo standing in shoulder-deep water, a bird perched upon its back. When the road swung southward at the coast, it became winding and narrow, with potholes and sheer drops to the sea. Here the Indian Ocean was treacherous, with huge rolling waves breaking over a coral beach, though after several miles we crossed a network of rivers where women bathed fully clothed and fishermen in orange-and-blue-painted dugouts fished the mangrove swamp estuaries with nets. One bridge bore the date 1914, but its pavement had been worn away, leaving only a bed of steel girders that clattered when we passed.

We entered one small village to discover a celebration in progress: at Tomy's suggestion we stopped. We were greeted by the village head, a man in his middle years with a stubble of beard and a lighted cigarette. Tomy spoke to him in Acehnese, and then the chief addressed me in Bahasa Indonesia.

"You are most welcome. We are having a wedding today," he said. "Please join us if you have time."

He led us inside a modest bungalow, where we were seated. Soon the entire village surrounded the house, peering through windows while we were served tea by handsome women in spangled veils who wore their hair in long, single braids. The chief was an affable man.

"I am fifty-eight," he said. "But I am an old man. As a boy I fight against the Japanese and then against the Dutch."

"How is it that you are head of the village?" I asked.

"The villagers elect me," he said. "Come."

In the next room a feast was being laid out: heaping serving plates of rice, with the meats to come later. Soon the mullah escorted in the bridegroom, a serious young man in his mid-twenties with a pencil-thin mustache, wearing a turban and dressed in a black ceremonial suit trimmed with red which resembled a military dress uniform. The mullah was a tall, bespectacled man with dignified bearing, and everyone, including the village chief, deferred to him.

"Would you like to see the bride?" said the chief suddenly. He led me through the small, bamboo-walled house to a small room, where the bride waited. At sixteen she had the bearing of a princess upon her throne. She was dressed in a red gown, her lips and cheeks rouged, a gold crown atop her bunned hair. Behind the two thrones, one yet vacant, hung a lavishly colored drape. Upon seeing me, the bride smiled, averted her eyes, and timidly covered her face with her fan.

"You stay for the wedding and feast?" said the chief.

I thanked him but declined, explaining that we had to take advantage of the daylight. I asked about a road through the mountains.

"Yes, there is such a road, but it is often impassable in the rain. That road runs through violent country cursed by hostile spirits, where we fight the Dutch and the Japanese. It is rough going, but these boys know the way. But be careful. You never know what happens in such a country, and *danau tawar* is an evil place."

Danau tawar was a lake deep in the mountains, and it became our destination. We turned inland, passing acres of marijuana plants, before gaining the highlands and the inland road, a dirt track the width of the jeep which swung southeast down the spine of the island through the rugged country of the Acehnese-Dutch wars.

When the Dutch declared war against the Acehnese in 1873, Holland was intent on quelling a rebellion, but to the Acehnese it was a holy war, which they waged for nearly forty years.

It was not a pretty story. A Colonel Von Daalen led a punitive expedition from Banda Aceh to Lake Toba along the Alas River, through some of the most inhospitable country in the archipelago. The Dutch were ill-equipped by any measure to prosecute such a war, and the Acehnese, who gave no quarter and expected none, were superb guerrilla fighters on a field they knew. The Dutch, nonetheless, were ruthless in their retributions, and carried out a number of wholesale massacres of the Acehnese. But the cost of the war to the Dutch was high: 250,000 lives and 50 million pounds sterling.

A practical outgrowth of the conflict was that the Acehnese earned the respect of the Dutch and special status as a territory that was reasserted contentiously in turn under the stewardship of the Japanese and then of the Indonesian military. Aceh strove to form an independent Islamic republic; that status lasted from 1953 to 1961, finally deteriorating because of conflicts between the clergy and military. But the Acehnese prevailed after a fashion. In 1967 Jakarta awarded to the province the title of Special Territory by virtue of the Islamic zeal of the Acehnese as well as their fierce spirit of independence.

At dusk it began to rain, and my drivers began chanting their hexes against the spirits that lay in wait for travelers.

During a brief lull in the rain, I suggested that we make camp. "No," they replied. "The spirits here are not good. They are all around us, in the trees, rocks, caves, and in the rain. We are helpless if we give in. It is best to continue."

So we drove the tortuous road for the entire night, as the jeep bucked and bounced across one obstacle after another: torrential streambeds, fallen trees, mud, rock slides. Often the vehicle became stuck and we were forced to get out and push, while my companions muttered their invocations. At daylight the rain abated, but there was precious little to see beyond the forest-covered draws and pockets where the Acehnese had humiliated and punished the Dutch.

The early-morning sun made me drowsy, and I kept nodding off as Tonku pushed the vehicle through the highlands that formed the eastern wall of the Alas River. Soon it became apparent that logging operations had entered the country of the Alas, and the jeep groaned through a portion of landscape cleared except for huge stumps and the orange residue of sawdust.

How odd it was amid such desecration to see suddenly a giant black orchid rise to tower in front of us. The cobra struck with such force that its spring and the upward torque of the jeep's hood had the beast cradled momentarily intact against the windshield before it slithered off on my side. We stopped and got out to watch its writhing dance of death in a murdered forest, a crazed whip flailing its crimson head in the ankle-deep sawdust that burned our nostrils.

We pushed on. Eighteen hours after we had left the wedding party, we sighted Lake Tawar, the northernmost of the string of freshwater lakes settled into Sumatra's interior. The rain had stopped, so we made camp and divided our few rations. Intent on a bath, I clawed my way through a tangle of spiderwebs to the water's edge and began to remove my wet, muddy clothes for a swim.

"No, tuan, you must not swim here," said Tomy.

"Why not?"

"You must not," Tonku said. "It is certain death to swim here."

"Good clear water. Too high for crocodiles here."

The boys conferred for a moment, then gave me a great, fearful look. "A spirit lives at the bottom of the lake," said Tomy, and Tonku nodded quickly. "This spirit wills itself into a woman, and all men who see her, desire her. When you swim, she invites you to follow her to her home in the deep. Men are seduced by her and do not return."

"She's not interested in me," I said and laughed, immediately regretting my flippancy.

"She is interested in any man, and it is not a matter for joking. She does yet not claim a white man, and she will not if we are here. Do you not recall the words of the village chief? That *danau tawar* is an evil place? No, tuan, you may not swim. We are so obliged to say this."

The driver fetched a bucket, quickly filled it at water's edge, and returned to hand it to me.

"You may clean yourself with this water," he said, "but please do not go close to the lake's edge."

I looked at the lake as the boys positioned their rugs for prayers. I did not dismiss their story as hopelessly romantic superstition. For them, such a connection between the visible and invisible worlds was all too real. Fear was legitimate because it was attached to nature's violent acts, to which they were accustomed, and to nature's hidden motives, which they could only respect. I envied

them. Unfortunately for me, I was far removed from the traditional Acehnese assumptions about the world and its mysteries
that had given them their mettle, their fierce pride, and their laws.

A few days later, after my return to Medan, I set out with Jake
and his driver to cross the island. Jake was making another expedition into the rainforest, and I was continuing south into West
Sumatra. We would stay the night in his head tracker's village,
and in the morning his driver would take me as far south as Lake
Toba on his return to Medan.

We set out after lunch. Our driver was a Javanese Muslim called
Tukiran, whose forebears had emigrated to the country around
Medan in the 1920s as indentured servants to work the Dutch-
owned plantations. Once clear of Medan we were in fine open
country, which soon gave way to foothills guarding the central
Serbeulang Range. By midafternoon we leveled out at the Christian Batak town of Brastagi, four thousand feet above sea level.

"How large is the wilderness you photograph?" I asked Jake
when we had cleared the town and resumed our climbing.

"Twenty-four hundred square miles," he said. "That comprises
the Gunung Leuser National Park. I've set up on a permanent
basis eleven cameras that operate electronically, the shutters released by trip wire or pressure plate. These are strategically placed
to snap the beasts that are simply impossible to stalk and shoot
with a hand-held camera. It's one thing to track an orangutan for
three days, but tiger, clouded leopard, spotted rhino demand more
ingenuity."

"A mountainous rainforest reserve on Sumatra larger than the
state of Delaware," I said.

"It is a vast area," he said. "You've got to have patience. I can
get to one particular camera only every fourteen months. But
there are other problems. You've got to safeguard the cameras
from weather, ants, elephants. Once a bull elephant in mating
season was so enraged by the flash that he ripped the camera from

its protective housing and trampled it. Months later I found the squashed camera, and the film was still intact.

"There are dangers, too," he continued. "Once, I was charged by a bull elephant and took refuge in a fig tree. I wouldn't be here if it hadn't been for the latticework of the hanging roots."

I knew about the fig tree in the jungle. It sounded innocuous enough, but its presence in the rainforest was a testament to the wilderness's strangling, poisonous beauty and its myriad inter-dependences, which wreak death out of birth in an unending cycle. Germinating in the upper branches of trees from bird dung, the fig sent tendrils to the earth to root there; it was a parasite that grew with astonishing speed and potency. Finally denying its hard-wood host sunlight and water, as well as food from the soil, the fig tree thrived, surrounding the host's moribund trunk. It was within the robust bars of this natural cage that Jake had found refuge from the attacking elephant.

"Do you see those?" We were climbing steadily through moun-tain forest, and Jake was pointing out steep limestone faces covered with vines. "My trackers and I have to scale cliffs like those to reach the habitat of a certain antelope."

"What do you wear when you go into the forest?"

"I try to pretty much meet the elements on their terms the way my trackers do. We dress in sarongs, go barefoot, carry native packs, use tobacco juice as a leech repellent."

Though Jake had a college degree in zoology, I sensed that he was more an autodidact in wilderness survival techniques. I re-called something Hank had said, marveling at Jake's gritty single-mindedness: "I'm a tough guy, but he's really tough. Trip after trip he's relentless."

Later we stopped on a plateau at the crest of the spine of moun-tains overlooking Lake Toba, which from where we stood stretched east as far as the eye could see, like a dream in mist. The only noise came from a breeze and a waterfall spilling five hundred feet into a limestone gorge that fed the lake.

"I thought this was volcanic country. Why are there so many limestone outcroppings?" I asked.

"This whole island is being lifted by the Indian Ocean plate," Jake replied. "You can almost see the Indian Ocean from here. Toba's quite a lake, isn't it?"

Toba represents one of the largest volcanic depressions in the world now covered by water. It is fifty-six miles long and nineteen wide, with a large island in its center. The peak of Samosir Island is covered with a sediment, suggesting that the island once was far below the surface of the lake, which plunges well over sixteen hundred feet at its deepest part. The present topography was structured eons ago and eons apart by two major volcanic eruptions. Now the area is volcanically quiet, with only hot springs on the west shore of Samosir.

We descended from the center of the island down the western slopes of the range. In the foothills I began to notice the desecrations of the logging companies. By late afternoon we were in the western lowlands, approaching the Alas River and entering Acehnese country. There were more signs of logging: idle bulldozers and felled, trimmed camphor trees. There was a transmigration camp and a village of ramshackle huts at the ferry site, and Jake stopped to buy cigarettes at a small toko.

"Cigarettes are a necessity, not a luxury, for my bearers," he said. "I'd have a desertion on my hands if we ran out of smokes. It's happened before."

The ferry consisted of four boats lashed together, with a deck of hardwood planking, and operated by a pulley cable. Ours was the only vehicle to cross, and Jake negotiated the fare. The Alas was brown and sluggish. "It's not always this way," he said. "At flood time buses slide off the deck into the water."

Before we boarded, he checked his list for any oversight, for this village on the Alas River was the last outpost of civilization.

(Notes from a Diary) By the time we cross, it is nearly dark. We have left the paved road that crosses the island many miles before. Now the road that lies ahead in the headlights is so heavily rutted, it is hardly any road at all.

"When it rains, this road is bloody impassable, even in the Land Rover," says Jake. "We're lucky this time, mate. I've had to walk in from here. Once I did and reached the village at dawn. There was a girl bathing alone in that very stream." He pointed out the window on the driver's side. "She was beautiful and totally unaware of me. I thought I'd entered the Garden of Eden."

We drive a full hour before the lantern lights of a small Acehnese village come into view. There is little to see in the darkness when we get out of the vehicle. Barely visible is a scattering of huts on stilts on each side and a narrow, slippery path leading across a stream and up a hill to the hut of Jake's head tracker.

Tukiran, the driver, usually stays in the hut of one of the bearers, so we leave him with the vehicle and begin the climb through the moonless night up to our host's hut.

After a quarter hour's hike up the precarious slope, we are greeted by a barking dog standing his post. Chickens cluck on their roosts under the house. Sarong-clad figures carrying oil lamps materialize like ghosts to lead us up the ladderway into the hut. We enter a small lighted room and take seats on the hardwood floor covered with woven-grass mats. To the rear is another room, where the family sleeps, and off this room is a smaller alcove with a dirt hearth, where food is prepared. That my presence is totally unexpected seems to make no difference to anyone.

Our host is known as *pawang*, a word literally meaning "guide" but infused with other meanings: "master tracker" and "one gifted with magical powers." A bony man in his mid-forties with sharp features and protruding gold teeth, he wears a sarong tied around a pitifully thin, bare waist. From his gaunt looks, I would have guessed him to be an old man. Once he had been near death from tuberculosis: Jake had had him hospitalized in Medan to be cured, and even now when they venture into the forest, he receives injections every Wednesday and Saturday night, much to the amused satisfaction of the other bearers. How deceiving looks are,

I am thinking. Here is a man who looks wasted, and he has the strength, stamina, and heart of a tiger.

His wife has borne him seven children, and though the older ones have moved into huts of their own nearby, four remain in the house, and together with Jake, myself, and the two bearers who will round out Jake's expedition, the room is filled for the meal pawang's wife and older daughter, a young woman, are preparing.

Jake and the others usually converse in the harsh Acehnese dialect of which I know nothing, but for my benefit they speak Bahasa Indonesia.

Pawang's wife serves us glasses of sweet, thick black coffee while we await the meal. Sumatran coffee is delicious, and it makes me light-headed. I wonder if it's been spiked with ganja buds, but I say nothing. I pass out kreteks, and the men light up, while the children watch in silence.

"Thank you for inviting me," I say to pawang.

"Thank you for coming," he replies.

"What is pawang's wife's name?" I ask Jake in a whisper.

"I don't know myself, mate. To us she is simply the wife of pawang. But to him she's the mother of his children. Soon he'll be taking another wife, a younger woman, and she's not too pleased about that."

The other two bearers are younger than pawang, perhaps in their mid-twenties; their names are Gadi and Samsul. Gadi, the leaner of the two, has the crown of his head shaved like a monk, and he explains that it is part of an elaborate cure for a headache, involving lighted tree bark, a glass, and two incisions made with a razor blade in his scalp to release the bad blood. Samsul, who is stockier than his companion, has a cast to one eye. The children, prepubescent except for the daughter in the kitchen, sit cross-legged, gaping at us.

With some ceremony Jake presents a small globe, the sort found in primary-school rooms, to pawang to unwrap. This accomplished, the tracker holds it up for general inspection, and there are murmurs all around.

"It is a globe, pawang," says Jake. "I bought it in Medan."

"A globe," responds the head tracker, seeming not to know what to make of it.

"It is a model of the world," Jake says, turning the globe. "Here is Sumatra, there is New Zealand, over there is California, and here is Mecca. It is best to use this magnifying glass." He takes a small glass from his pocket and hands it to pawang.

"Mecca is the holiest place on earth," says the head tracker, adjusting the glass.

"And Egypt?" says Samsul. "There is a rumor about a flood in Egypt in the market today."

"This rumor comes from television in a village with electricity," says Gadi.

"Egypt is here," says Jake, pointing, "not far from Mecca."

The glass is passed about, and each turns the globe and studies it for several moments. Finally, the glass is returned to pawang, who quietly continues his study. Gradually, his earlier look of bafflement gives way to revelation. He nods slowly. "It is yet another sign of the greatness of God," he says gravely to murmurs of approval.

"The globe and its glass will go with us into the forest," says the head tracker, "and it is part of our life there."

"I carry it," says Gadi.

"We take turns carrying it," says Samsul.

"Does this globe not tell of God's greatness?" says the head tracker, rising. He steps into the back room, and returns with two parang, the machete which is the indispensable tool of the forest. Both of these words, *pawang* and *parang*, so similar, are Indonesian words incorporated into Acehnese dialect. One of the parangs he holds is a rather ordinary tool, but the other is a thing of beauty: a finely tempered blade curved and weighted like a scimitar, narrow at the handle, with a sharp edge honed on its convex side. He presents this machete to Jake. Behind this gift lies a story that pawang, Jake, and the bearers all have a hand in telling.

"The first time I mount an expedition into the interior," Jake begins, "I have no parang. The native ways come gradually to me, and I learn everything from them. But after the first trip I know how essential the tool is. I buy the best I find at the market and take it along next time. We are a week out of the village. I am sitting on a rotten log and pawang opposite me. The log gives way and the cutting edge of my new parang is thrust as with a will of its own deep into pawang's foot, where it joins the ankle. It is crazy, a freak accident that never happens but does. The cut goes to the bone. You see tendons."

"The remotest country," says pawang. "No man visits this country since Adam."

"I am not certain that even Adam visits this country," says Samsul to me. "It is too violent a country for the first man."

"This country is not Eden," says Gadi.

"No, this country is Eden, where God places Adam," says pawang. "It is certainly that country. It can be no other."

"Then there is the woman," says Samsul. "Adam, his woman, and his children leave and do not return."

"After he is deceived by the woman," says pawang. "All the ills of the world are the fault of women. Since Eve tempts Adam, women mean nothing but trouble for men. They redeem themselves by bearing children."

Pawang's wife enters to pour more coffee. She looks at her husband with adoration and pride, but does not speak.

"It's the roughest country imaginable, jungle-covered mountains and steep ravines, and we have to get pawang out for medical attention," continues Jake. "Of course, he cannot walk, so Gadi and Samsul rig a stretcher, and we begin the long trek out. What good is first aid in such country? For the week's return to the village, I think only of infection and gangrene. That pawang loses a leg. But pawang does not blame me for the accident that was clearly my fault."

"I do not blame him," says pawang. "The spirits of the forest cause this accident. We are all at fault for not appeasing them when we invade their home. In the village we have the laws of the Koran. We pray at the mosque. But in the forest there are spirits with their own laws, and we are remiss in our duties to them. What happens, woman, when we come out of the forest?"

"When they emerge from the forest," says pawang's wife from the kitchen, "I weep and wail so that my husband becomes angry. 'Silence, woman, and make coffee,' he tells me."

"The wound," pawang says, "has a positive effect. Bad blood flows forth from it, thus aiding in the cure for tuberculosis."

"I take pawang to the hospital in Medan," says Jake, "and thanks to antibiotics his foot and leg are saved."

"But tell what we do the next time," says Samsul.

"As an infidel," Jake continues, "I am not privy to the deeper meanings of what we do. We carry a live white chicken. Certain other foods. The Koran. We return to the spot of the accident. We prepare a meal. We sacrifice the chicken. We read from the Koran. It's all done a certain way. The spirits are appeased by our rite of purification. The practical outgrowth is that nobody is at fault."

"We remain together," says pawang.

"This is the first parang I've handled in two years," says Jake, testing the balance of the machete.

Pawang's wife and daughter bring forth the evening meal: plates of rice with a sauce of chilis and a fish-stock base, the simplest meal imaginable, for these are poor people by any material measure. We eat in the local fashion, still seated cross-legged on the floor, with the fingers of the right hand molding each mouthful, and afterward cleaning the hand in a small glass fingerbowl of water. Laws of hospitality are scrupulously observed. Pawang's wife offers me more rice, which I decline for my hosts, who serve themselves almost apologetically.

"Please excuse me," says Samsul as he helps himself. "But we farmers have large appetites."

After the meal the younger children retire, and the woman and her daughter repair to clean the dishes, and afterward descend the ladderway by lantern light to walk down the hill to the stream for a bath, while we men smoke kreteks. Conversation turns to village matters.

"How does construction on the mosque go?" Jake asks his head tracker.

"It is finished in a month," says pawang. "Then we do not walk so far for prayers."

I speak to Jake in English. "Perhaps I can donate a little money, by way of thanks for their hospitality."

But Jake demurs. "I wish it were that simple," he says. "The fact is, pawang is feared throughout the community because of his magical powers. The question of gifts for the mosque and how they materialize is a touchy one. Pawang is the finest tracker of game in these parts, and that makes him two people as far as the villagers are concerned. A man of the village is one thing. A man of the forest is quite another."

"How is it that the villagers fear you?" I say to pawang.

"They fear what they do not know or understand," he replies. "This is a village of rice-growers on the edge of the forest. The forest is the unknown. As a tracker I see the unknown, and I see things no other man is permitted to see." He nods at Jake. "Tuan is not permitted to see the spirits and apparitions that I see. Some men say that I see what is forbidden for men to see."

"The forest is a threat to the village," explains Jake in English. "Tigers, for example. Not long ago a woman bathing at the stream was killed and dragged off. Tigers kill wild pigs near the village as a matter of course. That doesn't bother the villagers, who're forbidden to eat pork. But tigers trample their rice fields. They're not as rare as you might think. Several hundred in this area. So the natives bait them with poison and sell the hides. Eventually, they wind up in the hands of Chinese merchants in Medan."

"The forest is the unknown for good reason," says Gadi. "Men never go there."

"The forest has its own laws," says Samsul. "It does not like changes that men bring."

"When you blaze your way with a parang," says Jake, "you cut saplings that are apparent for years. If we find animal tracks and set up equipment, the animals often don't return for days or even weeks. As for us, our senses must become extraordinarily acute. We know when people try to follow us in. You sense it. But I'm afraid the forest is doomed. Indonesia is a nation of villagers and rice-growers, and we've got a Javanese farmer in office with short-range vision."

"It must not be so," says pawang. "The forest is unchanged since the time of Adam and must remain so."

The dog under the hut barks, and within moments we hear female laughter and talk. The women are returning from their bath, apparently sharing a great joke as they mount the ladderway and enter, chattering in the Acehnese dialect and laughing, their sarongs wet to the skin.

"It's Tukiran the driver," says Jake in English. "Apparently, he was about to take a shit, slipped in the mud, and fell in the ditch and got all muddy. His clothes, they say, are filthy, and he's really cheesed."

This is a source of great amusement for the women. It seems that Tukiran is extremely proud of his Javanese lineage despite his class, but the Acehnese are a proud, devout people who don't suffer outsiders gladly as a matter of routine. That the driver is in Jake's employ ensures his welcome here, just as my own status as guest is secure. But Tukiran wears his Javanese identity on his sleeve with a certain fastidiousness, and part of the delight of these women lies in his comeuppance. Still, there is more to it. Acehnese women, indeed almost all Malay women, possess alongside their demureness and piety a streak of elbow-to-the-ribs earthiness that is quick to surface: a refreshing mingling of the sacred and profane.

Jake and I are billeted in the rice barn down the hill, so we bid

our hosts goodnight and follow Gadi and Samsul with their lanterns, stopping after fording the stream to wash and drink water.
The water is sweet, so I fill an empty bottle with it. The rice barn,
a wooden hut with a thatch roof, is raised only a yard off the
ground, and there is a single step. Inside it reeks of dried fish and
chilis, but we are soon accustomed to the odor as we light a candle
and pitch mosquito netting over our grass mats spread on the
rough hardwood floor. Cats have the run of the barn.

I have scotch in a flask, so we mix it with the stream water in
our cups to sip while we smoke ganja weed. We talk for much of
the night, purposely eluding sleep until the false dawn, while pink
butterflies flutter about the candle.

"You know, mate, you're only the third person I've brought
here," says Jake. "The other two were Hank and my mother."

"She must be some kind of game lady."

"She lives in England now."

"How long have you lived in Indonesia?"

"Thirteen years. I came up on a sailboat from Australia. Was
going round the world, but I discovered these islands and decided
to stay. At first did some work in the oil fields. I've known about
cameras since I was a kid, but the rest I've had to pick up. I can't
really imagine living anywhere else. The exotic beauty of these
islands, the food, the women. There're no other women like Malay
women. If that's because I'm a white man and a racist, I'm guilty
as charged."

"Pawang seems a clever man," I say.

"The cleverest. Serpent-licked ears. He's steeled with native
cunning, but he's very loyal, too. Before he met me, he had only
a month or so to live, but by then he had sold the gold and artifacts
that were family heirlooms for unsuccessful cures. I pay him in
gifts and medicines as well as money. Now that his condition is
stabilized, his loyalty to me is total."

A soft breeze rises, extinguishing the candle, a signal to try and
sleep. The ganja and whisky do their work. Once I am vaguely
aware of a cat curling softly near my head against the netting.

Suddenly, an animal's terrible squeal pierces the silence. We sit upright.

"Tiger," Jake says.

"Jesus!"

"Killed a pig. You hear the neck snap? That popping sound?"

"I wasn't listening for it."

"We'll have a look-see when it's light."

Gradually, my ears are filled with the muted sounds of the night forest, quieter than silence. I am barely awake when dawn breaks, and can see the villagers moving about, insubstantial and ephemeral, while gibbons and orangutans sound the hour from the forest canopy at the edge of the village.

A boy's voice speaks softly at the door, summoning us to a breakfast of freshwater prawns pawang has netted in the half-darkness.

Outside there is a lot of excitement. The tiger circled the settlement stalking its prey. Behind the rice barn we discover several of the predator's large tracks in the mud.

"He wasn't twenty feet away, mate," says Jake. "He might have bounded in to pay us a visit. Our small cats must've scared him off," he says and laughs.

After breakfast I make my farewells and am ready to depart. The driver tends to the Land Rover, and Jake sees me off.

"As it turns out we won't be heading into the forest today," he says. "The women are making rice cakes for the market. It's a two-hour walk."

"What will you do?"

"Oh, I'll just take it easy. Sharpen parangs, knives. Stuff like that. You ought to be under way by nine to make Lake Toba." He extends his hand. "Safe trip, Chuck."

By ten o'clock we are midstream on the Alas River.

Sumatra: The Death of Muhammad's Grandsons

*I*T WAS A TWENTY-HOUR, bone-jarring bus ride south from Lake Toba across the equator to Bukittinggi, deep in the West Sumatran heartland. By midafternoon the vehicle entered the rolling, high country of the Minangkabau, whose green hills and valleys were dotted with ornate houses raised off the ground with horned ridgepoles and finely carved, painted wooden fronts.

The road followed an old cog railway that crossed a swift river under a bridal-veil waterfall and spiraled upward through a mountain saddle into a triangular hive of smoking volcanoes—Merapi, Singgalang, Sago—creating their own cloud formations over a cool, distilled country. We entered Bukittinggi and slowed for a group of schoolgirls dressed in white burnooses and caftans to cross the narrow, cobbled way.

This small, provincial city in West Sumatra's Padang Highlands is the capital of a people unique in the archipelago and in the world. Although converted to Islam, these Malays have retained their ancient custom of matriarchy, descent and inheritance through the female line, which is believed to exist nowhere in a purer form than among this tribe. The eldest man of the female line, called *mamak,* is the keeper of all family possessions.

By reputation successful in business and cunning in politics, the Minangkabau have managed to distance themselves from the rawer edges of existence experienced by other Malay tribes: the coarse Islamic Bugis of South Sulawesi, for example, who for centuries risked their lives in small boats on the open seas. Unlike the Bugis, the Minangkabau eschew the gross and base, and their shamans promote loftier superstitions. In this sense, too, they differ greatly from pawang and Jake's other Acehnese bearers: devout Muslims whose minds were compelled in certain rigorous ways by the rainforest and their intimacy with its sudden dangers.

I took a room in a small hotel on the edge of town, overlooking a deep wooded canyon and long-tailed monkeys swinging through the trees at its precipitous edge. Nearby, at the market square, the old clock tower built by the Dutch sounded the hour. There was a vibrant life in the narrow, cobbled streets: men played mah-jongg and dominoes at makeshift tables, but it was the women I noticed, and the town vibrated with their movement. Colorfully dressed from head to toe and immaculately groomed, they gave the shops and market stalls an elegance that seemed at odds with the town's down-at-the-heels charm.

Shop signs were ingeniously conceived. *"Dentis,"* read one sign above a painted set of upper dentures, and several doors away another pictured a set of uppers and lowers, poised to snap closed like a mousetrap. Balconies embossed with dates from the turn of the century hovered over the sidewalks.

At sundown lamplighters lighted the kerosene streetlamps, and on every corner men tending warungs grilled ears of corn. After dinner I walked back to my hotel to the music of the cicadas singing over the hooves of the ponies pulling the dokars with kerosene lamps swaying from their awnings.

`By day I looked for hidden patterns of Minangkabau life among the market's shifting colors. The market swelled to include the town center, with awning-covered streets and alleys running parallel and at right angles outward from a large public building that housed the permanent shops. The streets and alleys reached the main mosque on one side, and a wide flight of steep stone steps on the other that descended to the dokars, bemos, and buses.

For the locals, the market was a place where needs, real and imagined, were met. To the outsider, it provided clues to the attitude with which the Minangkabau viewed the world. Their market tolerated no indolence and radiated a steady fire. It was free of parasitic refugees, fugitives from upriver of the sort I had seen in Borneo's markets. Beggars, either crippled or blind, took their rightful place in the scheme of things, for Islamic law commanded that they be given alms. Typically, a little girl led her blind father, well dressed in a batik shirt, through the labyrinth, accepting gifts. Thus was the market infused with a vibrancy that gave the place the feeling of an organic whole, a vast human machine.

There were stalls of fruits, vegetables, dried fish, parangs, clothing, jewelry and other necessities and luxuries of life; but there were subtler presences than stock-in-trade. All through the market the hawkers and the folk-medicine doctors cried out for attention from the silent onlookers. One old man shrieked out the powers of dried reptile as a cure for skin and joint disease, and another had roosts of live fruit bats to cure asthma, two score or more dangling upside down like a rack of half-opened umbrellas.

Nearby a man sold bottles of honey, which he filled to order from a bucket, opening a mesh sack to dip a hand holding a plastic cup into the thick amber. The honey was guarded by bees clustered around a comb, along with a cutting of the tree flower that identified the source of the pungent, sweet liquid. The man's forearms were a mass of stings, swollen in a hundred different places, that might have killed an ordinary man. But he remained unconcerned, inured to sting and poison alike.

Squatting at curbside was a man selling an herb believed to induce fertility in barren women. His potential customers were sad-eyed females, including a nursing mother, who lifted her blouse for the infant. When I caught the eye of the other women, they laughed, distracted for a moment from the curse of infertility. Another stall featured a three-foot-high model of a mosque fashioned from exotic cuttings of fruit; there were other edible mosques as well, imaginative confections for West Sumatran household communions that nourished the body if not the spirit.

One stall offered nothing but brassieres of many sizes and styles; a crowd of women scrutinized these stays and lifts of the Western undergarment world. Javanese and Balinese women of the countryside often wore bras as external halters, but no women did so here. One young woman studied assiduously a black lace sample with cutouts in the center of each cup. At the adjacent stall a woman was selling statuettes of men and women reading the Koran, as well as other plaster-of-paris religious artifacts.

The second floor of the market building had permanent shops that sold almost exclusively fabrics, gold-embroidered costumes for weddings and festivals, slippers, and matching headdresses. These samples of ceremonial clothing were displayed on life-sized female mannequins, with sleek, black hair in buns. Bolts and drapes of cloth were exotically designed and dyed in every imaginable combination. With eager confidence women held their selections up to the light for close inspection.

As I left, the muezzin from the main mosque nearby sent up the call for prayers, and a shopkeeper alone with his wares knelt on his small rug to offer his own. Despite the underpinnings of animism, Islam's grip in these parts would never be relinquished. Its rules, codes, mores were unbending, while accepting ancient local customs seemingly aberrant in the Islamic eye.

I had lunch in the traditional Minang style at an upstairs café overlooking the big clock and enjoyed the curried chicken and buffalo simmered in chilis, turmeric, and coconut milk. When I paid at the door downstairs, the old woman who took my money tried her English.

"Too hot for you," she said. "Your face red. You have red face."

I told her I was an American.

"See ya later, alligata, so long Am-er-i-kan Christian," she cackled pleasantly.

Later that afternoon I walked through the old part of town and looked back over the rooftops of the entire city: the ruins of Fort de Kock, built by the Dutch during the Padri Wars in the early nineteenth century; the market; and the main mosque, the pastel sunset washing over its star and moon seeming the outward glow of an inward, impenetrable truth. After dark I took a different way through the kerosene-lighted streets, stopping at Fort de Kock to admire the mosque, stately and imperious under the ghostly-white full moon.

At my hotel I had learned of a young American anthropologist and his wife who were based in the city. When I called on them, they suggested that we have dinner, so we met at a small Chinese restaurant with red-checkered tablecloths and dined while a juke-box played Western rock.

"The Minangkabau are a flamboyant people," said Bob. "You see it in their dress. You hear it in their speech. They place great store in eloquence. Proverbs, for example. They have hundreds of them. 'I carry my son in my arms but lead my nephew by my right hand.' That sort of thing.

"We're talking about people with a great oral tradition," he continued. "They claim that their forebears sailed to Sumatra from Madagascar in the ninth century and that they're descendants of Alexander the Great. They call him Iskander. Both these claims are substantiated in old manuscripts. But practically speaking, the Minangkabau are inland people whose original settlers emigrated from the Asian mainland down the Malay Peninsula long before the time of Christ. Their origins are a curious confusion of mythology and history. It's all rooted in the extravagance of local legend and song."

"How did they become a matriarchal society?" I asked.

"It's really misleading to say that the Minangkabau are matriarchal," said Jill. "It's not a society of feminists. Matrilineal, yes, but you'd have to live among them a good while to appreciate how it all works. A wife remains in her kinfolk's house after her marriage. Her husband really has no house of his own. He's officially domiciled in his mother's house and simply visits his wife. Names, privileges, property derive from the mother's side. It's unique. They're clannish."

"Right, it's a clan thing more than anything else, and it predates Islam," added Bob. "They've fought wars to keep their ways. There are only two or three societies in the world that I know of that are even remotely similar."

"Primitive cultures as well?" I asked.

Bob smiled. " 'Primitive' is not a word we use in anthropology," he said. "But the Minangkabau are not immune to Western influences. If they have electricity and enough money, they watch television. They see 'The Cosby Show' but can't understand why a black man is so rich.

"No one really knows how the Minangkabau became a matrilineal society, but it's very deeply ingrained," he went on. "Again, it goes back to the clan thing. It keeps the clan together. You could never buy property in West Sumatra. It's owned by too many people. All very tightly knit. The wars we mentioned. Called the Padri rebellion. You saw the fort. The Dutch tried to keep a lid on things. Some Islamic fundamentalists in the early nineteenth century tried to impose stricter Islamic practices upon local adat. Relieving women of their lofty status, banning gambling, the drinking of alcohol. The Minangkabau are known gamblers. They bet on bullfights, and they drink at their festivals. So the coercion to a more conservative Islam didn't take, even though a lot of blood was shed. The Minangkabau call the Koran 'the compass of life,' but not at the expense of giving up their ancient ways. They've managed to integrate two mutually exclusive traditions, and that's why they're extraordinary."

Away from the city, the patterns of traditional Minangkabau life seemed equally resilient and practical. I hired a young man called Edy to guide me on his motorbike around the rolling, high countryside surrounding Bukittinggi. He made a chatty guide, and in his idiosyncratic English explained much of the local lore.

We passed a rice field where a man naked to the waist held two

large brown dogs on leashes, and Edy explained that they were
trained to hunt wild pigs. The villagers would mass as many as a
hundred dogs to pursue the beasts, which ravaged the farms. A
good hunting dog could fetch as much as the equivalent of $300,
and they were fed the meat of the pigs they killed.

Men harvested three rice crops a year in the carefully terraced
fields in the mountains, surrounded by groves of cinnamon and
banana trees. Peanut fields and jackfruit trees were worked by men
with parang and hand ax between the heavy rains, and palm trees
yielded a potent alcoholic brew. When he pointed these men out,
Edy remarked on the Minangkabau fondness for alcohol.

"We are a holy and obedient people but sometimes not so solemn. We make *arak* here from the palm tree that is very strong,"
he said.

"And it is drunk even though the Minangkabau are strongly
Muslim?"

"Yes, but it is drunk only as a hobby."

By late morning we reached an ancient Minangkabau palace,
the tips of its many gables shaped like buffalo horns. Outside,
royal graves lay under an old banyan tree, as well as a Sanskrit
stone with a snake image dating from the fourteenth century.
Inside, displayed behind the throne, was a portrait allegedly of the
last king, dating from 1814. He was dressed in a black suit with
gold and red sashes and a red crown on his sedate head. A holdover
from the bloody days of the Padri rebellion, when Islamic fundamentalists had placed a king on the throne, he had later been
deposed by the headstrong Minangkabau, eager to regain their
ways.

We stopped at an old wooden structure to watch a huge water-
powered coffee grinder whose workings resembled that of a giant
clock. Water was diverted from a mountain stream through a
complex of aqueducts to drive a waterwheel twelve feet in diameter. This cottage industry had been in the same family for centuries. Nearby villagers brought their coffee beans here to be
roasted and pulverized, a process lending the brewed liquid the

thickness of syrup. For a hundred yards around the air was infused with the deep, rich aroma of coffee.

The coffee mill was part of a larger holding, an entire village consisting of a farm of several old houses and rice barns with elaborately carved roofs, and beyond them rice fields and herds of ducks feeding on small fish in the irrigated ponds. We walked along the dikes to watch a short-tailed macaque on a fifty-foot leash scamper up a tree to wrestle loose a coconut. It fell with a splash into a moribund rice field. The Minangkabau were known for their skill in training these monkeys.

Edy knew the family here, but when we called at the main house, he appeared to have second thoughts and lost his earlier enthusiasm, growing reticent and shy. The house was a large building three centuries old, built off the ground, with a palm-fiber roof. We were greeted by a maidservant, and Edy was immediately deferential. The servant led us into a large common room, dark, airless, and dusty, where the matriarch, a toothless grandmother, received us under a large wall tapestry. Though her reception of me was courteous, she gazed with contempt upon Edy and then left us alone in the room.

Edy explained that the matriarch's brother was the village elder, the mamak, who was obliged to seek his sister's guidance in the administration of village adat. There were over two hundred members of this clan. A husband worked during the day and returned at night to his wife's mother's house. Boys from the ages of seven to thirteen attended the mosque in the evening to study the Koran and *pencak silat*, a form of self-defense like t'ai chi that had also evolved into a dance. Then Edy explained the process of circumcision, carried out by a traveling shaman, as central to a Minangkabau boy's life.

As we were leaving, a young mother was sitting beside the matriarch on the steps nursing her baby and smoking a cigarette. She was so elegantly dressed, in hand-stitched garments of cotton and silk, highlighted with gold and silver threads, the results of a painstaking local process called *stola*, that she might have been the tribe's crown princess. The effect, however, was at odds with the cigarette and the glower she gave Edy when she exhaled smoke.

"Is it common for Minangkabau women to smoke?" I asked.

"Not common," replied Edy. "But it might be her hobby."

We took a different route on our return to Bukittinggi, following a river where bamboo waterwheels turned at the banks to the rhythm of the stream, irrigating rice fields. These were ingenious contraptions, and like the elaborate, ancient machinery of the coffee mill, they seemed emblematic of Minangkabau industry and precision.

"You will see another side to the Minangkabau," Edy said, as we arrived at a large field with a hill on one side, giving it the look of a natural amphitheater, with at least fifty vehicles parked about and several hundred spectators.

The bullfight was actually a pitting of two male buffalo against each other, and could last a few seconds or a half hour. That afternoon there were two separate contests, and the bulls were kept apart by their owners or handlers while men inspected them and placed their bets. There was no bookie, and the bets, usually for large sums of cash, were made between individuals and sealed with a handshake.

Though gambling was anathema under Islamic law, the mood here was festive: there was much talk, and noise rose from the field as from a hive of bees, as the Minangkabau, each wearing a kopiah, and Chinese squatted in circles, puffing cigarettes and showing their money. Negotiations were intense.

"Suppose a man loses a bet but refuses to pay?" I asked Edy.

"Then there are fights," he said. "We may see."

As the handlers brought the first contestants together, Edy explained that a narcotic was fed the animals before the fight to make them more aggressive. Men pored over the bulls, massaged their noses, then twisted their tails before they were made to lock horns.

Whether the fight lasted seconds or minutes, the ending was invariably the same, with one animal suddenly turning, breaking through the moving circle of screaming spectators, and galloping off the field with the other in hot pursuit. There was no small risk of being trampled by buffalo or spectators when a bull broke free, but the safety of the hill or a tree afforded a poor view of the spectacle. When the second fight ended, I was knocked off my feet by the fleeing crowd as a cold rain started up.

When we arrived in Bukittinggi, Edy explained his discomfiture in the matriarch's presence.

"It is no hobby to have a broken heart," he said. "I am thirty-three and alone. The parents of my fiancée do not allow the marriage because I do not have enough money. But we are in love. So my fiancée comes to my home, which is the house of my mother. She stays for two days before her own mother comes to fetch her. I can do nothing. My mother can do nothing. Now the girl who is no longer my fiancée blames everything on me. It is no hobby to have a broken heart."

"What can you do?"

"I must leave," he said. "There is no honor for me here. Only shame. I must go to Jakarta and seek work. To enjoy a home is a hobby, and there is no hobby for me here. That is for certain. I am finished here."

At the hotel I left him with a long, sorrowful face, but without bitterness. He was poignantly resigned to his people's exclusion of him. How many of Jakarta's teeming millions were made up of exiles like Edy, hounded out of a dogmatic homeland?

"There are many men like me," he said with the look of a man suffocating, as he offered his hand.

(Notes from a Diary) Today I depart Bukittinggi by bemo for the village of Pariaman on the Indian Ocean. Quite by chance last evening, I learned of a event staged there only one day a year: the *tabut*, celebrated in the month of Muharram, the first month of the Islamic lunar calendar, honoring the grandsons of the Prophet, Hassan and Husein, killed in the Kerbala War. There is no more important festival for the Minangkabau. We depart under a bright sun with the promise of rain at the coast.

The route follows the old cog railway that winds through a twisting canyon of limestone cliffs to the coastal plain, fine farming country with men wearing pyramidal hats knee-deep in mud behind their plows. Duck herders mind their flocks in the rice fields, and naked children bathe in the irrigated ditches fringed with palm trees. Pursued by rain clouds, we cross a torpid, brown river and enter Pariaman, a seaside town of woven-thatch houses and low pastel-colored buildings of stone.

I walk toward the center of this small metropolis, which resembles a marvelous stage set with thousands of actors, for the festival of tabut draws natives from near villages and far. The Islamic roots of this festival are very deep, for Hassan and Husein perished in their efforts to override rival factions and consolidate Muhammad's legacy. In the Middle East this day is honored with passion plays, but here in this West Sumatran coastal town, the ceremony is infused with the pomp and splendor of another occasion: an ancient tribal schism that predates Islam's arrival on these shores.

Central to the day's events are two rival *bouraq*. These are huge, nearly inscrutable effigies, perhaps thirty feet tall, supposedly sent to earth from heaven to claim the souls of slain heroes. They are bizarre winged horses with the heads of women, as well as strange, mysterious symbols rendered in bright colors, mounted on two large floats that are borne like sedan chairs through the streets by the village's young men. These strange likenesses differ one from the other like the battle array of opposing armies.

The pony-drawn dokars can make little headway in the sea of people around the floats, whose green bases are shaped like elephants. The occasional sun illuminates a hundred kites against gathering storm clouds.

I remain in the vicinity of the floats, in front of the public buildings of the town square, where a grandstand of sorts has been erected. Here the local dignitaries are seated in folding chairs, and they invite me to cross behind the police cordon and mount the raised stage.

It's a well-dressed gathering, with the women in Minangkabau finery and the men in maroon sarongs, but the crowd is turning into a crazed mob. Drummers beat their drums frantically, raising the pitch of collective enthusiasm to a cacophony. One group of men lights a small fire to heat a drum, affording it a shriller sound, but the instrument catches fire and ignites the skirts of a passing woman. There are screams as men beat black hats against the flame, finally extinguishing it.

The incident incites the people to a new frenzy, and the mob swells, bursting the cordon. Policemen swing riot sticks and curse those trying to cross. The scene becomes uglier when rocks are thrown by the opposing participants. Tradition demands a mock-battle between the two sides, but it has gone too far. One of the floats topples into a nest of power lines. It's a miracle no one is electrocuted, and I can see that most of the highly charged crowd are drunk—if not on spirits, perhaps on ganja or religious fervor, or most likely all three.

Some prearranged signal is given, and the floats begin to move on their journey to the sea. Swept up in the throng, I have no choice but to follow. I receive many stares, some haughty and others merely curious, but even these are yielding. Once I catch the eye of a devout-looking old woman in a colorful caftan, and when I smile at her, she shoots me a bawdy, gold-toothed grin and digs her knuckles into my ribs. Two similarly dressed young women snatch my hat good-naturedly, and I pursue them a quarter mile before they return it, even then after much banter, for the Minangkabau love flowery speech and wordplay.

This procession to the beach relieves the atmosphere of tension, as people gorge themselves with warung food, send scores of kites aloft, exchange cigarettes in this animist-Islamic festival crossed with Mammon. Tape cassettes blare forth a weird amalgam of tinny Middle Eastern music and Western rock. Invariably, students seek me out to practice their English, but when I ask about the cultural and religious origins of this one-day-a-year affair, they provide only vague answers.

No doubt the town elders would satisfy my curiosity, but details of the past elude the public consciousness. The Minangkabau, like many other Indonesian peoples, are reluctant to dwell on the past, beyond celebrating what it has handed down to them. As the national language has only one tense, so the Indonesian people, as diversified a lot as any on earth, seem to live in the present tense with little thought of yesterday or tomorrow. Is there a correlation between the complexity, or sophistication, as it were, of a language and the way it induces people to behave, insofar as they regard cause and effect, the consequences of individual or group actions?

Whatever else it is or is not, tabut, like the Fourth of July, is a holiday and a grand excuse for a party.

By the time we reach the beach, it is raining, so I seek shelter under a rotted pier and watch the two fantastic figures being borne into the surf and the fierce dismantling of the floats in the water by the fully clothed celebrants, each intent on bringing away a piece of the wreckage as a talisman, while naked children splash in the surf.

On this festive day there are sobering images of deprivation. Beneath a wooden Ferris wheel a leper dressed in soaked rags sits with a cup for coins. She is a terribly disfigured pariah of a woman, with a mutilated mouth and stumps for hands and feet, who silently endures the rain.

Padang, the largest port of West Sumatra, down the coast from Pariaman, is a city of narrow provinciality, lacking Medan's worldliness. While the pony-driven dokars lent the flat, airless city a certain style, its streets were dormant and sluggish. I sensed a rigidity lurking in its antiseptic atmosphere that seemed anomalous to a coastal city built by trade, but the Minangkabau Muslims were far more conservative than Medan's Bataks.

But while the city seemed empty and lifeless on its surface, I walked the streets to hear the prevailing sounds of gambling, voices in dimly lit rooms behind drawn shades murmuring over the clicking of dominoes and the shuffling of cards. Prostitutes in bright yellow and green sarongs guarded the doorways.

Padang was bereft of Westerners, and whisky was contraband— surprising after the revelry of Pariaman. I found only two shops that sold scotch, but the bottles were kept in back rooms and purchases were made on the sly. One Indian shopkeeper wanted twenty thousand rupiah for a liter. A Chinese competitor undercut him by a quarter of that price, but kept a furtive eye on the door as she wrapped the container of White Horse in newspaper.

"Polisi," she whispered.

At the Pelni Line office I booked the next evening's passage on the *Kerinci* for the thirty-three-hour voyage to Jakarta. Oddly, the hotels were full due to an "international" bridge tournament, so I had to stay south of Padang.

The road south of the city wound along level with the coast at the foot of the Barisan Range before rising inland to cross a small peninsula. At its southern base lay a small, idyllic natural bay, which the driver said was my destination; but as we began our twisting descent, I was unprepared for the bizarre sight I saw. On the northern curve of the bay was a lumber mill belching clouds of black smoke. Huge logs of hardwood lay heaped on the beach and as many rode gently in the reef-protected surf, creating a solid floor of logs on the water's surface, held in check by the peninsula to the north and a wooden sea wall to the south that divided the mill from the hostelry's beach.

When we entered the hotel grounds, a wall of trees partially obscured the mill, though clouds of the black smoke rose over the canopy like sulphuric gas from a volcano. The incongruity from any standpoint bordered on sheer lunacy: a rustic getaway hotel of bungalows on a lovely bay renowned for sunsets conjoined to an aesthetic and environmental horror.

I took a room, and explored the hotel grounds, separated from the mill by a barbed-wire fence. A smiling middle-aged woman approached and wiped her hands on her sarong before offering one.

"What room are you in?" she asked in English. "Do you want anything?"

She behaved coquettishly, carrying on like an aging butterfly. Thinking she might be the hotel masseuse, I asked if she worked here.

"I'm the owner," she said.

"It's a charming place except for the sawmill," I said, "and I guess I'm alone here. Crocodiles?" I pointed at the water. "Is it safe to swim?"

"*Belum.* No crocodiles here," she said, nodding toward the sawmill. "It is safe."

The beach had a rise of dune fringed by a row of palm trees. I looked up the beach and down and saw no mangrove swamps. I entered the water and swam out a hundred yards or so. There was little surf, and the calm water was riddled with yellow sawdust. When the wind shifted, I caught the unmistakable acrid smell of trees being processed into lumber. Beyond the wooden breakwater at the mill's boundary, small motorized boats nudged the mammoth logs into position, while a tractor snaked them out of the water across the beach to the large corrugated-tin structure housing the saws.

When the sun flattened out on the Indian Ocean, I returned to my room to shower. The surreal elements here were so irreconcilable that this setting seemed more the province of Off-Broadway, its paradoxes fodder for the theater of the absurd. A charming hotel on a beautiful bay working in tandem with a misplaced factory, each despite the other as if it didn't exist.

The dining room was a cavernous place that could easily have handled a convention. Rock music blared from the speakers as a boy seated me at a table for eight.

"Ibu suggests that you like the grilled fish," the boy said in Bahasa Indonesia. "It is very fresh." He lighted a mosquito coil and put it at my feet, where a cat had already curled up.

I sipped a beer while I waited, hearing laughter from the kitchen. Suddenly, the opposite door opened and a young Western couple, German students, entered and joined me. Hans wore a stylish single earring, and Anya had a jewel implanted above the flange of one nostril, as worn by Indian women. They spoke excellent English, and I was glad for their company. The boy came to take their order.

"Can you believe this weird place?" said Hans.

"It's also expensive," said Anya. "We've been staying in losmens as our budget allows, unless we find a nice inexpensive hotel, as we did at Lake Toba. But here our room is simply not worth what we're paying."

"We're moving on tomorrow," said Hans. "Heading south. But what about this place? That beautiful bay's been ruined by that mill."

As we were finishing dinner, the owner, dressed for evening in a sarong and blouse with heavy makeup on her face, joined us at the table.

"How have you enjoyed your trip so far?" she asked. "What did you think of the Christian Bataks of Lake Toba? There's a joke about them. If there are two of them they play chess. If three they sing. And if four they open a church. Are you enjoying your stay here?" she asked the couple.

"The rooms are overpriced," said Hans.

"I agree with you," she said. "They are expensive, and do you know why? If I lower the price the prostitutes move in. Local girls. As it stands now, businessmen from Padang come down to have affairs. It has gotten to the point where I cannot or will not rent to local people. Now you young people are from Germany. I do not care that you are not married, because you are tourists. But I was born in Padang, and I know the customs here."

"When was the mill built?" I said. "Couldn't you do anything to prevent its being built?"

She eyed me quickly. "It was constructed at the same time as the hotel," she said. "I had it built. Or rather my husband did with my money and, how do you say, my blessings. But he had as a partner a Chinese as well as a Korean, and with the local West Sumatran government's approval, the sawmill and hotel went up together. But then something very bad happened. The Chinese and Korean cheated my husband, and he has since been removed from the partnership."

"You mean that you built the hotel and the sawmill together here on purpose?" I said.

"Of course. It's my land."

We looked at her in silence. To this woman's mind, the close proximity of the mill and hotel had made perfect business sense. They were both situated on her property, thereby realizing a dual financial yield.

"I will send a girl to wake you before breakfast," she said as we retired. "Please come to my house for coffee, and we shall together watch the monkeys being fed, and afterward I'll show you where we've begun new construction."

I was already dressed when there was a knock at the door at seven. I walked across the grounds bathed in the early-morning shade of the looming mountains and met Anya.

"Hans is still asleep," she said.

A maid led us through the house onto a patio in back that faced scaffolding for a building going up on recently cleared land. Beyond, the jungle rose steeply to meet the Barisan Range. Our hostess was in her morning robe and greeted us warmly. The maid served coffee and then fetched large bowls of cooked rice and corn, which she ladled out upon the apron of the terrace. In moments the food was set upon by two score long-tailed monkeys, who swooped onto the terrace from scaffolding and trees. They included an old patriarch, mothers with clinging offspring, and various siblings who hissed and fought over scraps.

Afterward, we admired the freshly poured foundations of the new buildings under their webbings of scaffolding, while our hostess returned to the previous evening's discussion.

"Land ownership here is very difficult for a foreigner to understand," she said. "It is almost impossible to buy and sell property because there are so many family members the land belongs to. One of the reasons Minangkabau custom requires that property descend through the female line is so that it will remain in the family. It's really as simple as that. Never mind that feminists come to us looking for something else. So while I still own the land in all respects, the controlling interest of the mill belongs to the Chinese and the Korean. If I cannot control it, I want it shut down. But my complaint goes only as far as the West Sumatran government. They will all squeeze me to death."

The upshot was that while she still owned the land, the controlling interest in the mill belonged to the remaining partners. While upholding the Minangkabau tradition of land ownership, the West Sumatran government was not about to shut down a thriving business. The result was that the saws whined by day, the smokestacks blackened the sky, and sawdust soured a formerly pristine bay.

But the supreme irony, which we tacitly grasped, was that it appeared the owner wanted the sawmill closed more out of spite than anything else. If she could not realize profits from its operation, no one should. Absent from the equation were any aesthetic or environmental considerations, the things we visitors noticed in dismay. Most bizarre was that with only three guests in the hotel at this phantom "peak" season, other buildings were under construction.

Anya and Hans flagged a bemo after breakfast and headed south, but because the *Kerinci* didn't sail until near midnight, I had the day to kill.

Late in the morning I had a coffee with the owner. She told me there were more Minangkabau in Jakarta than in West Sumatra, and I was sad to think of Edy's imminent exile.

"It's none of my business," I said, "but I really should tell you something."

She took off her reading glasses and looked at me thoughtfully.

"I'm sorry. It's just that if you want to run a hotel, that sawmill is a mistake. I don't think you're going to have a lot of the sort of business you want, as long as it's there."

She stared at me. Moments of silence passed.

"I do not understand," she said finally.

Epilogue

IT WAS THE THIRD of September, and the *Kerinci* steamed southward off Sumatra's west coast. Tomorrow would be a day of saying goodbye to friends. I would have a meal at the old Dutch mariner's restaurant of memories, and afterward air out my clothes and pack. I would shake out my seersucker jacket and tie my tie for the long flight back across the Pacific Ocean.

Through the late afternoon, under a declining orange sun, I sat on deck and read two successive daily editions of the *Jakarta Post*. The papers were several days old. A front-page story accompanied by a photograph caught my eye. "Jakarta residents thronged the Slipi flyover project site in central Jakarta yesterday after reports that these ancient palm trees are protected by supernatural forces. Two chainsaws were broken in the attempt to fell them.

" 'They are husband and wife,' Asmir, 66, a senior resident in the neighborhood said of the trees. 'The taller is the wife and the shorter the husband. The wife regularly produces the fruit.' "

I checked the next day's edition for a follow-up and found it on page three. "Controversy has grown as the authorities finally decided not to fell a pair of ancient palm trees near the Slipi flyover, while the number of people coming to see the two continuously increases. Hundreds of people of neighboring towns have been flooding the area to see and collect wood shavings from the trees.

The large number of people coming there has caused traffic jams even late at night.''

The episode seemed a parable of sorts: of primitive wisdom and hope, pawang's mysticism and primordial forces born of the wilderness now unleashed, a native affirmation amid urban decay and renewal, the handmaidens of Western corruption. I thought of ibu and her hotel and sawmill: ibu, successfully or not, walking a middle path.

Ahead of us lay the Sunda Strait, the narrow body of water separating Sumatra from Java, which we would cross in darkness to make Tanjung Priok, Jakarta's port on the north coast of West Java, by early morning. In that strait was Krakatau Island, or what was left of it, but we would pass these volcanic ruins in darkness. *Anak Krakatau*, or "the Child of Krakatau," was the legacy of the infamous explosion of August 27, 1883, that claimed thirty-six thousand lives, sent tidal waves past Cape Horn to the English Channel, eleven thousand miles away, and dust into the atmosphere that created darkness at noon in Batavia and fiery sunsets in the United States for three years running.

I stood at the rail, counting the flying fish skimming across the surface. A cool wind blew out of the south, carrying storm clouds that would obscure a final brilliant sunset. I walked around the fantail to the port rail to watch Sumatra's deepening green twilight, pausing at the stern to drop a coin in the wake for good luck.

Pawang's appeasement of forest spirits now seemed anything but arcane ritual attending quaint superstition. If natural forces played with the lives of men, the gods so willed it, and men must act accordingly and venerate what was finally unfathomable and unknowable and unchangeable. The realization burned in my heart like a beacon when it began to rain.

Acknowledgments

MY DEBTS IN WRITING this book are many. I am especially grateful to the many people of Indonesia, natives and expatriates, who shared their country with me, some of whom are mentioned in the text. Sometimes, to protect their privacy, the names have been changed. In addition, I would like to thank the following people for their time and advice: William Abrahams, Des Alwi, Barry Bailey, Mira and Carl Berman, Sam Chandra, Lovick Corn, Bill Dalton, Christopher M. Dawson-Roberts, Tom Dowling, Michele Dreyfuss, Dan Frank, Mike Griffiths, Daisy Hadmoko, Drg. Halim Indrakusuma, Eric Hansen, Dave Heckman, Loky Herlambang, Fred Hill, Burt Hoffman, Gerald Howard, Shari and Thomas Johnston-O'Neill, I. B. Kompiang W., Lekha Menon, Barbara Perris, Christine Pevitt, Sharon Silva, Frank Viviano, Douglas Weaver, Rosalie Muller Wright.

Collateral Readings

The following entries are not so much a bibliography as a short, hence incomplete, list of collateral readings, and at its head must be *The Malay Archipelago: The Land of the Orang-Utan and the Bird of Paradise. A Narrative of Travel, with Studies of Man and Nature,* by Alfred Russel Wallace, first published in 1869 and available today in a Dover edition. As well, on this shelf must reside the "Eastern" novels and stories of Joseph Conrad.

Barbour, Violet, "Dutch and English Shipping in the Seventeenth Century," *Economic History Review* (1930): 439–54.

Blair, Lawrence and Lorne, *Ring of Fire: Exploring the Last Remote Places of the World* (New York: Bantam Books, 1988).

Bonner, Raymond, "The New Order," *The New Yorker* (June 6 and 13, 1988).

Caufield, Catherine, *In the Rainforest: Report from a Strange, Beautiful, Imperiled World* (Chicago: University of Chicago Press, 1984).

Child, Josiah, *A Treatise Concerning the East India Trade* (London, 1681).

Dodge, Bertha, *Quests for Spices and New Worlds* (Hamden, Conn.: Archon, Shoe String Press, Inc., 1988).

Erlanger, Steven, Reports: *The New York Times,* 1988–90.

Griffiths, Michael, *Indonesian Eden: Aceh's Rainforest* (New York: Mobil Services Co. Ltd., 1989).

Hanna, Willard A., *Indonesia Banda: Colonialism and Its Aftermath in the Nutmeg Islands.* No date.

Haley, K. H. D., *The Dutch in the Seventeenth Century* (London, 1972).

Hansen, Eric, *Stranger in the Forest: On Foot Across Borneo* (Boston: Houghton Mifflin Co., 1988).

Hart, Henry H., ed., *Marco Polo, Venetian Adventurer* (Norman: University of Oklahoma Press, 1967).

Huizinga, Johan, *Dutch Civilisation in the 17th Century* (London and New York: 1968).

Irian Jaya: The Land of Challenges and Promises (Jayapura: Provincial Government Level I, 1987).

Jones, Clayton, Reports (Boston: World Monitor, 1990).

Koentjaraningrat, ed., *Villages in Indonesia* (Ithaca: Cornell University Press, 1967).

Legge, John David, *Indonesia* (Englewood Cliffs, N.J.: Prentice Hall, 1965).

Legge, John David, *Sukarno* (London: Allen Lane, 1972).

Loeb, Edwin M., *Sumatra: Its History and People* (Kuala Lumpur: Oxford University Press, 1935).

Mendes Pinto, Fernão, *The Voyages and Adventures of Ferdinand Mendez Pinto*, Introduction by Arminius Vambery (London: T. F. Unwin, 1897).

Morison, Samuel Eliot, *The Great Explorers: The European Discovery of America* (New York: Oxford University Press, 1978).

Neill, Wilfred T., *Twentieth Century Indonesia* (New York and London: Columbia University Press, 1973).

Nordoff, Charles, and James Norman Hall, *Mutiny on the Bounty* (Boston: Little, Brown & Co., 1932).

O'Hanlon, Redmond, *Into the Heart of Borneo* (New York: Random House, 1985).

Perelman, S. J., *The Swiss Family Perelman* (New York: Penguin Books, 1987).

Schneebaum, Tobias, *Where the Spirits Dwell: An Odyssey in the Jungle of New Guinea* (New York: Grove Press, 1988).

Zentgraaff, H. C., *The Aceh Wars*, translated into Indonesian from the Dutch. Jakarta. No date.

Among guidebooks, three publications stand out as informative as far as they go on this still mysterious and rapidly changing part of the globe: Bill Dalton, *Indonesia Handbook* (Chico, Calif.: Moon Publications, 1988); *Indonesia: A Travel Survival Kit* (Oakland, Calif.: Lonely Planet Publications, 1990); and *Passport's Regional Guides of Indonesia* (Chicago: NTC Publishing Group, 1990).